2017 Nautilus Award Gold Winner
2018 Readers' Favorite Gold Winner
2018 Whistler Independent Book Award Finalist

Certain people invite you into an experience that will alter your world view forever. They have gone so deep, searched so thoroughly, traversed territories that most would shun, and then they return and lay their soul at your feet. Toko-pa is one such individual and this book is her soul made visible. She reaches her hand out to you and asks you to take a journey with her. If you are ready, take her hand and prepare to grow.

—Clare Dubois, International Speaker and Founder of TreeSisters

An exquisitely crafted journey that explores the deep longings of the soul, the mysterious workings of our dreams, the bittersweet wisdom of the orphaned self, and the losses of our lineage that we would rather ignore. Toko-pa Turner speaks with poetry and practicality, pure compassion and profound integrity to the heart of what it means to belong to ourselves, to our people, to our communities, and to the earth. *Belonging* is the book I have been longing to read all my life.

—Lucy H. Pearce, Amazon bestselling author of *Burning Woman*

Belonging is full of profound insights that flower from Toko-pa's powerful life experiences and her resilient, compassionate spirit. To me the central message of the book is that, to be truly original, you have to experience some sort of difference or exile from the 'club,' and take that initiatory journey. It's a message I believe we urgently need to hear today, as there is such a strong cultural emphasis on fighting our differences rather than allowing them to bring us to a full reclamation of our own unique selves. *Belonging* is breathtakingly compassionate and surefooted!

—Michelle Tocher, Mythologist and Author of *How to Ride a Dragon*

I cannot recommend this book highly enough! Not only is it full of timeless wisdom and glorious insights, it's quite possibly the most beautiful book I've ever read. Toko-pa's voice is one of beauty and one of necessity in a troubled world. I consider her a vessel for genius, someone who has a direct line to the soul of the world and knows how to translate soul-wisdom into words that feel like home.

—Seraphina Capranos, Herbalist & Homeopath

Toko-pa is such a wonderful, imaginative writer. Her love, intelligence, and bright ideas are shining on every page of this book.

—Angela Gygi, Story Researcher for Paramount, HBO, Netflix

With astounding clarity and compassion, Toko-pa guides us to embody a humanity deeply rooted in our belonging and reverence for the grand dance of life we are part of. Through her exquisite word-magic, she midwifes the deep wisdom of our souls into incarnation.

—**Chameli Ardagh, Founder, Awakening Women Institute**

Belonging is something quite extraordinary. It's more than just a book; it's an experience. As I read Toko-pa's writing, I found myself being transported, not to some distant place, but to my deepest core. *Belonging* is a mirror to our true face, revealing the exiled threads of our being so that we may gently re-weave them back into the greater fabric of which we are all a part. This is a book that provides living nourishment for these times and will be a classic for decades to come.

—**Bethany Webster, writer and international speaker on The Mother Wound**

Belonging

Remembering Ourselves Home

Belonging

Remembering Ourselves Home

Toko-pa Turner

Her Own Room Press

Cover art and interior illustrations copyright © 2017 by Molly Costello, used with permission. Cover layout and design by Toko-pa Turner.

Author photograph: Morgaine Owens.

ISBN-13: 978-1-7751112-0-7

First paperback edition: December, 2017
Third printing: February, 2019

www.toko-pa.com

Special discounts are available on quantity purchases of *Belonging* for book clubs, organizations, and others at www.belongingbook.com.

For orders by U.S. and Canadian trade bookstores and wholesalers, contact the publisher at ordering@herownroompress.com.

10 9 8 7 6 5 4 3

For Craig —
who is the ground
in which my belonging
is rooted.

Acknowledgments

I wish to thank Terri Kempton, my friend and my editor, for walking with me every step of the way, masterfully midwifing the birth of this book; Angela Gygi who read the manuscript and offered me her rigorous and valuable feedback; Caoimhe Merrick for her lavish pages of enthusiasm; Michelle Tocher for encouraging me to put my story front and centre; Molly Costello who summarizes in one artwork everything I want to say; my late mentor Annie Jacobsen who, despite my reluctance, kept insisting I was a writer; and most especially Craig Paterson, my beloved husband, for showing me every day how belonging is made, through his unwavering presence, wise reflection, and the sheltering generosity of his tenderness. Finally, I want to thank Salt Spring Island, for holding me in its mystical branches, and lending its moisture to my words.

Table of Contents

For the rebels and the misfits, the black sheep and the outsiders. For the refugees, the orphans, the scapegoats, and the weirdos. For the uprooted, the abandoned, the shunned and invisible ones.

May you recognize with increasing vividness that you know what you know.

May you give up your allegiances to self-doubt, meekness, and hesitation.

May you be willing to be unlikeable, and in the process be utterly loved.

May you be impervious to the wrongful projections of others, and may you deliver your disagreements with precision and grace.

May you see, with the consummate clarity of nature moving through you, that your voice is not only necessary, but desperately needed to sing us out of this muddle.

May you feel shored up, supported, entwined, and reassured as you offer yourself and your gifts to the world.

May you know for certain that even as you stand by yourself, you are not alone.

Love,

Toko-pa

One

Something Greater

To this world you belong. To this moment, in this place where you already stand, something greater has ushered you. To the momentum of a long line of survivors you are bound. From their good deaths, succeeded by new lives, and to the incidents of love that seeded them, your story has been woven. With the wild jubilation of nature, you are in correspondence. By every season's conditions, and by the invisible holy inclination, your life has been hewn.

And yet you may feel, as so many of us do, the ache of a life orphaned from belonging.

There are many ways to be made an orphan. Outright, by the parent incapable of caring for you, or by the ones who neglected to understand your gifts. By the System, which demands your loyalty but trades away your uniqueness. Or by history which, through intolerance and war, has made you a refugee.

But we are also made orphans by a culture that, in its epitomizing of certain values, rejects others, forcing us to split off from those unwanted parts of ourselves. And this is perhaps the worst orphaning act of all, because it is an abandonment in which we are complicit.

With this meagre scratch to begin it, without so much as the acknowledgment of all that we've been lost from, we must fare a way. We must begin with absence—a longing for what might never be assuaged—and follow it deep into the heart of exile, to discover what, if anything, can be made out of nothing. To make a foundling of the orphaned life.

Though it governs so much, belonging is rarely spoken about in the open. Like grief, death, and inadequacy, we are led to believe that to feel unbelonging is shameful and should be hidden from view. The great irony is that modern culture is suffering an epidemic of alienation, yet so many of us feel alone in our unbelonging, as if everyone else was inside of the thing that we alone are outside of. And keeping silent about our experience of estrangement is, in large part, what allows it to perpetuate.

We are living in fragmented times, with racism, sexism, xenophobia and other systemic forms of "othering" on the rise all over the world. Never before have we experienced such seismic migrations of humans across our borders as we do today. And the challenges of settlement and integration are vast and complex, even several generations down the line. Today, we find ourselves at a critical juncture, divided on the fault lines of politics, class, gender, and race. In its silent way, belonging is the central conversation of our times.

Certainly, one of the most influential motivators of my own life, the longing to belong, was shaping me in ways that I was largely unconscious of, until it finally grabbed me by the hair and pulled me deep into its terrifying dimensions. This book is the travelogue of the initiation that took years and a passage through seemingly endless gates, each of which required the relinquishment of something precious to me. And so, I write to you not as an expert in belonging, but as an orphan who needed to discover that there was more to lose before I could be found.

There are many different kinds of belonging. The first kind that comes to mind is the feeling of belonging in a community, or to a geography. But for many of us, longing to belong begins in our own families. Then there is the longing we feel to belong with an intimate other in the sanctuary of relationship, and the belonging we yearn to feel in a purpose or vocation. There is also spiritual longing to belong to a set of ways or traditions, the longing to know and participate in ancestral knowledge. And, though we may not even notice how its severance influences us, the ache to belong in our own bodies.

There are also subtler forms of belonging, like the one we must eventually create with our own story, and the gifts that have been forged from it. And, if we take a broader view, there is a belonging with the earth itself, which is felt (or not felt) at the heart of us all. Finally, there is the great belonging, which may be the most nebulous and persistent of all, the longing to belong to that "something greater" which gives our lives meaning.

The Living Bridge

In north-east India, high in the mountains of Meghalaya, the summer monsoons are so heavy that the rivers running through its valleys grow wild and unpredictable, making them impossible to cross. Centuries ago, the villagers came up with an artful solution. They planted a strangler fig on the riverbank and began to coax its ravelling roots across the river until they took hold on the opposite side.

Through a slow process of binding and weaving the roots together, the villagers created a sturdy, living bridge that could withstand the deluge of the summer rains. But because it is a labour that cannot be completed in any one person's lifetime, the knowledge of how to bind and tend to the roots has to be transmitted to each of the younger generations who keep the practice alive, contributing to what is now a thrilling network of living root bridges throughout the valleys of Meghalaya.[1]

If we take the living bridge as a metaphor for the work of belonging, we can imagine ourselves being stranded on one side of a dangerous river, longing to be connected to something greater that lies beyond our reach. Whether it is the yearning to find our true place, our people, or a meaningful relationship, the longing to belong is the great silent motivator behind so many of our other ambitions.

In my years of working with dreams, I have found this longing to belong at the heart of so many people's inquiries. It is the longing to be recognized for one's gifts, to be welcomed in love and kinship, to feel a sense of purpose and necessity to our community. But it is also the longing to open to the sacred dimension of our lives, to feel in service to something noble, to live in magic and wonder.

Yet alienation, belonging's dark sister, is so pervasive that we might call it epidemic. We are more technologically connected to one another than we've ever been, and yet never more lonely and estranged. We are the generations who have missed receiving the inheritance of knowledge that will bridge us back to belonging. But what's worse is that, in our amnesia, we often don't even know what's missing.

More and more, our interactions with one another are being supplanted by machines. Whether it's through digital communication, customer service robots, or retail machines where humans used to be, we are becoming captives of the mechanical age. Designed by corporate interest, we are reduced to consumers, cogs in the very machine to which we are beholden. This larger, often hidden entity is a substantial part of what contributes to us feeling dehumanized, giving us the sense that we are expendable. We don't love the machine, and it doesn't love us back.

We try to get on, contributing our small piece to the mechanical choreography of things, but there is a sense of purposelessness which plagues us. We unconsciously feel that there is something greater to which we long to belong. And though we may not be able to articulate what it is, we perceive others belonging to this greater something while we look in from the outside.

We ache to have our absence from the circle of belonging noticed. It poisons us from the inside out. Though we try to stay busy, the hidden loneliness underneath is rarely assuaged. Given the first breath of silence, there is an upwelling of alienation so great that it threatens to swallow us whole. No matter how much we accumulate or accomplish, the pang of unbelonging continues to pierce from within.

And so we treat our lives like a project for improvement, attempting to become useful, admired, impervious or savvy. We work at cutting off any unwieldiness that may be preventing us from fitting in. But as this "self-development" encroaches upon our inner wilderness, our dreams and our connection to the holy suffers. As we harness every last resource in service to the unconscious longing to belong, we feel less and less at home.

This is our starting place: right in that raw fissure of our lostness, down in the ache to find our place in the family of things. Before we even ask ourselves how to heal our estrangement, we must first sink down into the wound itself and apprentice ourselves to it. We must enter into the question of what has been missing from us. Of what are we being deprived? Only when we lower ourselves down into that holy longing can we get a glimpse of the majesty we are meant to become.

Dreaming Ourselves Home

Human beings have a natural urge to worship that "something greater" which coheres us, but we, in modernity, are living in a kind of spiritual cul-de-sac where our gifts only serve ourselves. Unlike the many shamanic cultures that practice dreamwork, ritual, and thanksgiving, Westerners have forgotten what indigenous people understand to be cardinal: that this world owes its life to the unseen. Every hunt and every harvest, every death and every birth is distinguished by beauty-making and ceremony for that which we cannot see, feeding back that which feeds us. I believe our alienation is the felt negligence of that reciprocity.

Although every culture has its own mythologies, the animistic way of seeing the world is to know that spirit lives in everything. Not just the human people, but the people with four-legs, the tall standing ones, the far-seeing feathered ones, the strong and silent cliff people, those sleeping mountain dreamers, and the always-up-for-a-conversation river people. Sometimes you can even catch spirit in the curve of a ceramic cup.

While animistic cultures live in a reciprocity with what author and Mayan shaman Martín Prechtel calls the "holy in nature," we have become a culture infatuated with literality and rationalism. Divorced from myth and the symbolic life, our personal stories cease to have meaning in a larger collective momentum. Also atrophying in this separation, is our ability to imagine, wonder, and envision a way forward.

But each of us has a private gateway back into kinship with mystery—through our dreaming life. The practice of dreamwork is a powerful way of weaving back into intimate relationship with what the Sufis call the Beloved: that divine coherence, the holy in nature, from which all beings originate. As we remember it, it remembers us. Like the living bridge between two riverbanks, our conversation is the practice of belonging together. Throughout this book, I will be sharing dreams, my own and from those who have kindly given their permission, which beautifully illustrate the different gates on the path to belonging.

The way that I understand it, dreaming is nature *naturing* through us. Just as a tree bears fruit or a plant expresses itself in flowers, dreams are fruiting from us. The production of symbols and story is a biological necessity. Without dreams, we could not survive. And though it is possible to get by without remembering our dreams, a life guided and shaped by dreaming is a life that follows the innate knowing of the earth itself. As we learn to follow the instincts of our inner wilderness, respecting its agreements and disagreements, we are also developing our capacity for subtlety. This sensitivity is what makes us more porous and multilingual, bringing us into conversation with the many languages of the world around us.

Sensitivity is the privilege and responsibility of remembering. As Oscar Wilde wrote, "a dreamer is one who can only find his way by moonlight, and his punishment is that he sees the dawn before the rest of the world." As we come to understand the symmetry between the outer landscape and the inner wilderness, we can't help but grieve the ways in which our own nature has been tampered with, denigrated, broken into obedience, and in many cases eradicated from memory. We begin to face the ways in which we are complicit in this slow apocalypse, within and without. Only from such a place of loss and longing can we begin remembering ourselves home.

This book is an attempt to exalt what I understand to be the broader definition of dreamwork: the practice of weaving a living bridge between the seen and the unseen, an endeavour that can only be made with patience, an aptitude for grief, and a willingness to assume a stake in the way things turn out, even if we won't live to see the benefits. This is the practice of belonging.

With this writing I hope to spare you, brave wayfarer, some of the confusions on this initiatory path. I will introduce you, as I have been introduced, to the different faces of belonging and how we came to be estranged from them in the first place. We'll look at the influences that can cause us to become diminished versions of ourselves, which is also how we are seduced into taking up residence in "false belonging." We'll meet the archetype of the outcast, and then descend into the dimensions of exile, a painful but necessary attrition into true belonging. There, we will encounter the otherness within that wants to belong to us. This is the grand endeavour I like to call Remembership. Most of us think of belonging as a mythical place, that if we keep diligently searching for, we might eventually find. But what if belonging isn't a place at all, but a skill: a set of competencies that we, in modern life, have lost or forgotten? Like the living bridge, these competencies are the ways in which we can coax, weave, and tend to the roots of our separation—and in so doing, restore our membership in belonging.

Two

Origins of Estrangement

ike so many others, my quest for belonging was seeded in alienation. I remember a recurring scene at the dinner table when, after an episode of hurt, I would run upstairs to my room in tears, desperate for my mother to come after me and coax me back into belonging. But she never came. Instead, I would creep back onto the stairs outside the kitchen, secretly listening to my family going on without me while my belly rumbled with hunger.

And though we all have our version of *the waiting stairs*, at its heart this is what it is to feel outside of belonging. It is the excruciating belief that you are not needed. That life does not consider you necessary. When nobody comes after you with invitations, it confirms your worst fear and sends you pushing further into the province of exile, even towards the cold beckoning of death.

Symbolically speaking, I spent many years of my life on those waiting stairs: hungry for love, aching to be recognized as missing, wishing someone might call me back into belonging. And when leaving the table wasn't enough to make my family miss me, my departures became further, longer, and eventually total.

When I was nine, I found a condemned house that I tried to make my own. There was a small space between the two-by-fours nailed across the back door that I pried apart to gain entry. Over the weeks, I scavenged for things that could brighten up that dingy, rotting hideaway. I found a broom and swept up some of the debris, snuck away with snacks and drew pictures for the walls. Some broken furniture did well enough and, for a time, I played at being really gone.

This early impulse may have been the first sign that something in me wanted to separate, to distinguish myself from my family of origin. Even as decrepit and dangerous as it was, I was drawn to creating a new self. A life of my own. Of course, I was too young to take care of myself and when the house grew black at dusk, I would reluctantly return home without ever being noticed as missing.

When people hear that I was raised in a Sufi ashram, their faces light up. I can only imagine the exotic image it must conjure for people who come from a more conservative upbringing. Suddenly, it is as if I make some new kind of sense to people, as they call to mind whirling dervishes and the poetry of Rumi and Gibran. And it's true that for my young heart, living in a devotional community where music, prayer and poetry were woven into every day, was a brief time of belonging. But like many spiritual communities, it also cast a profound shadow.

We had eighteen rooms in our house filled with transient devotees, but despite its sprawling size, it was far from luxurious. It was an old tenement situated in the red-light district of Montreal, with bats scratching in the walls and prostitutes and drug dealers right outside our front door. We were very poor and made do with shared resources. I remember the bitter Quebec winter when we had our utilities shut off and had to sleep huddled together by a fire. But as a child, none of this bothered me. There was always some character to be entertained by—musicians, artists, gypsies and intellectuals—and every summer we retreated to a yoga ashram in the Laurentians, with visiting teachers like the Sufi master Pir Vilayat Inayat Khan.

More than anything, I remember the music. The Sufi songs were a mixture of Hindu, Sanskrit and Arabic devotions to the Beloved. They were invocations to open the heart, to give voice to our longing to return to the divine reedbed from which we human-reeds were plucked. We were always praying and chanting *zikr*, dancing until we were ecstatic.

I was eight when my mother and stepfather became pregnant with my sister, and my grandmother moved our family out of the commune and into a semi-detached house in the suburbs. Perhaps it was the sudden close quarters, the stress of a having a new baby in abject poverty, or perhaps it was the suburbs themselves which felt like an alien culture to us all, but it was as if I came to know my family for the first time. Home revealed itself as a place of volatility, conflict, and neglect.

My stepfather was considered a spiritual leader in the Sufi community, but behind closed doors he was emotionally detached and physically violent. And my mother, a yoga teacher and herbalist, was one of those people who could infect you with her creativity and enthusiasm; but as easily as she'd go up, she went down. Prone to severe bouts of depression and rage for which she never sought treatment, my mother's moods wreaked havoc in our home. Depending on the day or even the hour, she could swing from mania to despondency and meanness, so we all learned to walk on eggshells around her. In times of depression she was suicidal, deeply afflicted by her belief that nobody loved or valued her.

As a small person of eight, my heart broke for my mother. All I could see was her beauty and felt it was my mission to comfort and reassure her, pull her back into the shelter of love. But like a flash storm, her skies would darken and she would snipe at me in fits of cruelty. Perhaps because of her own unmetabolized grief, she was repulsed by any show of emotion. When I cried, she would keep a good distance from me and tell me I was being over-dramatic, or say that I'd brought it upon myself.

My earliest dreams were of my mother abandoning me. I dreamed she would leave me in a dangerous alley at night because I'd inadvertently wounded her. Or I'd be left to kidnappers who would tie me up to a bullseye and throw darts at me. Indeed, it felt like there were two versions of my mother: one who I felt responsible for, and the other who made me her target.

The more I tried to be loved, the more alone I found myself in the deepening dark. Soon I began to practice at withdrawal.

By the time I was eleven, I was preoccupied with thoughts of suicide. What I didn't understand was that I was internalizing the rejection I felt from my family. Suicide was the ultimate self-rejection; it was a way to 'make real' the deadening impulse that was closing in on my heart. When I was fourteen going on fifteen, I ran away for good. For a while, I panhandled for money, slept on floors, and made the worst kinds of friends. Eventually I was apprehended by the police who took me to a detention shelter where I was committed into what we called the System.

The System was an organization of government-run, ironically named 'care facilities' for orphans. Some of us were abandoned, some abused or neglected, some with qualities too strange to manage. Like myself, many orphans still had parents in the world, but for a jumble of reasons were cut loose, drifting on the margins, in various stages of physical and spiritual homelessness. Terrified and confused, with no meaningful source of guidance, most of the kids turned to gangs, violence, drugs, and self-harming.

The years that followed were the darkest of my life and yet somehow I understood that living in exile was an improvement upon the life of wishing myself dead. At least here I was in the company of orphans, and we were unbelonging together.

Healing the heart's contractions from love can be a lifelong endeavour. But for the many of us who have been fractured in spirit, it must be said that there is a medicine to be retrieved from exile. That medicine, the treasure lost and recovered, is one that might otherwise never be known. If you can stand fully in your own unbelonging and become friendly with the terrors of loneliness and exclusion, you can no longer be governed by your avoidance of them. In other words, you are on your way home.

The Origins of Estrangement

In considering the origins of our estrangement, we must begin in our personal stories. Though our experiences vary greatly from person to person, we share more similarities than differences. As children we are naturally inclined to wonder, dreaming, and discovery. We can live long hours in make-believe, consulting with nature, experimenting with sensations and ideas, assured in our own safety, confident in the impossible.

Like the Garden of Eden itself, it is a time of harmony, abundance, and the absence of shame. But at a certain point each of us, some sooner than others, experiences a gradual or sudden estrangement from our native relationship to magic. We may be told to get our head out of the clouds, that it's *only* in our imagination, or it's *just* a dream. We are asked to decide what we want to be when we grow up, told how 'a proper lady' should behave, thrust into public life at school, and otherwise initiated abruptly into the ways of consensus reality.

For some, this first estrangement may be shaped by trauma, abuse or neglect. Maybe you were made to care for the needs of others while your own inner life was dismissed, humiliated or ignored. Maybe you were made to feel necessary in only one way, while the true inclinations of your belonging were sent like fugitives underground.

Maybe you, and anyone like you, was maligned by the culture in which you were raised. Maybe the demands of your environment forced you to put your gifts out of sight while you attended to something more immediate.

Whatever the particulars of your first estrangement, you will have felt the rift being torn between who you really are, and who you had to be to survive. And so begins the work of moulding our qualities into this more acceptable version of ourselves. Over time, these efforts at 'passing' as normal become all-too-successful, until even we begin to forget our true nature.

As a kid, I remember being told regularly that I was too talkative, too loud, and too dramatic, so I began to practice at acting 'cool.' This coolness is something you recognize in most urban teenagers. Though their insides are a colourful explosion of hormones and passion, desperation, and longing, they do whatever it takes to pretend they don't care about anything. And it works!

After some practice at pushing my own expressiveness down, I remember being praised for having 'mellowed out,' as if the previous, authentic version of myself was annoying or embarrassing to others. But this suppression can take an enormous toll as we get older.

Those qualities and abilities that are banned from inclusion in our families, churches, schools, and other social milieus don't cease to exist because we ignore them. Rather they tend to turn on their keepers, like the bids for acknowledgment they are, taking the form of depression or illness, anger or rebellion.

The pathologizing of rebellion in teenagers is one of the great harms we inflict upon our children. As the future shapers of our culture, there is a reason why so many cultures perform ritual initiations into adulthood. Rebellion, if given proper reverence, is the necessary confrontation with society that ensures our sustainability. Just as any relationship must allow for the tension of conflict to deepen our intimacy, so must our young people be invited to contribute their disagreements to our shared aliveness. This is a threshold in a young person's life when the dynamic between elders and youngers reverses. No longer is the old one in the position to teach, but now must become the listener. After all these elders have imparted, personally and vicariously through culture, they now have the chance at hearing from the young ones how they've been doing.

It is here that the ache and rage of unbelonging is most needed. In the young person's disagreements and willingness to talk back to injustice, a wild storehouse of creative energy lives and thrives. While other cultures treat this transition with enormous significance, we make a tragic mess of it, treating our young people as aberrant and unruly, needing to be reformed and taught obedience. Instead of inviting the new adult into a seat of authority in our circle of belonging, asking them to galvanize our outdated structures, their passion is driven into shame and repression.

This rejection has consequences. When the emerging power, both physiological and psychic, is overtly rejected, it can never fulfil its purpose as the foundation of self-worth that it is. Without the welcoming ritual which says, "your blood is necessary, your anger is valuable, your pain is meaningful," the young person finds no place to commit his allegiance and drifts instead into greater distances of alienation.

The day I left home for good, it was in socked feet. My mother had hidden all of my boots and shoes before she went to bed. Determined as I was at fifteen years old, I left anyway, running down the street in my socks, hoping not to step on anything in the dark. A few days later the police tracked me down at my older boyfriend's house. Threatening him with charges, they took me away in the back of their patrol car. In a moment that will always remain frozen in time, one of the officers turned to me and asked if I wanted them to take me back home. And with all the certainty in the world, I replied, "No."

The alternative, I came to learn, would be a terrifying youth detention centre where I would be stripped of my belongings. Afraid that I might hang myself in the tiny cell with a slot for food and a single red button for alarm, they even took my belt away. I was sent to bathe with the other girls, given tiny issues of toothpaste and soap, dried with barely-big-enough towels. Quantities meant for people so small, they weren't really there. Water ran without taps in independent bursts, concrete doors locked themselves down and lights extinguished on timers without switches.

My mother did come to visit me once, but all I remember is how much like a wild animal I felt with her on the other side of the Plexiglas. Though I wanted nothing more than to be coaxed home again, I think she was relieved that I was finally being contained. Before I knew it, the various agencies were putting into motion a court case in which I was "voluntarily committed" into the System.

I wasn't sure why I was there. Because the things that I suffered with were the intangible, unnameable absences in my life, I lived for years with the invalidating belief that my experience of trauma wasn't significant. I believed, as my mother repeatedly told me, that I was being overdramatic and that I'd ruined our family. It would take decades to realize the little acorn of my destiny needed that awful soil to grow strong in. I needed to know real sadness and inhabit my aloneness, so I could discover that no love was better than halfway love. I needed to break from that which, in the name of love, despises, envies and resents.

The System tossed me around for months, from shelters to group homes, making it impossible to replant my dangling, thirsting roots. Just as I would begin to attach myself to an overloaded social worker, she would be reassigned. They never said goodbye. Nonetheless, I repeated the terrible ritual of unpacking my few small things only to be shuttled off again, usually in the night. This is how I learned about transience and how to shift my shape as a matter of survival.

In the attempt to belong, one can become masterfully adaptable, like a chameleon who changes her colours to blend into her environment. I learned to tune into my surroundings for any subtle threats, anticipate its needs and becomes useful where I'd landed. I would make myself quickly familiar with a place, learning its shortcuts and customs in order to appear as if I belonged there. But the irony is that in my adaptability, I could never earn a true sense of belonging.

Though the outcast learns to shift her shape to suit any habitat, it makes it harder to know her own true colours. She may feel free from imagined or

27

real constraints, but also yearn to trust a place, people, or vocation enough to invest her roots down into its soil. And that kind of aloneness, which knows no enduring home, can exact a toll over time.

Alienation continues to follow the person who burns bridges behind them. You may leave pieces of yourself behind in those places and times that you've made some cursory bond with. The more you leave, the more splintered you become. If you are such a person, you may even have achieved outer accomplishment but find that you are missing a sense of intimacy with the life you've built.

As a consequence of having exposed your true nature somewhere it was rejected, you become protective of those places. You can't bear to be hurt again, so you refuse to reveal who you really are anymore. You stop living from that place of truth and, over time, unwillingness turns into an alienation from your own nature.

Over time we no longer feel the acuteness of that which is missing from us. Instead, the absence itself becomes malignant and spreads like an indistinguishable depression or anxiety. Quite simply put, when we feel outcast, we are being shown the parts of ourselves we have cast out.

The Straight and Narrow

Our dreams are the first place where the alienated self will appear. Psychic energy that has been cast out can take many forms as it compulsively tries to re-belong to us. This is why I tell people that dark dreams are a validation, in and of themselves, because they mean that something is ready to come to consciousness. Nightmares are just dreams that have turned up their volume, trying devotedly to get our attention for something that is ready to be healed. But if we continue to ignore it, this rejected energy may take the shape of psychological symptoms like anxiety, panic attacks, rage, or depression.

Take Elaine, for example, a woman in her early fifties who grew up in a very traditional Christian family. Through a series of awakenings into her own values, she turned to dreamwork in order to come to terms with her longing for a different way of life. Because leaving the Church also meant breaking with community, livelihood, and family allegiances, it was an excruciating and gradual process. In the midst of it, Elaine had the following dream:

The Straight and Narrow, Elaine's dream

I am with my sister, a devout Christian, entering a shut-down mall to go shopping. The passageway to the inside is very narrow and when I am about halfway in, a terrifying dark figure who means me harm starts grabbing at me. I fall backwards and am stuck there,

28

restrained and screaming for help. A ghost-like figure then appears and gives me an injection to "shut me up." I feel calmer, but I am still stuck.

As we explored the dream, Elaine described the mall as a social place where everyone consumed what was given to them under the pressure to be "happy all the time." As she said those words, it struck her how similar she felt that pressure was within the Church.

That the mall was shut down, closed for business, seemed to reflect how Elaine had shut down many of those influences in her life. Yet there were still some deep bonds, like her relationship with her sister, which kept her 'shopping' there. Despite how 'straight and narrow' that world felt to her newly expanded perspective, she wasn't ready to leave it completely.

I asked Elaine what she remembered about the dark figure who grabbed at her and all she could recall was that he wore "fingerless gloves, like a beggar." Thanks to that small detail we began to understand that this figure, in the narrow transition between inside and out, was the archetype of the outcast. He was everything the mall-church was working to avoid. He was a lone wolf, rejected from society, without standing, wealth or belonging. And he was grabbing Elaine, like anyone's worst fear does, with the belief that if she didn't keep squeezing herself into that world, she might end up on the outside of society.

When I asked Elaine what it felt like to receive that quieting injection, she said it had a paralyzing effect on her. Struck by the contrast between how she'd been desperately calling for help to suddenly feeling anaesthetized, I asked her if she'd been experiencing any depression. "Yes," she answered right away, "I was feeling a huge upheaval of emotions a few weeks ago and then slipped into a kind of depression."

If we take all the figures in Elaine's dream as aspects of her self, then we might see the outcast character as the part of her that has been shunned, living outside of belonging. Dreamwork, for instance, is a subject she never brings up with her family or church friends though it is one of her great passions. But desperate for Elaine's attention, the outcast parts of herself became grabby and harmful, like any neglected or maligned being will.

As a result of their differences, the outcast is either banished from belonging or sometimes leaves voluntarily, no longer able to withstand the conditions of normalcy. Either way, they become a wanderer, perpetually seeking a place to call home.

Like Elaine, the hero or heroine in mythical tales must cross a threshold where she breaks from tradition so that she can know who she is outside the expectations of the kingdom. But without the help of dreams and fairy tales to navigate these symbolic departures, the outcast may get stuck in a lifetime identification with the unredeemed archetype.

Archetype of the Outcast

Like many other pack hunters, humans are guarded and suspicious of difference. Whether you have committed a crime, come from another country, possess different abilities, characteristics or orientations—or even because you are poor, sick or injured—you may find yourself identifying with the archetype of the outcast: an orphan, black sheep, rebel, outsider, dissident, scapegoat, weirdo, homeless, beggar, misfit. By whatever name, the outcast plays an important role in mythology and in life.

In every family, and in many folk tales, there is a designated black sheep. This outsider carries the shadow projection for the whole group. In their collective rejection of him or her, the black sheep is a uniting force. In other words, they become the carrier of the rejected, undiscovered and forgotten pieces of the family story and, by living life in their own way, the black sheep is often responsible for bringing the family to consciousness.

But as heroic as that may sound, it is a lonely, difficult path. Whether by abandonment or choice, being estranged from or without a family puts unbelonging at the foundation of our lives. A feeling of homelessness can live like a persistent condition in the psyche, colouring everything we do.

In some cultures, being an orphan means you'll be disowned from society. In Zambia, for instance, orphans are humiliated and called "goats" because they are considered 'cultureless' for not having gone through the proper initiations and customs of the collective.[2] Yet in other places, foundlings are considered special wards of the tribe, protected and even venerated. Among the Akan people of Ghana there is an old folk song called "Sansa Kroma" in which "children singing this song are reminded that if anything happened to their parents and they became orphans...they would be protected by the village."[3] When we examine the folktales of orphans from around the world, we find many of the same recurring motifs. "Orphans are at once pitiable and noble," Melanie Kimball, Professor of Children's Literature at Simmons College in Boston, writes. "They are a manifestation of loneliness, but they also represent the possibility for humans to reinvent themselves."[4]

Let us imagine for a moment that we could strip our varied stories of exile down to their bare essence to find what we have in common with everyone who has experienced something similar. This set of patterns and redemptions are what we call the 'archetype'.

Archetypes, from the Greek *archetupos*, meaning 'first-moulded,' are the blueprints of our innate, universal experiences. Like the Hero, the Wise Old Woman, and the Trickster, these common archetypes can be found in myths and fairy tales from around the world, seemingly unconstrained by geography or era, and their patterns appear in our dreams during meaningful transitions in our human lives. Archetypes show us that we aren't just leading insignificant lives, but stepping through the same gates with bravery and despair, awe and triumph, as the heroes and heroines whom we grew up admiring in our storybooks.

As Jungian analyst Ann Bedford Ulanov puts it, "As the instincts are to the body, so the archetypes are to the psyche."[5] In other words, archetypes are innate reflexes which get triggered by certain conditions in our environment and, whether for better or worse, determine how we react and behave.

By studying how dreams and fairy tales work, we can then follow their archetypal maps with greater agency into the unknown because they help us to see the meaningful dimension of our personal experience. They show us when we are undergoing universal rites of passage such as initiation, exile, symbolic death, and rebirth.

The Outcast/Orphan archetype appears in hundreds of folk tales, books of fiction, and even films. Literary characters like Cinderella, the Little Match Girl, Jane Eyre, Frodo Baggins, and Harry Potter are well-known Outcasts. The Outcast is often an orphan who lives outside of caste or social class. He is seen as different from or dangerous to the social customs and norms. He is the uncomfortable Other, unique and alone in the world, who reminds us how close we all are to being cut loose, to being without support. But from rags to riches, he also inspires us to remember that even the most tragic stories of isolation can be overcome.

So these archetypes are not just single images, or characters, but patterns of unfolding. The orphan in these tales always suffers some form of mistreatment, abuse, or neglect in her place of origin. Then there is a quest or journey put before her, which she must undertake to find her true place in the world. But to do so she must leave home, breaking from her established group or family, to endure a long period of exile.

During this time of wandering, she will at times be overcome with hardship and feel close to giving up. But if she summons the wit and virtue to hold her own standpoint, magical allies will show up to assist her. In the end, her triumph is a place of belonging in the world that is unimpeachable, not only because has she wrought it from scratch, but because it is large enough to shelter others.

Three

The Death Mother

*W*hen I was eleven years old, my grandmother gave me my deceased grandfather's wedding ring. I treasured it above all other possessions. It was made of white gold, etched with elegant carvings and, most precious of all, had his name, *Tadeusz*, inscribed on the inside of the band. One day, I made the mistake of going swimming with it and it slipped off my finger. I spent two hours diving to the bottom of the pool looking for it, but each time I came up empty and exhausted. I was too ashamed to tell anyone, but when we had dinner at my grandmother's house the next weekend, she noticed it missing. I told her I was so sorry that I'd lost it. My mother turned to me and venomously spat, "You can't trust Toko with anything valuable."

Taken on its own, an event like this could be seen as a mother parenting poorly in a weak moment, but as the latest in a steady stream of cruel occasions, it was the campaign that eventually convinced me that I was inadequate, untrustworthy, and undeserving of a place at the family table.

If, like me, you grew up feeling unseen, invalidated, or worse—with the unspoken communication that you were unwanted or wished dead—you may be the child of a woman possessed by the Death Mother.

The Death Mother is a term for this energy or archetype that resents, abandons, and even wants to destroy her child. Death Mother was originally coined by Jungian analyst Marie-Louise von Franz,[6] and later fleshed out by author, teacher and Jungian analyst Marion Woodman in her interview with Daniela Sieff, "Confronting the Death Mother."[7] As the Death Mother's target, the child eventually develops the conviction that she is living in a dangerous world and that her life is at risk.[8] But long after leaving the family home, the child is haunted by the Death Mother, who campaigns against her from the inside out.

Before you even think about attempting something new, engaging your creativity, using your voice, or stepping towards change, the Death Mother is there. Like Medusa, she only needs to raise a single eyebrow for your whole body to turn to stone. She is the paralytic energy that dismisses your creativity and demands your silence. She feeds on your shame and powerlessness and is provoked by any show of emotion or colour.

No longer able to withstand the pain of rejection, the child will stop offering her creative spark. She hides it away where it can't be criticized, believing, as she's been taught, that it's worthless. As Woodman puts it, "Her unique creative core is split off and buried in a hidden recess of her unconscious psyche."[9]

Instead, the child of the Death Mother does what he can to survive. He begins to perform the role he thinks will ingratiate him with his mother, attempting to behave in a way that might solidify his tenuous place in belonging. Whether this manifests in perfectionism to reach Mother's impossible standards, becoming fiercely independent of her, or becoming her champion and caretaker—even surrogate husband—the child attempts to be valuable in any way that he can to weather this hostile environment.

But no matter how we attempt to outsmart her, we inevitably internalize the Death Mother; we begin conflating her voice with our own. Operating internally, the Death Mother is devastating to a person's life. As Woodman writes, "If this child knew in the womb that it was not the gender the parents longed for, or there was no money for another child, or timing in the marriage was bad, or it barely escaped abortion, this child knows it is not welcomed into life...not wanted. Is there anything worse for a helpless infant to experience in its bones?"[10] And as the child gets older, she will project this being *not wanted* onto others, anticipating rejection from friends, authority figures, even life itself. Worst of all, the child will turn that stone-cold glare on herself.

Learning about the Death Mother was a revelation for me, because it explained why I had been suicidal at such a young age. Suicide, or the "yearning for the oblivion of death," was a way of taking up the Death Mother campaign against myself. Suicide was the concretized version of the rejection I felt aimed at me everyday.

I found myself living in what Sieff calls a "trauma-world," a parallel psychological reality characterized by fear, disconnection, and shame. Most of us think of trauma as something brought on by a physically or sexually violent event, or series of events, but researchers are now discovering that there are many subtle, insidious forms of trauma that evoke the same set of responses in the body and nervous system. Witnessing violence, chronic instability or chaos in the childhood home, emotional neglect, and lack of secure attachment with your primary caregiver because they are chronically depressed, mentally ill, volatile, or suicidal—all of these can create the conditions for emotional trauma in a young person.

We are fundamentally changed by trauma, not only psychologically, but at the cellular level as well. Internalized, the Death Mother takes the form of self-abdication, especially towards our own bodies. As Woodman describes, "When I am hungry, I am not fed. When I'm exhausted, I'm not allowed to rest. When I need to move, I'm forced to stay still." Sieff further explains, "In response to experiencing overwhelming pain and fear, biological changes occur that leave our minds and bodies extremely sensitive to potential danger…we see threats where perhaps none exist, and we over-react to these imagined threats in ways that create self-fulfilling prophecies."

I remember hitchhiking to a concert once when my car was out of commission, and I got picked up by a crone in a very dirty car. When I opened the door, I saw a pile of dog hair and debris on the seat, so I started to brush it off before sitting down in my white skirt. The driver sniped at me, "Just get in! This isn't some kind of a taxi service!" Suddenly I was frozen. I spent the whole ride unable to speak, consumed with anger and shame. As fate would have it, when I arrived at the concert, the crone was seated right next to me. I remember silently obsessing with thoughts of injustice, then immediately volleying to the opposite, attacking myself for being too precious. It was a replay of the chronic internal argument I had with my mother, as if always trying to make a case for the validity of my hurt feelings…and losing. Soon I was overcome with a feeling of being an exile, as if everyone at the concert was inside something I was outside of. By the time the night was over, I was deep in a shame spiral that took days to escape.

Amazing that such an insignificant trigger could lead me to such despair. But when you live in a 'trauma-world,' your responses are generated by a compromised nervous system, which assumes you are always under threat of being attacked or abandoned even if there's no real danger.

The Death Mother hits you in the body, stops you in your tracks, silences you before you can even speak. She is that paralyzing energy which stops you from participating in life. This is what Woodman calls "possum mentality," where "life is experienced as a minefield in which we are knocked down by explosions that are inaudible to others. If there is unconscious hostility in the environment, the inner body, acting autonomously, retreats and falls over 'dead.'" [11]

To heal the wound left by the Death Mother, it's helpful to understand her origins and how she came to be such a terrifying expression of nature. If we turn to the myth of Medusa, we learn that Medusa wasn't always a dreadful monster with a head of serpents who turned others to stone. Before she became the one who would persecute and *objectify* others, she was herself objectified.

Medusa was the most ravishing of three sisters—an enchanting maiden with golden ringlets. And while many suitors aspired to win her favour, Poseidon took her for his own, raping her in Athena's temple. Filled with vengeance for the desecration of her temple, Athena put a curse on Medusa, turning her beautiful hair into serpents and making her so ugly that gazing upon her would turn onlookers to stone.

For our purposes here, I'd like to focus on two aspects of this myth: how Athena persecuted Medusa for desecrating her temple, and how Medusa's terrifying form as a gorgon was the result of her own violation.

Athena was born from her father Zeus' head, in full armour, ready for battle. You could say she was the ultimate father's daughter, deeply identified with patriarchal values like reason, strength, and victory. Though we think of Medusa as the embodiment of feminine rage, she was once known best for her sensual beauty and loving relationship with her sisters. Taken symbolically, we could say these two women represent the cultural split of the feminine, between civic and primal, *logos* and *eros*, obedient and wild. It is the same split we see mirrored in other places, such as the biblical story of Mary and Mary Magdalene. As a virgin goddess, perhaps Athena was threatened by Medusa's life-giving, primal energy, so she cursed her to become a monster. But let us not forget that it was an act of unspeakable violence which was really at the centre of this split.

When Medusa was raped by Poseidon, and later murdered by Perseus, it is symbolic of the cultural subjugation of the wild and unruly feminine that she represents. The name *Medusa* (*Medha* in Sanskrit, *Metis* in Greek, and *Maat* in Egyptian) means 'sovereign female wisdom,' so her violation can also be seen as the vanquishing of Goddess religions by the male-dominated culture led by Zeus. To survive these conditions, women have had to become as Athena was, aligned with her father in order to thrive. But the consequence of being a 'good daughter' or a 'good mother' is that the darkness, represented by Medusa's banished fury, will rise up in unpredictable ways.

Have you ever noticed in fairy tales how often the protagonist's mother is either dead, missing, or supplanted by an evil stepmother? For example, in the tale of *Snow White*, the wicked stepmother is so jealous of the girl's beauty that she exiles her and sends a hunter to cut the heart out of her body. Or in *Hansel and Gretel*, the woodcutter's wife convinces her husband to send the twins into the forest in the hopes that they won't find their way home and starve. It is so inadmissible to us that a mother could be capable of such dark, even murderous acts towards her children that we have replaced her with another woman who feels no emotional attachment.

The truth is that many mothers struggle with feeling ambivalent towards their children, even to the point of wishing they were never born. We occasionally hear horrifying stories of mothers who have killed their own children. And while most women would never be driven to this extreme, many can relate to the rage, desperation, and exhaustion that can precipitate violence.

Though I am not myself a mother, I have many friends who are mamas and I see how hard they are on themselves for becoming impatient or angry with their children. I think this is because in our culture we deny the shadow side of mothering. We hold up an idealized archetype of the Good Mother who embodies unconditional love, compassion and nurturing. But the problem with this one-sided perspective is that it teaches both mother and child that anything less than a Good Mother is aberrant or unnatural.

In her fascinating essay "The Death Mother as Nature's Shadow,"[12] author and anthropologist Daniela Sieff looks at the dark side of mothering through an evolutionary lens, exploring how a few central factors, such as the availability of calories and social support, contribute greatly to the inclination (or not) of a mother to bond with her child. Sieff describes how in some traditional subsistence societies it isn't uncommon to abandon or kill an infant in the absence of those things. For reasons of survival, "she cannot commit to her infants indiscriminately; rather she must take account of both her own circumstances and the characteristics of the child when deciding whether to nurture [them] or not."[13]

In the Western world we are richer in resources and, thankfully, infanticide is quite rare. Yet in exploring these evolutionary underpinnings, Sieff helps us to see that however unsettling, destructive impulses are a natural dimension of mothering. While not every woman will be driven to the extreme of the Death Mother, if she feels unsupported, invisible, and stretched to her limits, she will be susceptible to possession by her own shadow. So long as we lionize the Good Mother and don't acknowledge her dark counterpoint, women will be doomed to act it out unconsciously.

Unless we recognize the barriers that mothers face, finding ways as a village to give them the support they need, the hidden shame of a woman's felt inadequacy to the Good Mother image eventually turns upon her, as unacknowledged shadows do, and begins to express itself destructively both internally and towards those who are in her path. The children of those mothers also suffer in our culture's disavowal of mothering's shadow side. It may cause them to question the validity of their experience with her darkness, creating the conditions to repeat the cycle of the Death Mother.

Scarcity and Worthiness

Scarcity is the underlying condition of the Death Mother archetype. It makes us believe that we never have enough, that there are always greener pastures to reach, instead of belonging ourselves to what is right in front of us. Most of us think of scarcity as a physical lack of abundance, affection, and belonging. And while we may certainly suffer with too little of these things, scarcity is most insidious as an inner condition.

Learning, as we do, from our parents, and them from theirs, scarcity can be deeply entrenched in our family lines. Scarcity is the belief that no matter how much (or how little) there is, it is never enough. Whether we are the workaholic who can never accomplish enough, or the perfectionist who has difficulty releasing anything into the world because it's not good enough yet, our entire lives can take on a feeling of not-enoughness.

You may have some money, but it isn't enough to do what you really want. You may have one or two friends, but you don't have 'community.' You may have an opportunity, but it'll take a miracle to make it real. You may have a lover, but you don't have a family. Like having a gorgeous view out of your windows and narrowing in on the peeling paint of the walls, we focus on what's missing rather than cultivating an attentiveness to the beauty right in front of us. This is Death Mother's campaign: to reinforce deprivation until it becomes normal.

My mother once told me that after I was born, my brother began to throw tantrums every time she sat down to nurse me. She would put me down to attend to him—but after a few weeks of these interruptions, her breast milk dried up. This always stood out to me as both a literal and deeply symbolic representation of the scarcity that characterized our relationship, and later, my lack of belonging in the world.

From this earliest experience of my own needs being less important than the needs of others, I learned to find my value in the family home through taking care of others, a role that women and girls are commonly made to feel is their only value in their home and their culture. But disregarding my own needs created an unremitting hunger to be seen, to be loved, to be valued. The Death Mother endorses the kind of femininity that claims we're valueless beyond our surface role in the family or culture. Without a mature sense of the value of her character, she needs continual reassurance of her worth.

This neediness is the wound we call scarcity. Indeed, the feeling of lack permeated all areas of my life—emotional, physical, and spiritual. I was perpetually driven to find love outside myself, to accomplish significant things, as if they would win me approval. I spent years disciplining myself to be more mindful, generous, and good; as if god's love, and my place on earth, depended upon it. It wasn't until I learned what was at the root of scarcity that I began to pull back its pernicious projections and change the way I was seeing the world.

The further distanced we are from our instincts and needs, the more unconscious they become. When we can't see or name the destitution we feel, it is projected onto the world around us. Life becomes the Death Mother and we, its ever-needy child.

To understand how scarcity forms, we must first explore worthiness. To feel worth means to feel significant, valuable, appreciated, and deserving. It is the state of feeling plenty. If we weren't raised to feel these qualities of worthiness, we may believe good things are outside of our deserving.

At times when you are identified with the Death Mother's voice, believing her invalidations of you to be true, you may dream of wandering in these dangerous, abandoned parts of your psyche where dilapidated structures crumble. What little life there is in these places scrounges and competes for scraps, and there is danger at every turn. I call these the Lost Zones: underneath bridges, the back alleys, and abandoned developments that symbolically correspond to the parts of our psyche which have been ravaged by scarcity and neglect.

These places develop from a lack of love, and without our attention to healing them, can become systemic. Like the part of a city that is neglected or ignored, it gathers more despair until it becomes an established place to which lostness is attracted. The psyche similarly gathers momentum. Given the right trigger, like seeing others enjoying the warmth of family or friendship that we are missing, we can be instantly transported into these districts of desolation within.

So how do we begin to revitalize our Lost Zones in a way that isn't cosmetic, but integral? Revitalizing these Lost Zones within our psyche is about looking directly at the damage, as we do with dreamwork, and stitch by stitch, bringing what has been torn from us back into belonging.

The first thing we have to do is really find out who we are and what we value. I love this word 'value,' because it has two meanings: that which we appraise with a sense of worth, and that which distinguishes our character. So we must first make a true appraisal of our gifts and abilities, and then we must learn how to stand up for them.

In her wonderful treatise, *The Gospel According to Shug*,[14] Alice Walker wrote, "HELPED are those who love others unsplit off from their faults; to them will be given clarity of vision." This language has such an impact on me because it suggests that faults, aberrations or oddities in our personality are part of our intactness, and that splitting them off is a disservice to others and to ourselves. But furthermore, in reconnecting with what I call the 'refugee aspects of the self', we can reclaim the ability to envision a way forward, not only for our lives, but for our collective future.

The habit of unworthiness is a kind of splitting-off, causing us to show up only partially for life; worthiness is felt in direct proportion to our ability to live an integrated life. Rather than outcasting the parts of ourselves which were once rejected, we work to reclaim those parts of ourselves that are afraid of being seen, hurt, or left behind. We allow and include them, moment by moment, strengthening our capacity for inclusion, for belonging. It is the practice of bringing the fullness of our presence to a moment, whether it's filled with rage or an upwelling of sadness, to say, "This too belongs."

A few years ago, I was taught an important lesson while staying with some friends of mine about how exiling ourselves can also hurt others. I was in transition, having left the town where I'd been living but without a new place to call home, and my girlfriend and her husband were letting me stay in their spare room. At first it was sweet to live in the home of this loving and thoughtful couple, but after a few weeks I began to hit my capacity to receive their generosity. Though they hadn't given me any overt reason to worry, I was nonetheless coming to feel like an intrusion.

I tried to be of greater service, buying all the groceries, cooking the meals, cleaning while they were away. But eventually even that didn't feel like enough. I began to stay out of the house for long periods, or literally hide myself away in my room, so they could have their privacy and rhythms without me. But the truth was that I was tumbling down that dark shame spiral into a Lost Zone again. Having to depend on my friends in a home that was not mine triggered all those old feelings of unbelonging. But below that awareness, I was recreating that feeling of abandonment as I watched from the proverbial stairs the life going on without me.

One morning my girlfriend asked me if something was wrong and at first I tried to shrug it off. But a few moments later, I shakily wrote down some words on a piece of paper because they were too difficult to say out loud: "I feel like I'm in the way." What ensued was a tearful conversation in which my friend, rather than comforting me, confronted me with my behaviour. She said by removing myself from life in the home, I was actually the one doing the abandoning.

These words were like a cold splash of water. In a single moment, I could see how many times over a lifetime I had similarly removed myself from life in order to spare others my presence, walking ahead before I could get left behind. It was an unconscious bid for love and attention. Just as it had been in childhood, absenting myself was really motivated by a longing to be felt as missing. And while this strategy helped me survive those early years, it was now outdated and revealing itself as lacking in real bravery.

So long as we keep aspects of ourselves hidden from view because we believe only an edited or presentational version of who we are will be accepted by others, we are depriving ourselves of belonging. But also—and here's the piece that takes some real practice to see—depriving others of belonging with us.

Death Mother Culture

For most of us, whether we want to admit it or not, the values we carry are the ones that have been transmitted to us by our culture and our families. One of the first terrifying steps on the way to belonging is to differentiate our indigenous voice from the voice of the Death Mother, both as she appears in our personal lives and how she expresses herself in cultural norms.

As we begin to understand the Death Mother's icy spread in our personal unconscious, we simultaneously come to see that she is an emissary for a culture which denigrates what the Jungians call 'the feminine.' So much about the way we live in modernity is hostile, even fatal, to the feminine. It's exhausting to keep pace with our growth-infatuated society and its emphasis on prestige, productivity, wealth, and power. Even when we are successful in these ways, the goal posts keep moving. Because the Death Mother is never satisfied.

While the Devouring Mother eats away at everything good within us, leaving holes of scarcity on our inner landscape, so too does she devour the outer landscape. She appears in the drive to plunder delicate ecosystems like the Arctic for more oil. She's the hunger that tolerates factory farming and monoculture agribusiness, even as it wipes out ecological diversity. Growth economics is like the cancer cell that reproduces endlessly without purpose until it kills its host. The Death Mother doesn't care who or what is trampled in her path, so long as she keeps growing.

She depends on isolationism, because so long as we believe that worth is something we can achieve by ourselves alone, then we'll continue to work hard, buy stuff and keep striving for that hyper-individualistic notion of success. Meanwhile, for an increasingly large number of people, success is a far-off mirage. Survival is the most that many can hope for.

But what if worthiness depends on our belonging together? Worth is really another way of saying 'plenty.' It is the resting state of abundance. This is our natural state when we live in solidarity with others and in harmony with our environment. When we each contribute our unique gifts and abilities to the whole, we always have more than we need. Conversely, when things go wrong, we shoulder it together, lessening the load for us all.

Only from a place of combined resources can we begin to defeat the Death Mother in our culture. As we dismantle those inherited values from our intrinsic dignity, we begin to make contact with a unique vision for ourselves and the world we live in.

Healing the Wound

Revitalization of the scarcity wound created by Death Mother culture is slow, important work. The first step to healing is the refusal to keep minimizing the impact that neglect and denigration of the feminine has in our own lives and in the world at large. For individuals, this may look like reclaiming those aspects of the feminine which are missing from the Good Mother: our disagreeability, our impatience, our anger, our isolation, our desperation for support. In these places lives a hidden power that, if wielded consciously, can become an ally to us instead of a destructive impulse.

When I was in my late twenties, I interned with the Jung Foundation of Ontario for a number of years, an organization through which all the great living Jungians travelled. It was a rich time in the company and tutelage of people like Marion Woodman, James Hollis, and many more. Though I was too young to be admitted into the analyst training program, I volunteered my time so I could absorb as much of their scholarship as possible. At a certain point, however, I realized that the prohibitive costs and requirements meant I would never be privileged enough to enter the program. I would always be outside of that inner circle, even though I had so much to offer the field.

Though I learned a great deal of theory *about* the feminine, I longed for someone to speak *from* the feminine. I began to feel like the analytical approach to dreamwork was too limited. I longed for indigenous, earth-centred practices, which put dreaming back into the hands of the people.

One day, in the middle of a weekend workshop, I had the following dream.

The Witch's Grave, Toko-pa's dream

I dream some of the male analysts from the Jung Foundation were deep in a forest, building a platform out of wood. What they didn't realize is that they were building it on the grave of a powerful witch, who was awakening in a rage. In what felt like an instant, she leapt from her grave and unleashed her fury, slaughtering the men and everyone else in sight. It was a terrifying bloodbath.

Startled awake by this dream, covered in sweat, my heart pounding, I knew something serious was trying to get my attention. That morning I took my trembling, pale self to the workshop and tried to listen to what was being said, but the witch's wrath was still rattling in my bones. It was so clear. She was pissed off that the Jungians were building a platform on her grave! What if there was an older way, a way that had been left for dead, a feminine way with dreams and magic that was a greater authority than the one I'd been following? I left that day and never returned.

The next year of my life was devoted to learning more about indigenous, shamanic dreaming practices. But more importantly, I recognized my dreams as my most powerful teacher. My dreams were the great, unsplit-off Mother.

Though we are led to think the opposite, I believe the self is the macrocosm through which the outside culture is shaped. So rather than thinking of inner work as selfish, we can see it as a service to the cultural consciousness. In order to heal the scarcity wound—created by the lack of nurturing both in our families and in our culture—we must learn to become the loving mother to ourselves that we never had. This 'remothering' is the ongoing practice, tremendously helped by a mentor, of learning to care for your body's needs, validating and expressing your feelings (even if they're unpopular), holding healthy boundaries, supporting your life choices, and most of all—being welcoming towards all that is yet unsolved in your heart.

The reason I love working with dreams to heal trauma is that dreams cast our problems into images we can relate to. They give our patterns form so that we can begin to understand them as psychodynamics. Like the poisoned apple that jumps from Snow White's throat with the Prince's kiss, the poison is no longer operating from within but becomes something we can actively work with outside of ourselves. From this tangible perspective, it becomes less fearsome and more approachable. And while this can be a terrifying process, every time we look it in the eye, it loses power over us.

To your remothered self I offer this future blessing:

> *Through trial and fire, against the odds, you have grown to trust that the world can be a safe place and you have every right to walk here. You have made parents of your instincts, intuition, and dreaming; you have allowed love into where it had never before been received; you have grown life where once it was barren. Your gifts and your goodness given is a boon for us all. With just a few found and trustworthy seeds, you have nurtured the greatest harvest there is in this, your humble life of belonging.*

Four

False Belonging

In the brave memoir, *Sun at Midnight*, author Andrew Harvey tells the story of his disillusionment from his long-time guru, Mother Meera. He believed she was an avatar of the Divine Feminine, and by the age of forty-one, Harvey had devoted a decade of his life to her teachings, helping her to gain a worldwide audience. But when he met the love of his life, a photographer named Eryk Hanut, Meera began pressuring him to marry a woman. For a while, Harvey tried to keep his two lives separate, but things came to a head when Meera asked him to write a book about how her divine force had healed him of his homosexuality.

Harvey refused to deny his sexuality and made a painful break from Meera, who he was coming see as a false guru. He refers to what happened next as "the annihilation," because not only was he harassed by Meera's group, with death threats and literal fire bombs in his apartment, he was cast into the despair of spiritual crisis, questioning everything he believed to be true.

For ten years, Harvey had devoted his life to what he thought was a place of belonging. Like many of us, I'm sure he could look back with hindsight on the moments in that decade when he ignored warning bells, shirking from his truth in order to be accepted. But when he met Eryk it was as if love emboldened Harvey to be his true size. The cost of stepping into his bigness was high, but the price for his remaining small was intolerable.

For some people, there is a single defining moment when an internal vow of smallness was made. For others, this cringing of the spirit comes from a repetitive and insidious rivulet of disapproving glares, mocking jeers, or shaming of their particular flair. Sometimes, it is the eclipsing nature of another's personality in whose shadow you lived. But we do learn it. We learn that if we want to fit in, we must split off, shrink down, and make ourselves silent or invisible.

We learn to live life with a limited palette of colours considered acceptable for public expression, while the darker, more vivid gradients of the human condition are stricken from the conversation. Driven into isolation, our secret grief, hidden failings, shameful desires, and vulnerabilities can survive the whole length of a life in concealment, refugees even from our own view. But by dissociating from the fullness of our being, we become much more susceptible to what the poet John O'Donohue calls "the trap of false belonging."[15]

Our longing for community and purpose is so powerful that it can drive us into joining established groups, systems of belief, or even employments and relationships that, to our diminished or divided self, give the impression of belonging to something greater. But these places often have their own motives and hidden contracts. They grant us conditional membership, requiring us to cut parts of ourselves off in order to fit in. Rather than committing to the slow accumulation of intimacy that it takes to weave a life of true belonging, we try to satisfy our longing by living in marginalizing places.

These groups may offer us membership, but only in exchange for our conformity to their conventions or goals. It may be a career that meets our security or status needs but requires us to put our creativity and feelings aside. It may be a relationship that keeps us from loneliness but excludes our anger or depression. Maybe it is a religious or spiritual group that binds us to its lineage, but expects our subservience to a guru or leader. Traditional, patriarchal groups have a clearly delineated hierarchy, where the whole structure is dependent upon a single leader or entity, and our membership is contingent upon our agreement with its views.

We have an innate longing to be of service to something larger than ourselves. Sadly, that devotional quality is often exploited by these kinds of organizations. For instance, the military uses our longing for kin and purpose to recruit for war. It is often much later that one realizes the group doesn't actually want their uniqueness but their conformity so that it can be manipulated for its own goals.

But everyone is born with a set of sacred agreements to a higher authority than those of this world. Like a pole star, there is a divine Self which directs and shapes our lives into what we're meant to become. Sooner or later, we must navigate by our star's light, or risk being lost in the dark night of the soul.

Often when your pole star begins to rise, people in your family or community will dismiss, underestimate, even criticize you at that pivotal juncture. One of the great silent contracts of false belonging is that you remain a follower. As soon as you try to step into a leadership role, you meet with resistance. The group feels threatened by the emerging sexuality, the charisma, intelligence, or creativity that shakes up the order of things. On some level your rising star may be interpreted as another's demotion or loss of relevance.

Your star's very existence brings the ranks into question. Can there be more than one star in the family?

And so the star in us declines to rise. Maybe from the fear of putting our belonging in jeopardy; maybe from the lack of resilience that comes from a history of being undermined or unsupported. But in many cases, we are the ones who put our star-self away. We do it not only once but perpetually, shrinking back from opportunities, from difficult conversations, from disagreements, even from a flashy outfit, a strong emotion, an awkwardness, staying in our cramped residence for fear of the alternative.

The difference between 'fitting in' and belonging is that fitting in, by its very definition, is to parcel off our wholeness in exchange for acceptance. Like the original Grimm's telling of *Cinderella*, her sisters literally cut off their own toes to fit into her tiny slipper. False belonging prefers that we hold our tongue, keep chaos at bay, and perform a repetitive role that stunts our natural inclination to growth.

We may live for a while in such places, leaving well enough alone, taking its benefits while ignoring the costs. But the difficulty begins when those hidden contracts begin to show themselves. Maybe we knew it all along and it's just become impossible to ignore. Maybe it started taking too much of a toll on us. Or maybe we are awakening through conflict, illness or loss. But there is always a threshold at which we can no longer compromise ourselves. While false belonging can be useful and instructive for a time, the soul becomes restless when it reaches a glass ceiling, a restriction that prevents us from advancing. We may shrink back from this limitation for a time, but as we grow into our truth, the invisible boundary closes in on us and our devotion to the groupmind weakens.

The Split-off Life

The moment something precious goes into concealment is difficult to pinpoint, but it is often a strategy for survival in too harsh a world. In the attempt to safeguard ourselves against vulnerability, we send our gifts underground. Later in life, this separation manifests in crisis or through lethargy and depression. A spiritual or creative paralysis can develop from the prolonged silencing of one's gifts. This self-imposed exile may once have protected us, but now the energy it takes to keep quiet drains us.

There are as many kinds of silence as there are voices in the world. There is the silence between musical notes, which is a gathering of good tension; the silence that comes on suddenly when it is captivated by beauty; the silence that invites another's story to be heard; the silence that waits for an opening to reveal itself. But the kind of quiet that is inherited or administered by shame is a darkening shroud upon the wholeness of one's sincerity.

If something important is left unsaid, everything in its wake is less truthfully spoken. Some lives are intricately constructed around remaining silent. Maybe there was a cruelty, a violence, a volatility which terrified us into silence; perhaps it is the quiet that grows out of being discouraged; or maybe it's because the private language of things feels too sacred to be exposed. Whatever the origin or collateral against which a silence may be held, over time it can breed an ambience of isolation from which we suffer, but in which we are also paradoxically complicit.

Silence is a power because it keeps what's tender, what's vulnerable, away from scrutiny, criticism, dismissal, interruption, and exile. The keeper of silence has tremendous control. What she keeps sealed away can never be harmed so long as it remains hidden. Silence is a power, yes, but when does silence turn upon its keeper and become the captor? When does it inhibit the natural impulse to speak, the urge to sing, the longing to contribute? So many wait for the express invitation to speak, for some permission to be granted, to be coaxed into contributing. But what if this invitation never comes?

When does silence stop us from fulfilling our purpose, or making connections with others? When does silence stop a healthy disagreement, like the one that names an injustice and invokes change? When is silence being complicit, when it should be calling on a revolution waiting to happen?

Silent Virtuoso

A young musician named Tziporah came to me some years ago in a deep depression. She described feeling creatively paralyzed, unable to even pick up her instruments for the debilitating unworthiness she felt. There was a room in her house reserved for her instruments and creativity, but she couldn't even bring herself to enter it. Almost every night she would have dreams of her instruments thrown in dumpsters, fallen in the subway gap, left in the rain. One dream in particular, however, brought us into the heart of her issue.

Silent Virtuoso, Tziporah's dream
I dream I am homeless, living inside the belly of a piano. I play on a plank of wood, hearing my virtuosity in my imagination but not making any actual sound. One day, someone comes along and clumsily plays a few actual notes on the piano. Eventually, through trial and error, the stranger stumbles upon some gorgeous, heart-wrenching chords, and I am so envious.

In this dream, we can feel how Tziporah is living only in the potential of her creativity rather than its actuality. So long as she holds the expectation of virtuosity over her own head, she can't even make a note. This is an oppressive sort of silence which, unlike the stranger, refuses to risk being clumsy. For Tziporah, who was raised by extremely critical parents, sounding "mediocre" (as she puts it) is terrifying because it opens her to ridicule and criticism. Instead, she refuses to begin. Yet the dream seems to say that only when one is willing to make a few mistakes can something beautiful be discovered.

Perfectionism is a virus, widespread in Western culture, which keeps us running on the treadmill of never-enoughness. It is inherently deadening for how it strives and never arrives. Failure is embedded in its very pursuit, because humanity can never be homogenized. And yet, we are constantly being harangued into sameness, the condition upon which our inclusion hinges.

It is only in Tziporah's willingness to bring her music to the outside, even in its early, fumbling state, that she will begin to find home. So long as she keeps abandoning her instruments, she remains in a state of spiritual homelessness; moving from potential into real-world action begins to build a shelter of belonging in the world.

Underneath the envy that Tziporah feels in the dream is a pure longing for her own inclusion, for an accepting 'beginner's mind' that allows her to tinker, to get it wrong, to creatively meander until she finds magic. The only antidote to perfectionism is to turn away from every whiff of plastic and gloss and follow our grief, pursue our imperfections, and exaggerate our eccentricities until the things we once sought to hide reveal themselves as our majesty.

We all have outlawed attributes in our lives—those things that have been driven to the margins of belonging, that starve for the leftover scraps of our attention. In avoidance of the things that make us different, we construct entire lives and personas around those qualities which, consciously or unconsciously, we understand to be acceptable and desirable to our families, congregations, and culture.

Looking at the cliques that form in grade school, when one particular group holds the social power over others, there are certain qualities that qualify you to be 'in' and others which cast you 'out.' Those who are in the 'in-crowd' are often carriers of privileges such as wealth and beauty, strength, heterosexuality, and whiteness. It is those privileges that keep you safe in numbers. If you're one of the chosen ones, you will be invited, included, and spared ridicule and harm. But being 'inside' also comes with a hefty price to pay: you will always be expected to match, as closely as possible, the look, language and values of the in-crowd. Like being stuck on the rails of train tracks, there is very little room for deviation, so there is constant pressure to maintain one's position in belonging.

For those who couldn't 'match up' if they tried, school can be a torturous time. Those young 'outsiders' who are sensitive, creative, or possess a differing set of attributes and abilities are often bullied, ridiculed, and otherwise marginalized. Blessed are those young people with a support system in place to remind and reassure them of their uniqueness. But for many, these early influences put them on the tracks of either striving for false belonging or defying the narrow norms of acceptability.

Defying acceptability by following your star is a huge risk because we know, even if unconsciously, that stepping out of false belonging means taking on the responsibility of leadership and independence. This can't be underestimated. As any entrepreneur or single mom knows, defiance means stepping out of the usual support systems, flawed as they may be, and doing it all yourself, at least for a time.

Like moving from a corporate job to an independent profession, we must do far more than just be creative; we have to generate the entire structure in which our offering is presented and delivered, requiring a whole arsenal of skills that may not come to us naturally. Or like leaving a loveless marriage, in which our basic needs like security and shelter are met, but we don't feel seen or heard. We are sacrificing outside support for our own inner resources, trembling as they may be. The toll for leaving false belonging can be great.

I meet so many women in my work who have gorgeous ideas but are terrified to release them into the world. This terror is a combination of things, but at the fundamental level it is the fear of criticism. The inner critic, a spokesperson for all the diminishing voices in our past and in our culture, is the first gatekeeper of true belonging. It barrages us with "buts." "But you don't have anything original to say." "But you can't prove that." "But you will look or sound ridiculous." "But you aren't as talented as X," and so on. When we look at these criticisms more rigorously, we begin to see that they are all based on the outer-measurement we've come to associate with patriarchal thinking. The challenge of this gate is not to measure up, but to use a different barometer altogether.

After more than a decade of her life in academia, a woman in her forties named Ariella was longing to share her own writing with the world. When she was in school, she never had difficulty writing a dissertation or essay, but she couldn't seem to get out of the starting gate with her personal writing.

Stolen Car, Ariella's dream

I dream I am supposed to teach a class, but it's eight hours long, which is much more time than I'm used to. Normally I would improvise, but now I'll have to plan ahead to fill the time. When the time arrives, I feel unprepared. I spend so long giving introductions to the material that I never teach the content. When I return to my car, which I've parked at a fraternity house, I find it stolen. I'm arguing with a young man who doesn't understand what it's like to be a woman in Judaism. I tell him I don't want to wear a yarmulke, like the men. There must be a different feminine way to worship.

As we worked with this image of the yarmulke in the dream, a powerful story emerged about Ariella's bat mitzvah, a Jewish coming-of-age ceremony. Traditionally, the young girl's father would read from the Torah, but Ariella wanted to do her own reading—something which had never before been done in her synagogue. As a result, many people in her community refused to attend her ceremony. At the tender, vibrant age of thirteen, Ariella was initiated into the losses that come with following your truth.

As we explored the image of the car being parked and then stolen from the fraternity house, Ariella associated this with her life in academia, which was steeped in the patriarchal writing style, always emphasizing factual arguments and being 'objective.' After receiving her doctorate, she felt that there was no place for her in that world anymore, and began to pursue a profession in energy healing.

But in this dream we found Ariella unprepared, never getting past the introductions. Indeed, she could relate to that feeling with her writing, which never made it past the idea stage. Her challenge was to shape that spontaneous energy into deliverable content. But although she had lots of experience with organizational thinking, she was symbolically parked at the fraternity, the logocentric 'boys' club' whose demands for objectivity were robbing her of her vehicle for movement altogether.

Ariella argues with the voice who says she must wear the traditionally male yarmulke, because in her dream-self's infinite wisdom, she knows there must be a feminine way to worship. There must be a way to write and engage in other creative endeavors that doesn't simply do as men before us have done, but turns to its own erotic authority. The feminine voice comes from the body's knowing. It is the writing of aches and ragged breath and dirty fingernails from climbing out of the underworld. It is the sonority of our words that is primary, not their definition. This voice is the howling of a child for its mother before language is even learned. It doesn't strive for objectivity, which is removed from feeling, but rather sinks us deeper into the muck of it. It takes things personally. And it gives things personally in return. There is no such thing as impartiality when you live in a body; it speaks from the flesh and bone rhythms of that first belonging. It knows the secret loophole: you can't argue with poetry.

As Ariella's thirteen-year-old self knew, and as she is coming to know again, she must be supportive of her voice while it is in its early stages. This self-support comes from the positive inner masculine. Without the tempering guidance of the feminine, the masculine can fall into its negative aspect. But when it acts in harmony with the feminine, it gives us an inner firmness. It provides structure for our ideas. It is our backbone; our follow-through in times of doubt. The masculine is our ability to perceive a goal and work with fidelity towards it. After all, there is only one way to penetrate inner criticism—and that is through discipline. When we hear the word 'discipline,' we immediately think of toil, sweat, and deprivation. Over the centuries, the once beautiful word has been distorted to mean something akin to punishment. But at its root, a disciple is someone who devotes themselves to something they love.

While it may feel like a lack of loyalty to break from the group, you are answering a higher authority which, paradoxically, may also be the life of the group wanting to grow through you. Though more often than not, existing structures don't listen to their constituents, because they want things to remain as they are or grow in a single, unsustainable direction. But the greatest leaderships don't create followers; they create innovators. The healthy circle of belonging welcomes conflict and dissonance as the early warnings they are: signalling change and calling for growth. Your rebellion is a sign of health. It is the way of nature to shatter and reconstitute. Anything or anyone who denies your impulse to grow must either be revolutionized or relinquished.

As Marianne Williamson famously wrote, "It is our light, not our darkness that most frightens us."[16] Ultimately, I think we're afraid of the demands it makes on our complacency. Nature is always calling us into greater gestures of bravery. And as we accept those invitations to our personal edge, we lose the ability to shrink into falseness.

The practice above all practices is to relinquish the immature desire to be taken care of in false belonging and to parent our own originality. Again and again, our dreams demand leadership from us, calling our life's vision forward into the world, step by tenderbrave step.

Five

The Inner Marriage

There is an ancient heartbreak living in the centre of each of us, between two unrequited lovers we'll call Eros and Logos. These divine counterparts have been separated so long that they barely remember they belong to one another. Though impossible to imagine, because they are like night and day, the whole world is waiting for their sacred reunion. If only we could introduce them, they might remember. They might finally fall in love, as destiny intended, in a holy union of opposites within.

With her beguiling beauty, Eros will possess you. She is a singer and a dreamer, whose elements are mystery, magic, and earth. Her voice isn't pretty, nor is it sweet, but rather scorched with honesty. And when she sings, the ache of being alive rattles and resonates deep in your bones. It's with her raw passion that she pushes blood into an idea, and makes it dance. Her home is in the wild, and she speaks the language of all untamed beings. She is the animal body, both fierce and graceful, who moves with the rhythm and sway of the soul.

Logos is a powerful emperor who rules the sky kingdom, a place vaster than anyone has ever seen. He is a brilliant mathematician whose elements are reason, law, and matter. He has devoted his life to logical inquiry, in search of absolute truth, and is a master at creating order from nothing. He builds complex systems and then he governs them with incontestable law. He likes to be alone in his tower of books, where he loses himself in theories and plans. He prefers others to speak rationally, if at all, and provide evidence for the worthiness of their position.

The truth is that Eros and Logos belong to one another, but for as long as any of us can remember, they have been estranged.

It all began when Logos discovered what he called "irrefutable truth," a method of deduction that could explain the whole universe. Driven by the power of his dominion over nature, Logos began to dismantle the mysteries that Eros served, exposing them for the puzzles of constituent elements that he believed they were.

Captivated by his charisma, everyone followed Logos' rule. Eros was sent, along with the magicians and the night-walkers, poets, and revelers, to live underground where she could no longer influence people with her dark, moist longing for the holy in nature.

Though many of us think of ourselves as either feminine or masculine, each of us lives with the Other within. In Western culture, we are still learning how to think outside of the binary model where many cultures have long accepted those who identify as *two-spirited*, trans, or gender non-conforming. By their very existence, people who embody *bothness* remind us to be in relationship with the inner Other. So I like to play with different names for these counterparts, like Eros and Logos, or yin and yang, because the traditional gender terms can be problematic for how culturally charged they are. To give you an example, we can simply hear the phrase, "be a real man," or "just like a typical girl," and suddenly we've conjured up a host of negative associations to both.

But it's important to remember that when I'm using these terms, I am not speaking about the sexes at all. I am talking about the archetypal feminine and masculine, like Eros and Logos, both of which live within our psyches. Women are not the sole custodians of Eros any more than men are the keepers of Logos. We are what you might call psychic hybrids, possessing the potentiality for the full spectrum of qualities contained in both, but most of us develop on a bias because of the cultural expectations and projections onto the sex we are assigned at birth. Regardless of where we fall on the gender spectrum, the world will project the qualities associated with feminine or masculine upon us. And without being fully aware of it, we may cleave off parts of ourselves to fall in line with those expectations.

You may have had the experience as a young person of being allowed to express your fully androgynous nature, whether it was climbing trees or playing dress-up, singing, or building with tools. For a short while, you may have felt unconstrained by the delineations of 'boy' or 'girl.' But at a certain age your body begins to change, you are socialized with other boys or girls, and you start to become aware of what is expected of your gender.

My grandmother, who was a Polish immigrant to Canada but more British than the Queen, was fond of starting sentences with, "A proper lady..." Some classic examples include, "A proper lady behaves as if she's always being watched." Or, "A proper lady never smokes in public."

In high school, I was always more drawn to hanging out with boys. They seemed easier to be around and interested in cool things like books and instruments. Girls, on the other hand, were always talking about boys, makeup, and celebrities. I remember feeling like a female impersonator, saying and agreeing to things that I didn't really feel because I thought it might help me blend in.

When we do what we can to match gender expectations, the 'opposite' gender qualities within may atrophy or feel altogether foreign to our lives. This is when we begin to search for the 'perfect lover' who might embody those things that we've dispossessed. This may offer some explanation as to why half of all marriages come unhitched. Most plunge in thinking they have found their other half, only to end up disappointed post-honeymoon, when they still only feel like half a person.

The real marriage must first take place within. The Inner Marriage is a slow process of first attempting to understand the true qualities of masculine and feminine, how they manifest in our lives and dreams, and then undertaking a courtship of the inner opposite, activating those latent qualities in our repertoire.

To drain the charge from these words 'feminine' and 'masculine,' we could also swap them out for the Chinese concept of yin and yang. The first thing we notice about the yin-yang symbol is that both black and white halves are interdependent parts of a whole. They also contain an aspect of each other within. And perhaps most excitingly, they interact with each other along an ebbing and flowing seam.

As many of us experience when working with the feminine and masculine archetypes in our dreams, we can never settle on a static definition of either: both seem, at different times, to borrow from one another's roles. We can only avail ourselves of the ongoing dance between the opposites within. Like the symbol, there is a fluid line between dark and light sides that appears to be in constant motion.

Yin is often referred to as passive, negative and dark, while yang is the active, positive, sunny counterpart. The words alone are not denigrating or aggrandizing, but through the lens of our dominant culture we certainly read them that way. Because language is so powerful, it's important to find ways to reframe some of these old notions that pit the opposites against one another. So instead of referring to yin as passive, we might use the word 'receptive' instead. Can you feel how that changes the dynamism of the word? For anyone who is practiced at non-action, you will know how paradoxically active and engaged receptivity can be.

Instead of negative, we might refer to yin as 'magnetic.' It is the realm of interiority, of holding, waiting, and invoking. Instead of dark, we might say 'reflective,' like the moon, or 'gestational' like the soil. Yin is the place of refuge and rest, of containment and acceptance. Darkness is, after all, the primordial womb from which dreams emerge. It is the origin of all life before it comes into being. Yin is the receptive, feeling, compassionate force within. It knows the wisdom of surrender and chooses to yield, even when everyone else is getting ahead. For yin, withdrawing is entering. It's there we refine our intuition and have a centre from which to interrelate.

Yin is the eternal, or what Rumi calls "the reedbed." It is the place from which all beings have been plucked and to which we will all, some day, return. Like an ecosystem, yin considers all components essential. Ideas that emerge from this level of imagination serve more than the individual cause—they serve the great togetherness unto which we are all responsible.

Yang is our direction, focus and backbone. With piercing clarity, yang takes a stand and sticks to it. It is assertive, analytical and works independently. It knows how to discriminate and cuts away the excess. It builds systems and follows through when something needs to be done. Yang is the arrow that speeds to its target, turning our dreams into realities.

But without the balancing influence of the other, both yin and yang have the potential to stray into their negative aspects.

Without the active, discerning objectivity of yang, yin can become stagnant, lost, paralyzed, and overwhelmed. This is when we might feel possessed by our fears and anxiety, allowing our emotions to 'get the better of us.' An overbalance of yin may cause us to react impulsively, become indulgent and possessive of others.

By extension, yang's sunniness can become a burning scrutiny without the tempering shade of yin. It can be so directed in its focus that it neglects to consider who it runs over, even if the victim is our own body. Without yin's consideration of the whole, yang's viewpoints can become fundamentalist and exclusionary. We see this in our culture that blindly follows yang, building outwards and upwards without any sense of the relational whole, inconsiderate of the needs of our communities, human and otherwise.

Perhaps reading these descriptions, you can already feel how much on a yang-bias we are as a species. We are all suffering to meet the demands of this yang-centric culture, while the feminine has been denigrated, disgraced and cast into hiding.

Suppression of the Feminine

The historical roots of feminine devaluation vary from culture to culture, but the most widespread European and North American campaign to subjugate women—and, by extension, the feminine—was a 200-year period starting in the 15th century that we now refer to as the witch hunts.

By some reports, hundreds of thousands of women were captured, tortured, and burned at the stake on even the suspicion of practicing so-called witchcraft, which included a wide range of activities such as midwifery, herbalism, divination, and the healing arts. Led by the Christian church and state, women were brutally scapegoated for any and all of society's problems such as ailing crops, cattle sickness, inclement weather, and even death. Far from being some 'craze' by the ignorant masses, the widespread extermination of women and nature-based practices was a methodical crusade by the ruling elite to force a new patriarchal order upon the people.

In her book *Caliban and the Witch*, Silvia Federici makes a direct connection between the persecution of women and the rise of capitalism. She explains how "the witch-hunt occurred simultaneously with the colonization and extermination of the populations of the New World, the English enclosures, [and] the beginning of the slave trade."[17]

Previously, women had significant economic independence through their trades and practices, as well as power in female community and belonging, but during this gruesome period women were turned into "servants of the male work force...where women's bodies, their labor, their sexual and reproductive powers were placed under the control of the state and transformed into economic resources."[18] The casualties of the centuries-long witch hunt were of course physical, turning hundreds of thousands of children into orphans, pitting villagers against each other, evicting peasants from their common lands and livelihoods. But perhaps most devastating to us all is the loss of an ancient feminine legacy.

This lost network of feminine systems of knowledge and practices is so vast, you could say we are living only half a life without it. Though this unclaimed legacy has countless iterations, some of which are just recently finding their way back into cultural esteem, like midwifery and natural medicine, at their core they have a common uniting origin: nature.

The feminine is in direct conversation with that which joins us to all living beings. It is the mystical path that turns us to our own senses, and to the living world around us for guidance and collaboration. We need no mediating authority to grant us permission or tell us how to heal or bring life into the world, because there is a greater authority, a vital impulse which is flowing through each of us at all times. And it is our network, our combined wisdom and experience, our dedication to belonging to one another, which is our true source of power.

But to this day the feminine is tolerated at best—and at worst, it is dismissed. I say at worst, because to dismiss something is to be impervious to its being brutalized. We feel this personally, in all the ways we've been prohibited and invalidated. The loss of the feminine on a collective scale has resulted in devastating consequences far beyond the human drama, into the reaches of all nature.

The loss of the feminine in our personal lives takes many forms, but many of us can live a whole lifetime without knowing what is at the root of our missing. It may be felt as a secret longing for a way of life, a feeling of inclusion, or a set of practices which are currently ridiculed in our culture as insipid, insubstantial, or even dangerous. Devalued for generations of patriarchal culture, our families and cultures are left with little to no recollection of how to esteem and tend to these qualities in ourselves or one another.

These qualities are what I consider aptitudes of the soul. The feminine values the intelligence of our feelings; recognizes the necessity of ceremony and rites of passage; teaches the power of listening and being witnessed; holds the significance of intuition and dreams; it is sensitivity itself, vulnerability, and it honours the body's wisdom.

But perhaps more grave than any of these losses is the overarching ability to consider and tend to our belonging with one another, and with the earth. Thích Nhât Hanh coined the wonderful term *interbeing* to describe how no thing can exist alone. Every thing lives in relation to all other things. So what appears to be separate is actually a combination of interrelated parts.

Take the physical form of this book, for instance, which is a bound stack of paper. The paper has been created from the flesh of trees that were once rooted in a family of other beings we call a forest. None of the forest could exist without the soil, water, light, and minerals to nourish it. In fact, we could explore an infinite number of paths contributing to the forest's life. Or we might take another route, tracing the centuries-old origins of the language that is written upon these pages, an often dark history of power and exile, or perhaps we could follow the ideas of this story, formed by me, your writer, which are a wild combination of constituent influences.

This related way of thinking is one of the great attributes of the feminine. It remembers us back to the elements from which we are made, and upon which we are dependent. Like a reciprocal roof, which is a self-supporting structure, we lean on each other from all sides. The centre is everywhere and if even one of us falls out of togetherness, we will all eventually fall. One of the great capacities of yin is the inwardness that enables our reconnection to the greater web in which we are but a thread.

It isn't that Logos and his world of order, reason, and word should be diminished in our estimation, but rather given direction by Eros, rather than the other way around. Eros can be difficult to speak about directly because, unlike Logos, it is not logical, direct and linear. It is something that is indirectly felt in our encounters with nature, in our experience of symbols and story, music and ritual, in our relationship with others, and in the feeling body itself. Eros is our desire to connect with life, to relate with one another, to share and feel our closeness. It is love, yes, but it is also a way of embodying our experiences and experiencing embodiment in others. Eros comes with a sense of security and well-being, a welcoming and acceptance of the split-off self. In the broadest sense, Eros is that quality of belonging that we so ache to feel in our lives.

When we go inwards at night, we are restoring ourselves to the multiplicity of our coherence. It is a kind of 'innernet' where dreams, visions and insights are transmitted. Here, we find a true centre from which to relate meaningfully to the rest of the world.

In our culture, we use the word 'dreamy' derogatively to describe someone who is unrealistic or without ambition. But what thrills and amazes me about dreamwork is how grounding it feels when we do it. One of the reasons this is true is that dreams are expressions of the larger ecosystem of which we are a part. And it has a design for our lives within that greater context.

Rather than taking our cues from consensus culture, which is predominantly ego-based and human-centric, we are instead listening to the mystery that gathers and coheres us. As Ann Bedford Ulanov says, "the Self is...that within us that knows about God."[19]   When we come together in dreamsharing community, we experience this very clearly; our symbols begin to heal one another as we work within our psychic commons.

We must remember that the feminine works in a nonlinear fashion. While many are impatiently looking in dream dictionaries for the bottom-line, the final answer, the key to their liberation, they rarely find anything enduring. This is because there is a greater genius at work, one that we could never understand all at once. Instead we must follow a mysterious trail of breadcrumbs prompting us to take greater and greater leaps into the unknown, to build our trust in that which is parenting us. One day, sometimes years down the line, we finally understand how the symphony resolves itself.

One my favourite examples of this meandering genius of the feminine is the story of a young woman named Nicole who came to me with the following dream.

The Red Dress, Nicole's dream

*I am nannying at my employer's home where there are many children
I'm responsible for. I am also a maid and must serve a meal to a
large group of people with only a few ingredients. It is chaotic and
demoralizing. Off in the garden, there is a man painting and I am
drawn towards him. When I get there, I realize it is a painting of
me in a red dress!*

Struck by the passion of this image, I asked Nicole to paint her dream before
we even spoke about it. In that act of putting red paint to paper, she discovered
a forgotten longing to make visual art and, more generally, an urge to paint her
life with more vivid colours.

Raised in an extremely traditional family, Nicole had been taught that
creativity was for children only, and that at a certain age she had to behave more
responsibly. And so she embarked on a career as an *au pair*, working just to stay
afloat. Over the years, she became increasingly anxious and lonely, feeling stuck
and drained of vitality but not knowing how to move forward.

As we entered the subtlety of the feelings evoked by the painting, Nicole
described a loneliness for the wilder, expressive side of nature that had been in
deep remission for as long as she could remember. And with nothing more than
the small encouragement in red that the dream provided, Nicole found herself
again possessed with the urge to paint.

She worked for months until she had a small portfolio of paintings she was
delighted with and, through a series of synchronicities, ended up submitting
them to a local art school. Beside herself with joy when she was accepted, she
quit her nannying job and began to study painting in earnest. It was there that
she met and fell in love with the man who would become her future husband.
Together they would go on to travel and make a life of their combined gifts.

From a single dream we could never have known all that was set to unfold,
but if you listen to the contrast between the exhausting call of duty versus the
vibrancy of the red dress, you can sense the energy gathering there. And when
you follow that energy in whatever way you can, it always grows in potency and
consistency. To restore the feminine in our lives we must follow where the energy
wants to go. Like digging down into a bucket of ice cream, following the caramel
ripple, the strength of our remembering gets fatter and sweeter the deeper we go.

The Great Forgetting

As we explore the feminine, we encounter a vast storehouse of gifts that
have been ignored, rejected and fallen into disgrace. Dreaming is seen as

unproductive, communications from the body are medicated away, feeling has no voice in boardrooms, ritual has become empty and disconnected from nature, and of course the earth is treated as a resource for profit. We have constructed an elaborate culture in denigration of these things that, over the course of many generations, has become so commonplace in our religious and social systems that it would take a startling event of awakening for us to even recognize them as missing.

This is what we might call the Great Forgetting. It is the rupture that each of us feels in our lives; that place of wounding where we override our bodies, ignore our intuitions, and supplant our inner knowing with 'other people's information.' What we call dreaming is treated as illusory, while the false constructions of consensus reality are taken as real. In Nicole's story, she abandoned her creativity because she was told that it wasn't responsible. And in Tziporah's case, her music went into hiding to find shade from the critical scrutiny of her home. For both of these women, however, the real wound is in their forgetting.

This forgetting is a kind of self-betrayal, when we take up the original betrayal of our family and culture as if it were our own, continuing to uphold the devaluation of our heart's longing. You might say we are living someone else's story for our lives.

A number of years ago, I heard a guru tell a story about a dinner party. Everyone arrived in good spirits and a feast was laid out in front of them. A lively conversation began to flow around the table, but underneath that conversation each person was repeating the same silent mantra: "What about me? What about me? What about me?"

The guru was using this story to say what a narcissistic people we have become, that we are so self-focused that we are unable to listen to or care about one another. But I believe there's another way of looking at this—that there is an important story needing to come through each of us. We are longing to be seen, to be necessary, to belong to our community. But the only way a community can heal itself is to draw out the story coming through every individual. Only when we recognize the events of our lives, and of those who went before us, as leading us in a meaningful direction can we pick up the threads of our story in present time and weave it forward with common purpose.

Like this book—which is more than itself, but the culminate offering of trees and sunlight, minerals and language—your story is a contributing piece of another great culmination. As you salvage all that's been shunned in your heart, embodying it back into its rightful belonging, you are one of the gentle multitude who are restoring Eros to our world. Through every act of following the feminine, giving her the authority to guide Logos, yours is the great love story of heartbreak being redeemed.

Six

Initiations by Exile

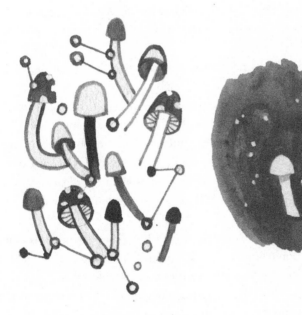

hough we may think of belonging as a static place of attainment, it is actually dynamic. If you've ever watched flowers filmed with timelapse photography, you've seen how they don't open in a single, continuous movement but contract right before opening wider. Belonging must also allow for alternating phases of contraction and expansion, apartness and togetherness. Even the forms of belonging that are enduring, such as a good marriage or engaging vocation, only perpetuate through our willingness to allow them to grow and change shape. The healthiest forms of belonging allow for, and even require, periods of exile or separation in order to mature into greater capacities.

When the individual's needs are at odds with the group or relationship, they must break into new ground, either by choice or by divine intervention. More often than not, we either resist, ignore, or reject these calls to attrition. We leave our roots planted in the shallow soil of false belonging for whatever benefits they might be affording us. But if we haven't been listening to the early warning signs of restlessness, doubt, and longing, one day a strong gust of fate will blow through our lives and knock us right out of that soil. Whether by way of an accident, a physical illness, or a sudden loss or crisis, life will have its way with us.

The door slams shut on your old way of life. The way home is completely lost. By 'home' I don't just mean a geography or culture, though that is an excruciating form of exile that many millions of people are facing. I also mean 'the way things were' in a broader sense: a golden era, a cherished relationship, a role in your community or family, a career track, or even in the ability of your own body.

These are what I call Initiations by Exile because, as we discover in myths and fairy tales, every hero or heroine must endure a period of their own exile if they are to be initiated into the true medicine of their calling.

For me, one of these initiations came some years ago after moving to a new town. I was having a difficult time making friends, feeling extremely lonely, until one day I met a woman named Jenna. Jenna shared so many of my values and interests that without knowing each other very well, we dove right into what you might call a romantic friendship. Our courtship was brief but grandiose, filled with lovely gestures and promises of devotion. We both felt like we'd found a deep sense of belonging in one another's friendship.

When I heard that Jenna belonged to a larger spiritual community, I felt instantly—and without knowing much about it—that I wanted to be a part of it. One weekend, I joined Jenna's group, and sure enough, the community I met was full of intelligent, soulful people whom I liked right away. But the group was also centred around a smooth-talking guru who rubbed me the wrong way. I'd spent so many years on the feminine path, where the emphasis is on circular leadership, that the implied hierarchy of this group didn't sit well with me. So, with a heavy heart, I decided to leave the gathering, a choice for which my friend Jenna warned "there would be consequences."

Leaving the gathering I experienced intense anxiety to the point of hyperventilating and developed a blistering migraine. In the weeks that followed, Jenna, who was devoted to her guru, wouldn't answer my phone calls. I drifted into a depression, feeling as if I'd ruined my chance at community. Months passed and I began to suffer a number of mysterious physical issues that grew into a serious pain condition that kept me in isolation for almost two years. Though I was of course hurt and disappointed by the events, it surprised me that I would have such an extreme reaction.

As I worked with my dreams and the memories they evoked, I began to understand that in my decision to leave this tight-knit community, I was being initiated by exile.

The Closed Path, Toko-pa's dream
I dream there is a magical forest path between my house and Jenna's. I find the way by singing a song, which the birds echo, and I follow their voices in the right direction. But suddenly the birds stop singing back to me and the path closes up. I take a wrong turn, ending up in a dodgy part of town where all the homeless people and criminals live. It feels dangerous. I'm hungry and there is nothing but a convenience store with junk food for sale.

When I woke up from this dream, I was struck with awe by how the birds had sung back to me, as if that call and response numinously opened the secret path to belonging. Indeed, in the initial stages of my friendship with Jenna, I felt as if my deepest longing was being answered. And isn't it so for us all?

When things fall into place, we begin to feel part of a larger coherence, as if nature itself is communicating with us, bringing us into its rhythms. But when my literal calls were no longer returned, my relationship with nature—or what some people call god—also felt forsaken. It was as if the magic went out of life altogether. I found myself in one of those Lost Zones, where everything feels hopeless and I was unable to find any real nourishment.

Whatever your form of exile may be, the ache of separation is like having ties cut from all that's familiar, and every cell in your body is bewildered. It remembers the old way, with its smells and textures, vistas and seasons. And it wants nothing more than to return to that intactness. But there is no going back. You may try, you may even dream nostalgically about your old life for years, but when you wake up you remember that the way home is closed to you. For many people, exile is permanent. Reconciling this can be a long and complicated undertaking. For refugees who've had to flee their country, or First Nations people recovering from the decimation of their culture through colonialism, it may take generations to find a new way forward. By comparison, my own exile seemed banal, so I couldn't understand why it was so traumatizing for me.

As I explored the severity of my reaction to this fairly new relationship with Jenna, I discovered there was a much older wound that was being triggered by these events. It echoed my experience of running away from home, a decision for which "there would be consequences." Indeed, estrangement from my family of origin changed the entire course of my life. While my peers were graduating from high school and going on to college, I had a full-time job at the age of sixteen, working to support myself. I never did the regular things others did, like learn how to drive, or have my health cared for, and holidays and milestones passed without acknowledgment.

Initiation often brings us into the core wounds of our past, inviting us, through a portal in present time, into the unresolved traumas of our own lives and those of our ancestral lines. When I met my friend Jenna, the whole of my longing for attachment was unconsciously projected onto this new 'family,' but it came with a silent contract: to gain acceptance, I would have to give my authority over to its father figure. After all I'd been through to find my own voice in the world, this was a compromise I knew I could not make.

The compromise you cannot make is often what leads to initiation. It says, "Will you stand by this? Will you bear the process of attrition? Will you find what's true within and vow to protect it? Will you trust in the unknown enough to let it carry you into new ranges of belonging?"

Exile may be self-chosen, like Siddhartha leaving the castle to live amongst the poor; or forced upon us, like the Ugly Duckling who is rejected by his brothers and sisters, or Quasimodo and all the aberrant weirdos who are sent to live in towers or to wander the world alone. But exile is an important and necessary separation from the group or society, meant to bring us into relationship with our resilience and originality. Sadly, in Western culture we don't have any ceremonial rites of passage to help our young people feel necessary, so they may turn to violence to express their unacknowledged power. If not done consciously, life will find another way to initiate us. As Jung so eloquently put it, "When an inner situation is not made conscious, it happens outside, as fate."[20]

For me, initiation was long and painful as I unpacked the compound issues scarring my childhood. Most significantly, I learned that a part of my soul was locked up with guilt for leaving my family, believing the hardship I suffered was my own fault. On some level, I believed that if only I'd stayed and been more tolerant that I might have had an easier, more *normal* life. But this central distrust of my instincts became the breeding ground for a constant inner doubt of even the simplest interactions. I was unconsciously attracted to abandoning relationships, in which I replayed the refrain, "It is all my fault. I should have done more."

My physical pain, it took some years to discover, was finally diagnosed as a degenerative autoimmune disease called rheumatoid arthritis. Though it can live dormant in the body for decades, it is notoriously triggered by stressful events. RA is when the immune system turns on the body, mistaking bones and cartilage for intruding pathogens, attacking them until they disintegrate. Just like my compromised immune system, which treats itself as a threat, I spent a lifetime under the constant oppression of contrition and self-punishment. Pain is the appropriate response to persecution, so my body produced it in scores.

What I really needed to do was stand by my young, runaway self who knew there was a better, more wholehearted way to love and be loved. I needed to release myself from the unnecessary guilt that was always seducing me into settling for crumbs of affection. So I began to practice the opposite of chronic contrition, which was to allow my everyday disagreements into the open. I began to work with the belief that I could still be lovable even when at odds with others. As my family's black sheep, I needed to recognize my voice of dissent as powerful, and fateful, to everyone involved...and deeply necessary to my own leadership in the world.

Though exile can be the end of an established way of life for the initiate, through the mythic lens it is a beginning, a turning towards the soul. In many shamanic traditions, healers are initiated by way of extreme crisis and illness. The 'healing crisis' is considered a rite of passage for shamans-to-be. To even the most reluctant of initiates, it is a calling to the inner life, the world of Eros, dreams, and mystery. The process is long, involves a rigorous series of tests, and brings a slow retrieval of the lost or captive parts of the wounded healer's soul. But if the initiate enters consciously into this initiation, he or she will learn its landscape well and become a skilled guide of these thresholds for others.

Joan Halifax describes the initiation process in *Shamanic Voices*: "As the person accepts the calling and becomes a shaman, their illness usually disappears... The concept of the 'wounded healer' addresses the necessity of the shaman-to-be entering into extreme personal crisis in preparation of his/her role in the community as a healer."[21]

Descent into the Underworld

Nobody goes willingly into initiation. By its very nature, initiation is a humbling of the will. It comes as a tsunami would, wild with nature, shattering us on all levels. And though every part of us may mount resistance to being changed, we are not meant to emerge intact. We are not meant to re-cover what has been revealed. Rather, we are meant to be *dis*illusioned, *dis*solved, *dis*appointed before any thought of rebuilding can begin.

The oldest known myth about descent into initiation is the Sumerian story of Inanna. Predating male gods like Zeus, Inanna comes from Babylonian times when the Goddess religions were still alive and well. She was the Queen of Heaven who descended into the Underworld to see her estranged sister Ereshkigal. Her sister insisted that she pass through seven gates, as anyone entering the Netherworld must do, until she was "naked and bowed low." When finally the sisters met, Ereshkigal killed Inanna in a state of wrath. But then in her grief, Ereshkigal handed the body over to Inanna's consorts, who brought her back to life. This story is about surrendering our "upper-world" regalia and making true contact with our darkness and the grief that accompanies the loss of our illusions about another, and ourselves.

In exile, we must do as the goddess Innana did, surrendering layer after layer of armour and adornment, until we are bare. We must then undergo a symbolic death of the old life in order to be reborn with greater resilience and a holy assignment to carry forward. The initiated adult has learned to withstand uncertainty, has paid a debt to the gods through his loss and his grief, and has decided to make beauty with his life as the future ancestor that he is.

One of the big reasons that so many of us cling to false belonging is that braving into a more genuine life requires a terrifying initial descent. There's a gripping scene in the documentary *Touching the Void*, a film about two climbers in the Peruvian Andes, when one of the climbers falls 300 feet into an icy crevasse. He is dangling there, suspended by a rope, unable to climb out for more than twenty-four hours when finally he decides to cut his own rope and fall into the darkness. To his amazement and disbelief, not only does he survive, but he finds a tunnel at the bottom of the crevasse which leads into the open where he is eventually rescued.

It is this lowering down into the very isolation you feel, coming to know its proportions, that enables you to tunnel outwards into a greater intimacy with your life. But like cutting the rope without any sense of what lies below, you must first come to terms with the potential costs of severing ties. As our climber must have considered, cutting ties can mean a final, gruesome death. As lovely as *awakening* may sound, it often means the complete obliteration of life as you knew it. As Jung famously wrote, "there is no birth of consciousness without pain."[22]

Whether you meet with the ravages of grief, the anger for all that's been taken from you, or the bitterness that refuses to trust love again, there is much to be learned from the gatekeepers of the underworld. As they make themselves known, you may not be ready to welcome them, but if you recognize them as the threshold guardians that they are, you might at least be willing to pay them your curiosity.

The feeling of disconnection and numbness that afflicts so many people's lives comes from habitually absenting ourselves from our difficult experiences. Like the climber who'd rather die dangling on his rope, we are terrified of sinking down into those places we refuse to inhabit. The grief for what we've lost or never had, the longing for a worthiness we don't feel, the unknown of it all threatens to swallow us whole. So instead, we live in an anxious suspension above our fears and loneliness. But as the Persian poet Hafiz warns, "Don't surrender your loneliness so quickly. Let it cut you more deep. Let it ferment and season you as few human and even divine ingredients can."[23]

Like circling vultures, some of our most frightening adversaries have been waiting for this moment. We are at our most vulnerable when we're in defiance of the status quo, and they can smell it. All that has been controlling us from the shadows now comes into the open, rearing up twice as fiercely at the threat of dethronement.

For many, this means facing dreams of predators, rapists, landlords, Nazis, and imperious bosses. These are the henchmen of stasis, sent to ward off any threat of growth. They are what regularly keep us from our connection to Eros.

Rapist in the Path, Julie's dream

I am in an open field which turns into a maze of bamboo. My goal is to cross the field to the other side in search of a new house. I start my journey walking along when I have to take a turn, and then another. I realize I'm going to have to remember my way back. I turn around to find rocks to set in the path to help find my way. That's when two guys show up, acting friendly but giving me a bad vibe. One guy starts coming my way, and I feel like he wants to rape me. I feel timid and awful.

This dream came to a young woman named Julie who had just embarked on the path of inner work. We can think of the house she is reaching for on the other side of this maze-like field as the Self she is becoming. She knows there is a distance to travel and much to negotiate and is afraid she might lose her way. Not quite ready to 'cut the rope,' she puts anchors in place to find her way back. Indeed, the descent into the underworld is disorienting and part of us may feel like we need anchors in place before we go there in earnest. But the truth is, we are meant to be disoriented. If we think of ourselves as a ship that is navigating using a point on the horizon, a fog descends all around us in initiation. We must learn that in disorientation we are being given an opportunity to discover a different knowing, an inner compass.

I like to say that every moment in a dream gives birth to the next moment. So if we are unsure as to why something happens, we can look to the moments before it to see what precipitated an event. In Julie's dream, it is perhaps this act of reliance on the old way of going which betrays her lack of commitment to the path. Part of her is still attached to things remaining the same, and it is this timidity which evokes the predator. He ambushes her in the very moment she doubts her ability to navigate the way. He seems to say, "Remember your place, woman."

Our dreams often cast us in the most sympathetic role so we can learn to view ourselves with compassion. But the real bravery of dreamwork is then stepping into our adversaries' shoes to see how *we* are also the cruelty that victimizes us. There are malevolent forces both within and without that are invested in us living marginally. And the moment we step out of line, their status is threatened, so they make themselves known.

For Julie, this dream revealed how she was undermining her own efforts to move forward by indulging in doubt and believing the voices who violate her with their underestimation. Part of her would rather remain in timidity and fear of her becoming self, because to walk the maze to her next self she must face all that she's neglected and abandoned—everything she pushed away instead of grieved, all the impulses she never followed—and relinquish the things that no longer serve her.

Endurance and Relinquishment

There is always a sacrifice to be made on the way to belonging. Whether it is breaking with friends, family, security, or convention, something of real value that you've depended on must be relinquished. This is a ruthless phase of elimination—it strips you of everything that is not alive and growing so that you can find your true way of going in the world.

The word 'sacrifice' is not really about self-denial, as we've been taught, but comes from the root 'to make sacred.' In order to make an honest encounter with the unknown, something of great value must be given up, lest we cling to an old version of ourselves. And in making that sacrifice, there is a transfer of a power. In naming and releasing it, we own that which used to own us. The energy locked up in our conformity is liberated for our benefit and conscious use.

Sometimes the sacrifice is of our own willfulness. In exile, we are invariably made vulnerable for a time so that we can perceive a more mythic calling. The challenge is to surrender our own plans for getting ahead so that the greater good can come through. If we can take a step outside of time, renouncing our ego's urgency for progress, we have a chance at being danced, being sung into the greater song of things. This free fall is the turning point in the story when the heroine sees what she's been missing.

Sacrifice is a show of trust in the unknown. It is the pruning that redirects your energy toward the life of becoming. Like quitting a job only to have an opportunity appear the same afternoon, or breaking up a bad relationship only to meet your true love, there is magic in sacrifice. Life is calling you toward it, and your severance of the tethers that bind you to outgrown forms is the answering of that call. Your willingness to step into the emptiness from which all life springs is a show of devotion to your own belonging.

The reverberations of a previous or false belonging don't instantly cease because we've decided to relinquish them. Depending on how deeply and authentically we entered into those relationships, our tethers may be tenacious and painful to release. They continue on as echoes in our dreams long after we've moved on, and they can make us feel ambivalent about our choice. There is nothing wrong with this ambivalence—it is one of the necessary lengths of grieving that we must endure for anything we've loved dearly.

Our old belongings have been necessary in every way to our becoming: they've prepared us to know our own love. They have shown us by example or by contrast what makes our heart soar and where it feels deprived. And before our old life will release us, it must be thanked for its great service to our becoming. It gave us a taste of what it could be like, even in our idealism, to be in union with others: to contribute to a shared dream, to live for something greater than our life alone.

At the very heart of 'belonging' is the word 'long.' To be-long to something is to stay with it for the *long* haul. It is an active choice we make to a relationship, to a place, to our body, to a life because we value it. Even knowing that it may not be all that we hope it to be, we are keeping the *long* view of what is possible, and our life becomes an offering to making it so.

But when we lose or break the commitment to our endurance through periods of hardship and growth, belonging is cut short. We fall out of the fugue-like familiarity we've woven from our shared history. We must then contend not only with that loss, but with beginning again from scratch, building trust out of unfamiliarity. This is where many can fall into despair, because it seems so far off and impossible. But after initiation, the foundation on which a new life will be built is one of greater integrity, because we have been through the dynamic process of shedding the falseness of our previous selves to reveal our core values.

Take Carrie, for example, a woman who came to the realization that her relationship with Ella, her childhood best friend, no longer *met* the person she was becoming. Carrie described Ella as the kind of friend who, when she shone her light on you, made you feel like the most special person in the world. But then she would disappear from communication for long periods of time, leaving Carrie feeling lonely and unsupported.

When she was younger, Carrie tolerated Ella's tendency to withdraw because she adored their moments of reunion, which were spontaneous and full of excitement, and she would make herself available whenever Ella showed up out of the blue. But one year, Carrie underwent a profound transition through the death of her father, grandmother, and her cat of fifteen years—all within six months of each other. This cluster of losses initiated Carrie into a new level of vulnerability. When Ella wouldn't respond to her emails or phone calls during that time, Carrie was heartbroken into yet another loss. With nobody else to turn to, she realized she'd been clinging to her friend, despite their unhealthy dynamic, because a part of her believed that was the most she deserved.

Being stripped of so much all at once put Carrie in touch with a powerful need for intimacy and consistency, values she was prepared to offer in return. As she articulated for herself what she needed, she knew she had to end her relationship with Ella. As painful as it was, Carrie knew that she needed to make room in her life to cultivate meaningful relationships with more reciprocal friends. Though the loss of that friendship took a long time to recover from, Carrie immediately began to attract more steadfast people into her life. She knew that her decision was like a stable cornerstone in the home of her future.

Necessary Rebellion

Though we think of rebellion as warrior-like, it is really about making the self vulnerable in a heavily-armoured world. The act of rebellion is to expose, and be exposed, in those places that have been kept hidden for too long. Because the rebel chooses to speak up with her voice or her action against tradition, she risks her life and the security of false belonging for the chance at being truly alive. In so doing, she incites aliveness in others.

There is a pivotal juncture in every Heroine's Journey when she stands alone. She is led by the depth of her convictions to take a stand, to name the unaddressed, to call out of hiding the secret malaise in her community. She arrives at a standpoint not without doubts, but in spite of them. And sometimes there is a hefty price to pay, like being the target of criticism, or worse, rejection from the group which is at odds with her truth.

The willingness to rebel from the expected norms, roles, and silent contracts of establishment comes out of knowing that one cannot afford to build resentment. Resentment, which comes from the decision to go against one's truth, embitters the self. It somaticizes in the body and takes on the burden of pain as if it were ours alone. The whistleblower, on the other hand, reveals a shared complicity. It says, "I expect more from myself and from you." And in that stance the pain becomes, in a sense, communal.

The dissenting voice speaks for the voiceless. And in some ironic plot twist, it is in the revolt against outdated belonging that real solidarity can be born. Your willingness to speak the truth about something that disagrees with you is what allows for the undamming of communication, giving all involved a fertile place to grow and the chance to build a real village.

Though I never could have predicted it, years after I left my friend Jenna's gathering I was approached by several members of that community. They confided in me that they too felt at odds with the group's leader. Whether or not my decision to leave inspired them to do the same, a new togetherness was formed between those of us who were willing to stand apart.

While every mythic journey requires us to make painful separations from the group, it is so we can learn to hear and follow our originality. We discover that the very things that make us different are attempting to distinguish our lives. Those aspects of yourself that you discarded, set aside, ignored, and discouraged are the very things to which you must cling. The collective depends on the aggrandizing of your rejected qualities. The sooner you begin adopting your own difference, the sooner love can rush in to support you in raising your voice above the monotonous hum of the mainstream.

We think of rebellion as something we put to external service in the world: we become activists in protest of some wrongdoing, some injustice we must speak against. But I think there is a rebellion before the rebellion—a more intimate form of protest speaking from and for the devalued feminine.

The feminine has nothing to gain. She doesn't vie for leverage. She doesn't want to prove anything or achieve dominion. She does something infinitely more rebellious. She strips falsity and stirs up feeling in the anaesthetized heart. She awakens a kind of long memory throughout and beyond ages. She gives shape to the swelling and collapsing heart. That is all; but it is so much. Because when we sing with her voice, anyone who hears it remembers what they too have forgotten: that we are noble, and beholden to each other.

Rebellion is the pushback on that long-standing amnesia. Like nausea rejects a poisonous substance, rebellion wants to see what is beneath falsity. What is really enduring when all else is stripped away? What longing, if we undam it, might pound through our lives, bringing life to the dryness of an over-harvested creekbed within? What if there is a story coming through us which is trying to find its way into the world? If we can withstand the trials of exile, can we have the chance at turning that story into something that shows others that they aren't alone?

Rebellion can make us feel ostracized from the group, turning us into the 'black sheep' of our family or community. But the black sheep are the artists, visionaries and healers of our culture, because they are the ones willing to call into question those places which feel stale, obsolete, or without integrity. The black sheep stirs up the good kind of trouble. Her very life is a confrontation with all that has been assumed as tradition. Her being different serves to bring the family or group to consciousness where it has been living too long in the dark. As the idiom implies, she is the wayward one in the flock. Her life's destiny is to stand apart. But paradoxically, it's only when she honours that apartness that she finally fits in.

The world needs your rebellion and the true song of your exile. In what has been banned from your life, you find a medicine to heal all that has been kept from our world. We must find the place within where things have been muted and give *that* a voice. Until those things are spoken, no truth can find its way forward. The world needs your unbelonging. It needs your disagreements, your exclusion, your ache to tear the false constructions down, to find the world behind this one.

The Black Sheep Gospel

1. Give up your vows of silence which only serve to protect the old and the stale.

2. Unwind your vigilance, soften your belly, open your jaw and speak the truth you long to hear.

3. Be the champion of your right to be here.

4. Know that it is you who must first accept your rejected qualities, adopting them with the totality of your love and commitment. Aspire to let them never feel outside of love again.

5. Venerate your too-muchness with an ever-renewing vow to become increasingly weird and eccentric.

6. Send out your signals of originality with frequency and constancy, honouring whatever small trickle of response you may get until you reach a momentum.

7. Notice your helpers and not your unbelievers.

8. Remember that your offering needs no explanation. It is its own explanation.

9. Go it alone until you are alone with others. Support each other without hesitation.

10. Become a crack in the network that undermines the great towers of establishment.

11. Make your life a wayfinding, proof that we can live outside the usual grooves.

12. Brag about your escape.

13. Send your missives into the network to be reproduced. Let your symbols be adopted and adapted and transmitted broadly into the new culture we're building together.

Seven

The Symbolic Life

There is a world behind this world. The old cultures used to be in constant conversation with it through the sacred practices of storytelling, dreaming, ceremony, and song. They invited the Otherworld to visit them, to transmit its wisdom to them, so that they might be guided by an ancient momentum. But as we succumbed to the spell of rationalism, the living bridge between the worlds fell into disrepair. As fewer made the journey "back and forth across the doorsill where the two worlds touch,"[24] we forgot how to find the Otherworld.

Let's consider the word 'matter,' which comes from the Latin root *mater* meaning 'origin, source, mother.' In pre-Socratic times, *mater* was used to describe the underlying nature of the visible world. We still use it in that sense when we say, "This is what matters most." Though we may not be able to articulate why, we use it in this way when we're near the essence of a thing. But in the modern usage of the word, matter is the concrete stuff of objects composed of atoms, mass, and molecules. So in the evolution of our relationship to matter, we have gone from considering our fundamental nature to be limitless and unknowable to nothing more than corporeal elements.

Though we often think of materialism as the drive to consume, purchase, and accumulate stuff, these are really just the symptoms of an underpinning, rationalist belief that nothing exists beyond the physical world. Intangible things like spirit, intuition, and visions aren't considered real, and there is no relationship between our thoughts and the world around us. We are so accustomed to this way of thinking that it can be difficult to see how profoundly crippled we are by it. But it dominates every corner of our social, political, and economic systems in a wide range of cultures around the world. It is what underlies our judicial and penal systems that focus on punishing crimes rather than rehabilitating the systemic issues that fomented them. It is what exalts literature over folk tales, and rewards academic credentials over wisdom-keeping.

Materialism is the opposite of animism. Instead of believing that there is soul in all things, it reduces everything to what's observable: how things look, how they work, and how useful they may be to us. Stripping things of their spirit makes it easier to exploit them as 'resources,' and liberates us from our accountability towards them. There is no sense in the materialistic paradigm that living beings, or ecosystems, are any more than the sum of their parts. The Western medical industry is a great example of materialism for how it treats the human body not as the miraculous, interrelated organism that it is, but as an organic machine of aggregate parts. In its veneration of the physical, materialism dismisses meaning and magic, or what we might call the mythic dimension of our lives. It says that everything is random and happens to us by chance, therefore, there is no such thing as destiny, purpose, or a greater intelligence.

So much of the alienation we feel is from our loss of the symbolic life. We have displaced our natural impulse to worship from the symbolic to the literal. We accumulate wealth instead of strengthening our values, we're addicted to alcoholic spirits rather than aspiring to know the holies, we feed our bellies instead of nurturing ourselves, we accumulate information instead of insight, and we chase status instead of belonging.

It's amazing when you begin to consider the dilemmas of our world in these terms, looking at the ways in which we concretize or make literal the symbolic yearnings of our souls. Television, for instance, has taken the place of storytelling around a fire. There's a wonderful story that Joseph Daniel Sobol tells about a Westerner's trip to a small village in Africa where electricity had just been installed and the first television had arrived. Life seemed to just stop as the whole tribe was glued to the set. But after two weeks, they got bored and abandoned watching it altogether. The Westerner was confused by the abrupt disinterest and asked the leader what happened. "Oh, we don't need it. We have the storyteller," he replied. The Westerner then asked, "But didn't it have so many more stories to tell than your storyteller?" And the villager replied, "Yes, the television knows many stories, but *the storyteller knows me*."[25] Though we don't always recognize it, it is this reciprocity we long for. We still have that urge to be fed by myth, through our communion with elders, but because these ways don't exist in our culture, we turn to the material facsimile.

Materialism breeds emptiness and anxiety because it promotes the idea that we are expendable and that life itself is flat, nothing more than its visible surface. To assuage the meaninglessness we feel, we commit ourselves to the constant pursuit of physical success. But there is never any upper limit to how successful or attractive we should be, so it leads to more despair. Though huge numbers of people suffer with these feelings of despair, they are medicated and treated as aberrant, rather than as a valid reaction to this manic, one-sided way of living. And through a broader scope, this materialistic pathology leads to the objectification and commodification of the natural world.

Meanwhile, the inner life is left to atrophy. The things that truly *matter* are abandoned to neglect, and the heart can only long for something it barely knows. We are occasionally touched by this true mattering in myths and music, dreams and beauty, but most of the time we feel that greater meaningfulness just beyond our reach like a disappearing dream, always slipping away.

Felt Shoes, Sophie's dream

I am setting out on a ferry journey across a stormy sea. I am with some cousins and my best friend from childhood. As the winds pick up and the water gets choppier, I begin to panic and I don't think I can handle the crossing. I am relieved to discover there is a stopover where I can take shelter. We are in a tiny strip mall with one shoe store. I try on some funky, colourful felt shoes that I like but when I turn to my cousins, they say, "Those are ugly." I know that I can't buy them.

Sophie grew up in a very close-knit community with traditional, mainstream values. She had known the same group of friends all her life, most of whom followed the expected route: active members of their church, married with children, or established in business right out of university. Sophie, on the other hand, always had an intensely creative and sensitive nature that was scorned and belittled until she learned to keep it hidden so she could remain in belonging.

When she was in her late-twenties, a traumatic brain injury launched her into a protracted and painful period of her life. Seen through the mythic lens, this was a descent into the underworld, a kind of creative illness initiating Sophie into the true mattering of her Self.

After many years of healing work, including dreamwork, Sophie began to contact the neglected parts of her Self that had been locked away for so long they were barely alive. She began to tentatively nurture them, listen to their promptings, and even experiment with bringing them out into the world in safe company. She let herself be who she really was, rather than who she was expected to be.

Like the ferry sailing, this tumultuous crossing into a new but ancient way of life is not for the weak of spirit. It helps enormously to have someone on the sidelines, cheering, "Keep going! You're getting there!" But occasionally, we may need to stop and take shelter, ask ourselves which inner companions we are travelling with and if they are true allies or just dead weight, representatives of the old way.

When asked about the cousins she was with, Sophie said, "They are my polar opposite and make me feel like an outsider; homeless. My childhood best friend was someone who just stopped talking to me one day for no reason." For Sophie, that old friend is the temptation to abandon the crossing. She is the internal turncoat who loses sight of her worth and allies up with the cousins. It's important to notice that the cousins aren't even individuals, but the groupmind from which Sophie is escaping. They are the inner influence that says, "Without us, you aren't worth anything. And if you try to walk in that weird and colourful way, you will no longer belong with us."

While part of Sophie might say, "I don't want to belong with you," another part says, "But can I survive alone?" So she takes refuge for a moment and finds these wonderful felt shoes. These are symbolic of Sophie's hard-earned progress. They are the felt-sense of finally knowing where she stands, and what matters. I love these felt shoes because they represent the complete reversal of the outside-first approach. Instead they are a way to walk feeling-first, a new kind of listening to the impulses of the body, the longing of the heart, the agreements and disagreements of the instincts and the nervous system.

The voice saying those shoes are ugly is the reductionist attitude that also says your path is nonsense, it doesn't go anywhere, it isn't pretty. Before creativity can take its first breath, the rational voice frightens it away with its impulse to homogenize things until they are drained of mystery. You will know this strangling influence by its automatic quality. It is the invalidation that rears up the moment we step outside the line, questioning our legitimacy, scrutinizing our every note and movement, holding us to a deadening and unreachable perfection. It tells us we're too *woo-woo* and dismisses our feelings as sentimental, our dreams as illusory, our ideas as unoriginal.

Rather than pitting matter and meaning against one another, consider that they are simply in a backwards order of priority. If we come back to our guiding metaphor of the living bridge, we can see that what makes the metaphor so lyrical is the teaching of how we must come into collaboration with nature herself.

It is the strangler fig's tendency to send out its roots which, without any guiding influence, would choke the host for its own growth's sake. Materialism, like the strangling vine, is not evil—but left unmitigated by a higher purpose, is dedicated only to its own invasive spread. It requires our intervention, a participatory weaving with the soul's longing for beauty and meaning, so that it can become exalted in its service to the whole.

In the end, Sophie came to see how she still sometimes turns to the external world for approval. Though she had made great progress in finding those felt shoes at all, now she had to learn to walk in them, despite what others might say. And as she learns to give more relevance and value to her dreams, feelings, and creative life, a true sense of purpose and belonging will be rekindled in her heart.

Tending the Well

Most of us feel an agonizing longing to contribute something meaningful to the deficits of our time. But weeks, months and even years can disappear in just keeping up on the treadmill of life's demands. We are in a constant state of being responsive to the world's requirements of us. Whether it's our everyday to-do list, which never seems to shrink, or how we wait to be notified of opportunities and invitations, this 'call and response' relationship with the external world is such a deeply ingrained habit that we barely know another way to live. But the truth is, if we really want to make an eloquent offering of our lives, we have to step out of that dependency on the external world and locate our source of guidance within.

In some spiritual traditions, externalization is put to good use with the creation of symbolic places for you to visit where you can restore your relationship with the sacred. In Ireland, for instance, you can find hundreds, maybe even thousands, of holy wells located all over the country. Usually set in a grove of trees, at the edge of waysides, and other places of wild beauty, these elaborately built stone wells—where water springs from the earth—are considered sacred and supernatural. Holy wells which predate the arrival of Christianity in Ireland, are said to be the early sites of devotion to the Earth Mysteries, and were appealed to for divination and the curing of illness. Still today, these wells are the destination of many spiritual pilgrimages.

Traditionally, the pilgrim would offer gratitude to the holy well for the riches of village life and petition the well priestesses and fairies for healing. If someone slept near one, they might even receive dreams foretelling the future. In Celtic mythology, the holy well is considered the source of all life—certainly because it is the concealed origin from which water springs, but also because it is a gateway between the worlds seen and unseen.

What I find so enchanting about this Irish form of worship is how these external sites of reverence for nature are also considered gateways to the holy helpers of the hidden world. It was understood that if one of these wells would fall into disrepair, the village was at risk of losing not only their literal life source, but their connection to the Otherworld.

While most of us weren't raised with such a life-giving mythology, I believe we share a Grandmother Well that springs inexhaustibly with wisdom, insight, and guidance for our healing that we can access from the holy grove within. Especially in times of exile, when our anchors are pulled up and we're no longer taking cues from the outside world, we have a chance to find that inner well and reinstate our connection to the sacred. We may find it overgrown, or hard to reach through the brambles, but each of us faces a time when the well within needs tending: when we're no longer able to bestow blessings on others because we've over-given, or when something precious has been taken from us, or life's demands have been too taxing on our fragile system. When the moisture goes out of our lives, and we're no longer able to see beauty or converse with magic, we must ask ourselves how we can replenish our well-ness.

Too often, we fall into the misguided belief that the outside world is our source of vitality. We wait for its cues and its permissions and forget to honour, petition, and receive from the well within. Unconsciously, we're terrified to turn away from the world; we think we're putting our 'heads in the sand,' or that we'll lose everything if we don't keep pace. But the truth is that there is a different rhythm trying to temper us from within. If we shift our responsiveness from the outer to the inner world, allowing for a periodic ebbing of our external effectiveness, we come to see that it's in service to a more harmonious way with our own bodies and with our greater earthbody.

To hear the rhythm of your indigenous song, to fall in step with the poetry of your unfolding, first there must be a clearing away: a *temenos* of simplicity in which to dwell. *Temenos* is a Greek word, which has no English equivalent, meaning 'a piece of ground surrounding or adjacent to a temple; a sacred enclosure.' Strike a holy grove of silence where you can listen as you long to be heard, see as you long to be seen, recognize where you long to be relevant, needed, and necessary. Sink down into your estrangement, and let the grief of your disappointment be the moisture that baptizes the seeds of your potential so they can finally break open.

And as you are tending to your inner well, know that your work is part of a larger mission that is attempting, through our combined experience, to come into harmony. In other words, our individual well-being is also the well-being of the whole. Rather than thinking of the external world as the 'real reality,' you begin to see, as the Celts well knew, that psyche and nature are intrinsic. There is a conversational relationship between the inner and outer worlds, a dynamic reciprocity which can be strengthened by our tending to their equivalence.

This as-above-so-below thinking is one of the great capacities born of dreamwork. If we're doing it well, there are always two parallel conversations taking place: the personal individuation process, and the context in which that soul-work is being done. Traditionally, psychotherapy was focused on the individual's personal history alone, but over the decades, it has evolved to consider the context of human culture. A person's despair or anxiety cannot be tended to without considering the values, or lack of values, in which we are bred, such as poverty, racism, patriarchy, and capitalism. Conversely, the work we are doing at the level of the Self is contributing to our collective evolution.

As we dethrone our inner tyrants, we are contributing to the emancipation of people power in the world. As we replenish our inner scarcities, we are helping to create a culture that values and provides for its visionaries and outcasts. As we smash the influence of the patriarchy within, we are giving rise to Eros in the world. We are changing consciousness from the inside outwards.

Tending the inner well replenishes our devotion to the deep feminine aquifer for which our world is thirsting. When we recognize ourselves as a tributary of that greater upwelling, we allow things to be decided, spoken, and created not by us, but *through* us. In shifting our responsiveness to the inner call, rather than the outer one, our mission finds a sense of nobility in its service to the whole.

There is a world behind the visible surface of things which is pulsing vitality into our lives. It is the birthplace of dreams, the workshop of imagination, the source from which all creation arises and unto which the ancestors have returned. At any given moment, we are either turning away from or coming into congruence with our kinship with mystery. Only when we wrestle to keep the endangered language of beauty and sensitivity alive do we have a chance at becoming necessary to the urgency of our times.

Eight
Trekking the Creative Wild

There is a wilderness in every person. A way of walking, a set of spots, an inclination, a blinking impulse that silently draws us forward. Like an elephant finding water in a desert it has never travelled, or a bird coming to fly with brand new wings, we all have this instinctual capacity. It is the animal in us that knows what it knows, and it's the origin from which all creativity is expressed.

Instinct is the part of us, as in all animals, that knows without thinking what and when to do something, how to respond, which way to go. Like the salmon that swims its way across hundreds of river miles to its birthplace, we too have inborn impulses that don't require thinking to get us there. Instinct is our 'right responsiveness' guiding us towards our yesses, and away from our noes.

It is through this instinctual nature that our soul's medicine for the world flows. For many of us, however, this wilderness within has been so domesticated and harnessed for its resources that we barely recognize its call. But just as a plot of land can be rewilded by a kind of *leaving it alone*, so too can we rewild our psyches by ceasing 'self-development' and allowing mystery to work upon us.

For survivors of neglect and abuse, the relationship to the instinctual life can be especially damaged. An instinct is injured when your responses are repeatedly overridden, dismissed, or ignored, often by adults who have a wounded instinct themselves. For instance, you may have been criticized for overreacting when you were having an appropriate response, or perhaps you were told to stay quiet when you knew you should speak. Maybe you had to care for another's needs before your own. Whatever form the wounding of your instinct might have taken, over time the result is the same. It is the sense of distrusting your own responses, questioning the validity of your feelings, and giving power to another's information over your own.

On an intuition that she needed to work with her dreams, a woman I'd never met named Marika came to me with nothing but a few fragments of a dream. The dream was brief, and she was ready to dismiss it, but there was such potency in the image that I encouraged her to go deeper into it with me.

Blindfolded Horse, Marika's dream

I dream there is a black horse who has been blindfolded and beaten.
The horse is anxiously moving around in too narrow an enclosure.
I'm trying to lift the blindfold from his eyes.

The first thing I asked Marika was if she ever had a relationship with a horse before. Instantly, she remembered that when she was a small child, she briefly had a horse who was as black as the one in the dream. She proceeded to tell me how the horse was wild and trusted nobody but Marika to ride him. They had a very special relationship, and she described him as a lively and expressive spirit. Others, mainly her father, didn't know how to communicate with him. One day, Marika overheard her parents negotiating with a man in the kitchen downstairs and before she knew it, her horse was taken away and she never saw him again.

The story hung in the air between us like the life-changing event that it was. As we explored Marika's relationship with her father, it turned out that as a small person, she too had a wild and expressive nature that was often reprimanded. I asked Marika how the horse must feel being blindfolded, and she said his eyesight was a huge part of his instinct. Without it, he became anxious and full of restrained energy.

I asked Marika if she could relate to a similar feeling of being anxious in her current waking life, and she recognized it immediately. She described working in a corporate environment where she felt like she was living in disguise with her creativity completely restrained. She made the connection back to childhood, where she learned over time to keep her opinions to herself, to avoid talking about the "'weird' things that interested her, and eventually made a life in false belonging. Of course there was a price to pay: Marika was experiencing debilitating bouts of anxiety. The dream seemed to be leading us to discover the source of that suffering, which lived in the extinguishing of her expressive instinct. Like the dark horse, she was living in too narrow an enclosure for her life, and had been blinded to how it was affecting her.

Instead of being taught to protect yourself from things or people who might do you harm, like Marika you may have learned to distrust your own feelings, boundaries, and reactions. If you grow accustomed to overriding your responses, as you get older, you stop being able to recognize intrusions and violations. Over time, you may have delayed reactions to poor behaviour if you were taught to be accommodating above all else. You may have even found yourself dwelling for years on a moment in which you wish you'd said or done something differently.

But having a wounded instinct is becoming more common as a direct result of our disconnected culture. The more we live in virtual realities, where our connection to others is mediated by technology, and the more we subscribe to a human-centric way of life, the less we are in direct conversation with each other, our own bodies, and the natural world around us. As we fall out of touch with the physical world, our impulses for even basic things like hunger, thirst, and touch are ignored for long periods of time, often resulting in mental distress and physical disease.

While a wounded instinct can take a serious toll on our personal lives, at the collective level, our disconnection from the other-than-human life around us is devastating to our environment. Most of us carry around an indistinct grief or trauma about the consequences of our disconnection from nature, but few of us know what to do about it.

I believe we have more than enough creativity to solve the problems of our times, but we have to make a perilous trek into the wilderness within to reclaim it.

There is a stand of undeveloped jungle, a place of *indigeneity* within each of us, that can never be domesticated. It is a borderless land, beyond personality and convention, even beyond thought, where pure creativity arises. Like the signature song of a tropical bird, the spiralling of an arbutus tree, the evening scent of a jasmine bush, there is an essence in each of us intended to be expressed. Few make the trek into this creative wild, because the path requires great vulnerability. To come into our true originality, we must surrender the layers of numbness we use to protect our hearts.

In my practice I work with many medicine people who have sent their gifts for dreaming, seeing, and creativity into exile. These gifts are often forged in the belly of trauma, then sent into hiding because the world feels too hostile to use them in the open. The problem is that in armouring our sensitivity, we're in danger of numbing the whole spectrum of our feeling.

When we are thrust into exile, we are suddenly flooded with the backlog of unfelt feeling. This is why it can seem like one heartbreak joins with every other heartbreak you've ever felt in one mass of insurmountable grief. And though we may want nothing more than to distance ourselves from it, I believe we are being offered a chance, through the opening grief makes in us, to rehabilitate the relationship to our instinctual creativity. In exile, away from the hungry mouths and grabby hands that crowd in on our lives, we have a chance to come into conversation with our wild self again.

At a pivotal point in his career, an entrepreneur named Brian came to see me when he started experiencing serious health issues. It didn't take long to discover that he was tremendously stressed after a several-year undertaking to get his business off the ground. Exhausted now that he'd finally released his project into the world, Brian had strenuous plans to market the project over the course of the upcoming months. Since his work was already receiving a tremendous response, we spoke about where the urge to keep pushing came from. Brian recognized that a part of him couldn't trust that what he gave was ever enough, even at the expense of his own health. As we explored it in more depth, Brian recognized a lifelong feeling of not being supported and having to do everything on his own. Tears sprang to his eyes as he made this realization. Maybe, I suggested, he could give up this next leg of his plan and place his trust in something greater to carry it forward. Though he bristled at the thought of abandoning his elaborate strategy, his whole body relaxed at the prospect. That night, he had the following dream.

Undamming the Flow, Brian's dream

I dream I am at a big outdoor event to ceremonialize the decision to remove a long-standing dam. When the moment arrives, the officials open the dam and a rush of fresh water flows through the channel. Exotic tall birds, like herons and pelicans, have gathered at the mouth of the river to catch the new fish that, previously inaccessible, are now swimming in this water. I am standing in the water with my friend in awe, when I see baby orcas swimming alongside me!

When I asked Brian what he thought of the dam, he said dams are used for "harnessing wild water for power." In a sudden flash, he could see that his own drive for power was exploiting his well-being. But the moment he decided to dismantle that rigid way of thinking, giving up his ambitions to the wild force of nature, a rush of life flooded through him. He could finally see that there was already so much support trying to reach him. Like the heron, who is a master at waiting for the fish to come to him, the dream seemed to say there was much greater potential in letting things take their own course. Now that he'd done all the hard work, Brian needed to learn how to follow his instincts, listen to his body, and trust himself to be carried by the undercurrents.

Here on the west coast of Canada, the dwindling communities of orca whales are endangered by the encroachment of oil tanker traffic through the Salish Sea. Not only does the thunderous noise of vessels disorient orcas' ability to feed via echolocation, but oil spills devastate their habitat. Given all of this, the baby orcas in Brian's dream are deeply encouraging. There is a sense that something sacred has come to life in this new attitude. Perhaps we could even say that nature agrees with the rewilding of Brian's approach. Interesting to note that orcas are half black and white, just like the yin-yang symbol. Perhaps there's another clue in this dream about balancing the active side of Brian's nature with more receptivity.

Many take the path well-worn, but they are only given a half-lived life. To those willing to brave the unknown path, the dark thicket, a remembering of love, magic, and purpose returns. There is a wild woman under our skin who wants nothing more than to dance until her feet are sore, sing her beautiful grief into the rafters, and offer the bottomless cup of her creativity as a way of life. And if you are able to sing from the very wound that you've worked so hard to hide, not only will it give meaning to your own story, but it becomes a corroborative voice for others with a similar wounding.

There are many practices that can stimulate our reconnection to the instinctual self. Anything that involves us with the natural world—like digging in the dirt, walking in the woods, learning ancestral skills, eating food we've foraged or grown, and hanging out with undomesticated animals—can mirror for us how to get back to our own animal bodies. Dance and somatic play are especially wonderful in rekindling pleasurable ways to be in our bodies, which are so often treated as utilitarian machines. So is playing with art supplies; not to produce art, but to enjoy colours and textures and find the shapes of our feelings.

My favourite entryway into the instinctual wild is through the dreamtime. The first necessity of dreamwork is to receive a dream. In this far-from-passive act, receptivity is the central feminine principle that invites mystery to approach us. In dreams, the mysterious wild Other must be courted by the right conditions—coaxed out of the *metaphorest* with gentle cooing, indirect attention and steady remaining stillness. If you're lucky, you might catch a glimpse of her gleaming feathers, a piercing gaze, her glistening coat, and realize that she's been watching you all along—waiting for you to get quiet and brave enough to remember her.

When you dream of a wild animal, you are touching the part of yourself that can never be domesticated. The animal heart lives according to an ancient set of laws. She doesn't care about politics and politeness and never takes more than she should. She reminds you of your nobility, your physical magnificence, and the unselfconscious power of instinct. The animal heart sees clearly what the intellect cannot because it follows the innate knowing of the earth itself.

The animal heart lives behind logic, below reason, underneath the armour of objectivity. She has lived longer than any of us can remember because it was from her belly that we were born. Half-sighted as we are, we forget and deny her, building our platforms on what we think is her grave. But she is far from dead. She stays hidden not because she is timid, but because she is wise. And if she comes out to greet you, know that you are trustworthy of her approach.

The animals in our dreams are the keepers of our feeling life. More than just *affect*, feeling is the total capacity of the human organism to experience the world. The more we feel, the more sensitively we engage with the world around us. If we are overriding our instincts, our dream animals might appear wounded, starved, or neglected. Like a dog or cat we've forgotten to feed, consider that a part of us is craving the same nurturing intimacy that we feel in relationship with our familiar. This is to show us how to have compassion and reverence for our animal body and heart.

Letting Mystery Approach You

One of the greatest challenges in working with dreams is allowing mystery to work upon us. In this age of instantly answerable questions, there is very little left to the imagination. We take everything from that place and subject it to analysis. Governed as we are by the great scientific quest to pull things apart to get at their mechanics, we find ourselves asking, "Yeah, but what does it *mean*?" As if a dream could be summed up in a bottom line. But the truth is we aren't moved or changed by the fast and dirty definition. What we really want is a relationship, a dialogue, a conversation with that place within us which always remains essentially mysterious.

Rather than answering everything, it's important to remember that there are certain questions that should be cherished. In dreamwork, there is a complex alchemy that brews in our not-knowing, which is essential to our becoming worthy of a dream's revelation. As Dr. Clarissa Pinkola Estés tells us, there are those who used to refer to the dreammaker as the "Riddle Mother"[26] because when you carry your question into sleep, she responds to it with a riddle. Like any good fairy tale, the task is not to find a direction, but to let the quest shape you into the kind of person who knows which way to go.

If you feel dissatisfied with dream dictionaries, which reduce your symbols to mean something other than they are (like "if you dream of a butterfly it means new beginnings"), it is because your living mystery is being objectified.

While there are such things as universal symbols, even those vary greatly depending on the person dreaming them. It's more engaging to think of our symbols as living, breathing beings who are choosing to visit us. As James Hillman puts it, "Like the fox in the forest is not mine just because I see it, so the fox in the dream is not mine just because I dream it."[27]

So much of dreamwork and, conversely, belonging, is about making ourselves hospitable to mystery. Hospitality is the art of opening a space in our home for someone to arrive there. Rather than forcing the expectation that our needs be met, we make a courtship of that which we are curious about or admire. So let us make our lives alluring. Let us stand with a respectful distance and make an invitation of ourselves, that wildness might decide to approach us. Let us re-member ourselves to the mysterious unknown, even when we hear nothing back. Let us keep returning to that uncomfortable silence and allow ourselves to be shaped by our yearning for answers.

Just by turning a dream's symbol over in your hands, looking at it this way and that, walking with it throughout your day, maybe journalling a poem or sharing it with a good friend, you will come to understand why it is approaching you. Maybe it's an animal come to remind you of a power you've been shrinking back from, or maybe it's a tyrant who is helping you to find your "No." But as you live into relationship with each of your dream visitors, notice the parallel ways in waking life in which you feel similarly hindered by invalidation, criticism and restriction—or brought alive by that which fills you with energy. Understanding the nuances of your inner culture strengthens your instinctual response. You learn to trust that, even as you are honing the ability to express them with grace, your feelings have an intelligence worth following. And as your instincts get stronger and clearer, your creativity begins teeming again, like a river undammed.

Creative Originality

Creativity is one of those intimidating words, like artist, musician, writer, and so on, which has been co-opted to mean something rarefied and unreachable. We think of ourselves as being 'a creative type' or not, as if it were a quality bestowed on the chosen few. But if we decolonize the word and take it back to its true origins, we find the Latin root *crescere*, a word which means to come forth, spring up, grow, thrive, swell. Like the crescent moon, creativity is the living impulse in each of us which continually begins again.

Whether we are inventing a new recipe, combining outfits, or simply looking at things in a new way, we are compelled to recreate our world again and again. When things get too stagnant or comfortable, we begin to feel restless and wild. Our vitality is inextricably bound up with creativity. The instinct to create is what keeps life pulsing through our veins. Like Kahlil Gibran writes about trees in an orchard, "They give that they may live, for to withhold is to perish."[28]

As children, these impulses are strong and intrinsic. We leap wholeheartedly into what amazes us, and disagree loudly with anything we don't like! We can also spend hours lost in make-believe, creating something from nothing, morning to night. At that age, we have a clear and unhindered relationship with the imagination. Beguiled by wonder, creativity isn't yet thought of as something we *do* so much as an unimpeded continual flowing through us. Creativity is our instinct to find and express new perspectives. And these idea-animals don't come from the mind, nor do they come from a highly trained skill set: they come forth from the unconscious.

Whether through dreams or 'gap time' in our schedules, creativity is something that natures through us when we give it the room it needs. "It takes a lot of time to be a genius," wrote Gertrude Stein, "you have to sit around so much doing nothing, really doing nothing."[29]

From this perspective, originality is not something you invent so much as an utterance through you by your origins. By origins I mean that Grandmother Well from which every human being drinks. That which is dreaming us. You might call it god, nature, source, instinct, but whatever word you use, it is an act of great unfolding through us.

Originality then becomes the practice of unhindering what's already there. This work is essential to belonging because your creative offering is like a holy signal to those who carry a similar vibratory signature. In hearing or seeing what you've created, they will find a sense of belonging with you and, by being found, so will you.

Even when the creative impulse is strong, many people get stuck in the swamp of invalidation before they even leave the gate. The Death Mother is always haranguing us with accusations like, "Your offering is not good enough. Others have done it sooner and better than you, so don't embarrass yourself trying." Unable to penetrate the density of those blocks of perfectionism and comparison, we may sink back into hiding, our divine longing to sing into the great song silenced.

Perfectionism and Comparison

Perfectionism is one of the great pillars of patriarchy, used to stem the rise of the wild feminine. Like we saw in Tziporah's dream, it is an impossible standard that, when we strive for it, guarantees our failure because it's ultimately unreachable. Perfection is a counterfeit form of beauty which, as you're strengthening your instincts, will ring with dissonance despite its seductive surface.

True beauty always contains a delicious dash of chaos. It has a wild or unpredictable quality that takes you by surprise. Perfectionism tries to stamp out that quality in pursuit of an impeccability that strips a thing of its spontaneity. If we are seduced by it, it can choke all the life from our offering, turning it homogenous and agreeable. As I was learning to distinguish between surface beauty and true substance, I had the following dream.

Flowery Chocolates, Toko-pa's dream

I dream of beautifully crafted chocolates in the form of a bouquet of flowers. I want so much to eat them, but am discouraged with the thought that they are sickeningly sweet and floral tasting. I know I'll regret it if I do.

I received this dream after comparing my music unfavorably to a musician I know who has the perfect soprano voice. The kind of music she makes is pretty and accessible, while my own is guttural and, for better or worse, often described as "unique." While my friend went on to win awards and sell records, I kept getting rejected for gigs and recording deals. Over time, I started to believe that unless I could learn how to make prettier music, I would never succeed. The day before this dream, I'd been listening to one of my friend's tracks, thinking how perfect it was in every way. And yet, if I'm honest, I would never buy an album like this because the artists I admire are 'unique' weirdos like me. In fact, the whole era of music I love most is analog and full of beautiful 'mistakes.'

The chocolates in my dream were symbolic of the shrill kind of beauty that I was ingesting with that formulaic, mainstream music. The dream warned me that if I bought into that 'sickeningly sweet' quality, I would regret it. On some level I was being seduced by the perfection of that genre, which is always being given accolades and airplay, but the truth is that creativity for me, like chocolate, should be a combination of dark and sweet, with a good dose of bitterness.

This bittersweet quality is what the Spanish call *duende*. Duende is thought of as a goblin or dark daimon that possesses the artist in a moment of pure, magnetic honesty. The artist must, as the poet Federico García Lorca says, "rob herself of skill and security, send away her muse and become helpless, that her Duende might come and deign to fight her hand to hand..."[30]

Psychically speaking, there is no such thing as perfection. In dreams, we come to learn that as soon as a room is perfectly tidy and clean, someone tracks dirt in, or a rat begins scratching in the floorboards. In other words, the moment we give into the belief that we've reached attainment—or that we're done with personal work and have risen above suffering, pain, or shadows—darkness will come calling. Nature will always take what is too high and bring it down to earth.

In some aesthetic traditions, like the Japanese concept of *wabi-sabi*, artists will go out of their way to put a flaw into a creation that is too perfect. As the author Richard Powell explains it, "[W]abi-sabi nurtures all that is authentic by acknowledging three simple realities: nothing lasts, nothing is finished, and nothing is perfect. This Buddhist approach is wonderfully respectful of darkness and the wisdom it can bring into our creativity, lives and relationships."[31]

Nick Cave further explained, "All love songs must contain *duende*. For the love song is never truly happy. It must first embrace the potential for pain. Those songs that speak of love without having within their lines an ache or a sigh are not love songs at all but rather Hate Songs disguised as love songs, and are not to be trusted. These songs deny us our humanness and our God-given right to be sad and the airwaves are littered with them."[32]

As you begin to dance with a safe dose of chaos, be wary of any influence in your environment that dismisses or judges your enthusiasm. Without it, you would become anaesthetized to life itself. Anyone who demands this smallness of you is in danger themselves and may have contracted this insidious, deadening monotone. Enthusiasm is the vitality of spirit, expressing itself through us, and its grace in our voice should be welcomed and cherished. The word originates in the early 17th century, from the Greek *enthousiasmos* meaning 'possessed by god.' Now, more than ever, the world needs your enlargement, your weirdness, your fiery crescendos of rebellion from boring.

If creativity is doing its job well, it should bleed for us and, in bleeding, allow us to touch the ache of our own wounds. Similarly, our own creativity should draw upon the wisdom of our wounds if it wants to reach others in a meaningful way. So long as we are unwilling to brave towards our personal edge, we won't be drawing creativity from our origins but simply imitating those who have gone before us. There's nothing inherently wrong with imitation. In fact, for many people it can be a great way to test the waters of creativity. But if we stay in imitation too long, it can breed a habitual state of comparison to others. This is because we're not tapping the true origin of our creativity, so our touchstones are external rather than coming from within.

I actually believe that some comparison is an important and necessary part of finding your original voice and becoming whole. To compare yourself to another is an organic impulse vital to the unfolding of individuality. In our admiration of someone, we encounter the undeveloped qualities we have yet to step into, while in our healthy disdain, we come to know our refusals. Projection gets a bad rap because people use it almost accusatorily to say that when we admire or dislike another, it is just a reflection of our unintegrated shadow. But projection is the first and prerequisite stage to integration. As Rumi's beloved teacher, Shams Tabrizi, wrote, "We can't find the truth only listening to our own voice's echo. We can find ourselves only in someone's mirror."

The next responsibility of comparison is to then withdraw those projections and begin cultivating the qualities of the admired other in ourselves. There comes a time when the falsity of a borrowed voice is outweighed by your longing to sing truthfully. Perfectionism and imitation are really attempts to keep the unknown at a distance. To enter the authentic origins of our creativity, we must be willing to make a real encounter with the unknown.

Initially, there is a dark fog you must pass through. I like to think of that fog as a curtain which obscures the outside world and turns us towards ourselves. Like the bowl that has yet to be filled, there is an emptiness that precedes creativity that is alive with potential. With ordinary eyes, it's easy to mistake this emptiness for stagnancy. We may think, "I have nothing of substance to offer! I have no original ideas!" But down at the invisible base of things, there is a holy dance taking place. Though we may want to run from the tension, the polarities are in constant motion, readying themselves into harmony. Far from dormant, this dance is the *active receptivity* that calls things into form. We are such a vessel. These times of 'nothingness' are actually busy with living into a new capacity.

Originality comes when you stay close to that emptiness, making it a welcoming place, adorning it with your divine longing, learning the shape of it, and filling it with your questions. Every great artist I know is obsessed with a question, and their artworks are less attempts to answer that question than they are exaltations of asking. As Jean Cocteau says, "The poet doesn't invent. He listens."[33]

By moon and starlight, abilities you don't use during the day come alive. Like cats and owls, you may discover an ability to navigate the dark with a different kind of seeing. There is a deep knowing that lives in our bones, our bellies, and in the earth itself. Like the wisdom of the gnostic goddess Sophia, this inner knowing is what lights the way, even if distantly and dimly at first. If you can touch the exhilarating side of fear, you are touching your instinct. The mystical pull of your feeling begins to lead the way. You can sense the density of objects around you, hear the songs of stones, and know things are coming even before they've left to meet you. Once you find this way of moving in the dark, you are no longer a follower but a wayshower.

We need more wayshowers, who have penetrated the fog of their own uncertainty to find something truthful. Something human and tragic and beautifully lost, something small but utterly true. Like cupping your hands around a tiny flame, if you can protect the young embers from the harsh winds of your dismissal, it may become a real heartfire. That fire then becomes a beacon for others to sail towards. Not to imitate it, but to emulate its quality of bravery, which has been left like a vibratory signature on the thing you've made. Paradoxically, there is nothing new in eternity, but what *is* new is your alchemical encounter with it.

Vibratory Signature

There is an energetic stamp or vibratory signature behind every act of creation. Though difficult to perceive, it is like the wind blowing through a valley, touching everything we do. Although we create in a multitude of ways, it is what's felt first by others.

My partner Craig is a master flute maker, and though his creations are incredibly beautiful to listen to and behold, people often receive one of his flutes and are struck by the instrument's kindness. Because of the man he is, committed to a life of heart, every simple thing he creates and attends to carries this signature of warmth.

Inasmuch as we are searching for our purpose and occupation in the world, the more salient pursuit is in the *who* we are becoming. It is the vibratory signature behind our enterprise that has the most impact. So the real art form is a kind of open question to the needs of the larger Self: How can I serve you? Do you feel understood? Where is your rapture? What are the conditions necessary for your expression and well-being?

Though we may think of questions like this as self-absorbed, they are actually what lead us to our greater nature that is in service to the broader inclination of the whole. Artful questions such as these penetrate our daily, surface concerns to take us into the deeper quest of the world, carried within our soul's code.

As long as we are attending to the well-being of the Self, purpose then becomes a thing as simple as flowering in all its stages: from dormancy to emergence; the slow, almost imperceptible unfurling; and eventually the trumpeting colour of your truth.

Make no mistake—this temple of originality is not yours alone, but something we're building together. After all, we share the same origins and one day we will, like all our ancestors, return to them. In the meantime, creativity is essential to belonging because it serves as a way for us to recognize each other. We listen for that pulse of originality coming through us, giving it the unique form that comes from our particular encounter with it. And as we make beauty from our origins, we find networks of people just like us, adding their voice to a thing we're all trying to make real.

As extensions of nature, we need our differences to thrive. Some people will be the fire of inspiration you need to inch you closer to your edges, and others will look to you for that push. Originality needs many emissaries with different voices to get its message across. Like a choir, every voice is necessary to make a grand swell. With this in mind, we can remember that creativity is really an act of devotion to that which is creating us.

Our indigenous voice feels no self-consciousness because it is devotional. It is an ancient song that emanates from our gratitude and sings to keep the stars in the sky and the seasons turning. It sings to keep the moon rising in its arc across the night, and the sun giving its healing warmth. It recognizes itself as necessary—an essential note in the great choir of being.

I offer you the following invocation I wrote in honour of Sedna, the Inuit Mother of the Sea, who was once an orphan but became a powerful goddess ruling all ocean life. As water is the source of all life, she is also our mother.

Sedna's Signature

Great Ocean Mother, I call upon you to grace my shores.
I make myself as still as sand,
who knows the patience of millennia,
having been ground down to my essential parts.
I wait my turn at the edge of known things
that you might soak me with your rising swell.
I wish for nothing but to be dislodged by your power
perhaps even carried into your depths
for the chance at a glimpse of your underlife.
May I be taken into your possession, even for a moment,
to know the absence of my gravity
and participation in your rhythms and contractions.

May my body be for what it was intended:
an expression of your grace.
And what small ways I make with this poetry —
what songs and friendships I form —
what migrations and ripples I disturb in the world —
may they have something of your signature on them.
May the you that has touched me
go on multiplying in your phenomenal mathematics
until we are all suffused with awe
at your vastness within us.

Nine

The Dark Guests

*W*e cannot speak of creativity without exploring its dark counterpoint, the destructive hand of nature. For consciousness to have movement, the intactness of belonging must be broken. The force that casts us into exile is an undoing in service to a more elegant reconstitution. This dynamism is the threshold upon which the work of belonging takes place, between what we already have and accept in our lives, and what feels distant or 'other' than us.

Dreams call us to better inhabit our feelings, which is another way of saying *belonging* to the true breadth of our experience. This can be very difficult to do if the dreams we are having are full of anxiety, fear, and sadness, because we are taught in modern culture to distance ourselves from difficult emotions. We are told they are aberrant, and that we should medicate them into oblivion. Even in many spiritual circles, there is huge emphasis on 'staying positive,' and anything that falls outside that border of acceptability is considered 'unspiritual' or negative.

While the New Age movement has awakened many to the power of creative intention, it has simultaneously pathologized the so-called 'negative emotions' and stricken them from our social palette of acceptability. We live under a kind of hegemony of positivity which emphasizes pleasure over pain, gain over loss, happiness over sadness, and the creative over the destructive. We are taught to 'rise above' things like anger, anxiety, sadness—and by whatever means necessary, stay in bliss and light. This kind of bypassing is dangerous because it teaches us to not only dissociate from the multiplicity of ourselves but from the magnificent spectrum of life itself.

What if the 'negative' emotions aren't wrong, but totally in their own right? What if they have something essential to communicate to us and each other, and the real problem is the misguided attitude that negative feelings make us less evolved and need fixing? In the same way that we hold others at an arm's length when they are too different from us, we avoid the inner encounter with otherness, excluding anything that doesn't fit the image we've been building of ourselves.

'Negative emotions' don't cease to exist because we ignore them. They just find other ways to express themselves. Sometimes we lash out inappropriately, have confusing crying fits, or feel protractedly numb. Most commonly, we slip into depression and anxiety. And if we leave it too long, we become prone to accidents, crisis, and even physical disease. In our dreams, this is when we have dark figures chasing us—because there is something quite literally trying to reach us. When we dream of violence, it is so often because we are enacting a kind of inner violence upon our less valued qualities.

If not addressed in a person's life, these issues can harden into ideologies which are then passed down through generations. When you add to this equation a loud or charismatic leader, movements like Nazism will be born from the corroborative fear of *otherness*. Nazism was fomented on the notion of a 'pure race' and, capitalizing on people's unintegrated shadows, convincing a nation to murder millions of people who were the unfortunate bearers of this shadow projection. We think of Nazis as evil, but the truth is we all have the potential for this kind of evil, which is ultimately the act of turning away from the suffering of others and ourselves.

Most of us have been raised to be moral, good, and agreeable, putting all of our 'unacceptable' qualities in what Robert Bly calls "The Long Black Bag" we drag behind us, or what Jung termed the personal "Shadow."[34] The Shadow is the place where everything we have forgotten, denied, rejected, or not yet discovered goes to live. But when we try to live up to the impossible image of a spiritually enlightened, knowledgeable, selfless, patient, forgiving, easy-going, supportive, generous superhuman, the dark side of our nature just gains in power. Like shoving a beach ball under water, you may succeed in disavowing your unsavoury bits for a while—but it's so destabilizing that, when you least expect it, the ball bursts out from under you, especially in the form of dark dreams or nightmares.

This is where dreamwork and belonging almost become synonymous. One of the basic tenets of both dreamwork and of belonging is to learn how to become hospitable towards the dark, repulsive, ambiguous figures that appear in our dreams. Instead of running from difficulty, we practice at turning towards what is chasing us, even inviting it to intensify its expression, so that we can find out what it really wants.

While learning to understand the language of dreams is an art form that takes years to master, there is one question that can almost always take you into the heart of a dream's meaning: "What is the strongest feeling in my dream?" While so many aspects of our dreams are dressed in symbol and metaphor, feelings are never disguised. They are honest representations of the feelings you are having, or *not having*, in waking life. Even if we don't have associations to a certain dream figure, we always know how we feel about them.

To the degree that they've been starved, ignored, or humiliated, figures may appear in our dreams as angry, desperate, neglected or even timid characters. They may take the faces of people who have wronged us. They may be terrifying and reckless. They may be hurt and appear beyond hope. They may be ragged and starving.

In the Taoist way of understanding creation, there is a nuanced spectrum between the polarities rather than a clear-cut boundary between positive and negative. And like any continuum, the opposites are always in a conversation with each other. Negative doesn't mean bad, it simply means opposed to the way things are. Like stones in a river, there are obstructions that arise in the flow which must be navigated. In mathematics, negativity is the space between and around matter. As we explored in the Chinese yin-yang symbol, negativity is the open, yin-like receptivity between actions. So if we remix those definitions, negative emotions are a disagreement with how things are and, if we are receptive to them, they can change the way we are navigating our lives.

There is no such thing as a life free from suffering, but we can change our relationship to pain in the way we choose to walk with it. In the Hindu tradition, the goddess Kali is worshiped as both the creative and destructive, womb and tomb aspects of the Great Mother. In one of her four hands she holds the head she's just severed, which fills a goblet with blood. She is often wielding a scythe, surrounded by a snarling fire, adorned with bones, dancing on a bewildered corpse. Far from the flaccid suggestion that when something isn't working we must "let it go," Kali is the ruthless power behind 'negative emotions' that clears the way for new life. She is the boundaries Anger wants. She is the pounding of Grief's river, rushing us to new vistas. She is the freedom Anxiety shakes for. She is the siren of change that Boredom signals. She is the expansion into which Fear longs to cross.

Just as fire can transform food from its raw form into something digestible, our darknesses are radical transformers. Instead of airbrushing our personalities, we should practice at exaggerating our blemishes, leaning into our stagnancy, wounding, and discomforts. If we really want to evolve, all we have to do is be more expressly where we are.

As an Ambassadress of the Darkness, my message to embrace these uncomfortable emotions is sometimes misinterpreted as an invitation to wallow, or let your base impulses run wild. But what I'm really talking about is getting out from under spiritual override long enough to acknowledge the validity of your feelings. Yessing your conflict doesn't mean staying in it. It means making a compassionate encounter with your difficult feelings until they reveal their hidden intelligence.

For most of us, enlightenment isn't a sudden awakening, but a slow process of shining the light of consciousness onto those rejected, forgotten, and denied places within.

At first, triumph may look like simply not running away, but eventually we will be curious enough to turn to face our pursuers. As we learn that redemption is always on the other side of shadow work, over time we become braver and more hospitable to the darkness. We learn that nightmares are in and of themselves a validation of something that is ready to come to consciousness. Eventually we may even attempt courtship of the dark visitors, recognizing them as clusters of energy that have fallen into disuse or malevolence but which, through our cordiality, reveal themselves as a pulse of vitality inclining us towards wholeness.

Most extraordinarily in this work, we discover that the lion's share of our shadow is pure gold. Hidden in the dark we find our creative endowments—those things that make us uniquely beautiful or powerful—and little by little, our divine inheritance can be fully claimed. A huge amount of energy can be locked up in our unexpressed feelings, but by acknowledging them, they can be liberated for our empowerment. That which used to chase us can be claimed as a source of power.

Learning to welcome our dark guests is a source of great personal potency, but it also changes the way we move in the world. In learning to love the entirety of ourselves, we come into contact with a far vaster compassion for others. As Alice Walker says, "Helped are those who love others unsplit off from their faults; to them will be given clarity of vision."[35] A symmetry begins to reveal itself on the outside as we welcome the Other within. We become increasingly accepting, not only of the diverse otherness in our fellow humans, but porous to the other-than human world around us. The work begins here; it is the molasses-slow acknowledgment of each of these unwelcome guests into our house of belonging, as Rumi describes so well in this exquisitely translated poem by Coleman Barks:

The Guest House

This being human is a guest house.
Every morning a new arrival.
A joy, a depression, a meanness,
some momentary awareness comes

As an unexpected visitor.
Welcome and entertain them all!
Even if they're a crowd of sorrows,
who violently sweep your house
empty of its furniture,
still treat each guest honorably.
He may be clearing you out
for some new delight.
The dark thought, the shame, the malice,
meet them at the door laughing,
and invite them in.
Be grateful for whoever comes,
because each has been sent
as a guide from beyond.

Anger

Anger is one of those emotions that's been long stricken from acceptability, especially for women, who are taught that being angry makes you unlikeable— and being unlikeable is a kind of rejection from femininity itself. You may have set about a lifetime of unspoken penance to becoming 'a nice person.' You turn down your volume, soften your step, retract your talons, and acquiesce. Or perhaps you had someone in your life who used anger inappropriately and you vowed never to be like them, swinging the pendulum to the opposite extreme.

But a terrible thing is severed in the suppression of anger: your relationship with one of your greatest allies. Anger appears on your doorstep when your heart has been offended, your values have been wronged, your beloveds are threatened, or somewhere, justice has been denied. Anger is the catalyst to the impotence you may feel in these situations. It sets your heart racing, elevates your blood pressure, and quickens your breath. Adrenaline surges through your veins and poises you for action.

This profound physical transformation can make you feel out of control, but that may be in part because the incisiveness of *power* has become a stranger to us. When we suppress our anger, it often results in one of two outcomes: it turns inward and takes the form of depression, sometimes somaticizing into disease, or it bursts out of us in an exaggerated and inappropriate way. If you're too quick to anger and later regret that you've lashed out at others, consider whether this is the result of chronically ignoring your own needs and feelings.

To give you an example of how this might express itself in dreams, there was a woman named Ginny who once came to me with a dream of being chased by a grizzly bear. She was wracked with fear in the dream, but when she woke up she couldn't relate to feeling fearful in waking life at all. But there was one detail in the dream which stuck out to me: Ginny was running away with a friend she described as "very spiritual" who was always "in love and light."

Rather than exploring the fear, to which Ginny had no association, I asked her to inhabit the bear instead. I invited her feel into what she imagined him to be experiencing. She described the hugeness of being in his body. A detail emerged in which the grizzly bear was eating a deer so small it seemed insubstantial by comparison. As the bear, she described how devouring she felt towards the deer. And as soon as the words came out of her mouth, Ginny had a sudden "A-ha!" moment in which the dream became clear to her.

She remembered how the day before, her husband told her he was feeling depressed and unmotivated. This was a chronic condition for him over the years they'd been married. Even though she felt a devouring anger growing in her for the stuckness he couldn't break out of, and which was holding their family back, instead she was gentle and reassuring towards him. The bear was the part of Ginny who was consumed with a grizzly rage that she was terrified to face or embody.

The redeeming medicine Ginny received from this dream was that instead of running away from conflict, taking a solely 'love and light' approach to the relationship, she should embody some of what she considered to be her un'bear'able feelings. And in expressing her anger more directly, she would not only feel more authentic, but perhaps help move her relationship out of stagnation into a more genuine intimacy.

Maturing your relationship with anger means developing respect for your limitations, no matter how much further ahead you wish you were, and using discernment in how you wield your personal power.

In the early days of befriending anger, it's important to explore it in a safe environment. The next time you find yourself growing upset, try taking a moment alone where you can 'run your anger' in private. Running your emotions is a practice, done in solitude, where you allow the feeling loose in your body. Rather than trying to push it away, or 'rise above it,' you go more fully into it. Call the feeling on stronger, amplifying it in whatever way feels right for you in the moment. Let it course through your veins—feel the power of its presence in your body—let it invigorate you. Maybe give it a voice and let yourself roar. Or perhaps you'd like see it in colour by splashing paint onto a canvas. Maybe you need to stomp it out, or dance to your favourite Metallica record. Whatever you decide to do, make sure the emotion gets to have a voice without being judged as selfish or bad. Listen to what it has to say. Let it know that you support it, that anger can trust you to have its back.

Though it may feel like chaos when you first run your emotions and listen to what they have to say, you are acknowledging their validity and restoring the damaged relationship to your instincts. Once you know what your instincts are telling you, you can begin to make necessary changes in your life. You may find that anger is protecting a hidden hurt or fear. Or you may get clear about asserting your boundaries, setting limits against other people's behaviour. Maybe you'll find you need to defend yourself or others in a constructive way. Or perhaps you'll discover that the real source of your anger is from keeping your needs silent for too long.

Sometimes anger runs deeper than the immediate situation in which it's being triggered. Especially for those who have suffered trauma and abuse, anger can be a constant companion over which you feel you have no control. In these situations, it's important to cultivate a support system around you where kindness towards all your feelings can be modelled for you to eventually emulate.

In the practice of belonging, anger is essential. It shows up to protect us, like a fierce sentinel, guarding what is still too tender to be seen. But it also shows us where our disagreements are with the status quo. It is the voice that needs to raise its volume because it feels unheard. It is up to us to listen to that voice, to dignify it first with our own attention. With enough practice, you will recognize your sacred disagreements sooner and not allow them to be swept under the rug, left to fester. Anger can become a sword of discernment, which doesn't lash out to hurt another but is uncompromising in its defence of your boundaries, teaching others to respect you as you respect yourself. As Maya Angelou puts it, "Bitterness is like cancer. It eats upon the host. But anger is like fire. It burns it all clean."[36]

Disappointment

Disappointment appears when somebody or something has let you down, or when you feel as if you've missed your own mark. Things have fallen short of your hopes and expectations. And with too many of these experiences, life itself can feel like a disappointment, never turning out as you wished it to. But this guest also has a concealed medicine for us.

Like anger, disappointment has a way of becoming overgrown. Without our attention and intervention, it can spread a drabness across the whole of one's life. Ironically, we may even find ourselves swearing off hope, expecting things to go wrong as a way of outsmarting disappointment. But that let-down feeling from things falling short of their promise can be a good fire. Inside the failure of the situation burns our longing for something better. Disappointment says "I expect more."

There is often a hidden falseness that reveals itself in disappointment. Like disillusionment, our tinted view of a thing comes into sharper focus. We realize that something was not up to meeting us well, or sometimes it is us who is not fully up to the meeting. We saw this earlier in the story of Ella and Carrie, the two friends who weren't meeting each other authentically. Ella showed up only sporadically for Carrie, suggesting that she didn't value the friendship—but Carrie tolerated it out of fear of losing her. In a sense they were both contributing to the falseness between them. Rather than staying in chronic disappointment, we could bring that conversation into the open, risking the loss of that relationship for something more meaningful. Though revealing falseness in a situation can be painful, it's good to grieve that which has disappointed us, because our heartbreak draws us more deeply into the longing we have for our lives.

Sometimes the things we think we want are lacking in imagination, when life has something far more interesting in store for us. Other times, commitment is strengthened by disappointment. In the example above, disappointment put Carrie in touch with what she really wanted. The absence of a great friend was better than the presence of a poor one, because it prepared a space in her life for new connections to arrive. Without support or momentum, are you still faithful to what you long for? Or do you give up too easily on what you've pledged yourself to? Disappointment is the secret teacher of devotion. It calls forward your unwavering fidelity to the path.

Disappointment can also take the form of boredom. Like a recurring dream, we are tired of meeting the same challenges with the same strategies that land us with the same results. It's marvellous to grow bored of a pattern, because it means you're ready to sidestep that old strategy and meet life with who you are in present time. Likewise, when you're feeling disappointed and let down by life, I believe you're really being given an invitation to create.

The opposite of disappointment is satisfaction. One of the practices I love most for dancing with disappointment is writing about that which I long for as if it's already happening, describing in great detail the well-being I have inside my new creation, looking around and saying what I see and why it's splendid. I like to sketch these out in drawings, however feebly, and fill them with poetry, focusing less on the form itself and more on the refinement of my feeling in that creation. I can't tell you how amazingly powerful and precise this exercise can be. It helps move us into the actualization of what we long for while also allowing for life's collaborative input to surprise us.

Depending on how much resistance we have to receiving satisfaction, a creation may materialize overnight or gradually come into form over months or even years. But the greater our devotion to that creation, the more our nighttime dreams behave like a North Star. As Meister Eckhart, explains "When the soul wants to experience something, she throws out an image in front of her and steps into it."[37]

Restlessness

It starts as a hairline crack, a seemingly harmless dissonance in the surface of our well-being. But over time, the crack gains momentum into a network of irritations. Forging ahead with a vague sense of needing to catch up, restlessness is the guest who is constantly in motion. It has a mission and is determined to run its course, but left unexamined it can become a persistent state.

The gift of restlessness is that it provides an oculus into our ways and habits. It serves to undermine those places where we might be struggling, mimicking, or falling into false belonging rather than moving with the rhythms of our inner life. As Jungian analyst Marie-Louise von Franz explains, "Restlessness is caused by a surplus of bottled-up energy, which makes us fuss around all the time because we are not connected with the dream world or the unconscious."[38]

Even as our lives take on excellent forms, we can easily fall into the habit of taking our prompts from the outside world, responding to its demands and invitations, instead of beckoning things towards us from a place of presence. At its deepest core, restlessness is the sacred question that asks, "Whom does the Grail serve?"

The Holy Grail is the part-historical, part-mythical vessel found in the Arthurian legend of Perceval. Perceval sets out on a quest to retrieve the Grail, said to have life-restoring powers, to save his dying King. Though his journey is long and rife with failure, there is a pivotal moment when Perceval must ask the question, "Whom does the Grail serve?" This is the moment when Perceval must confront the value of his quest. To what or whom is my life in service? The story is symbolic of our individuation process. We are each a holy vessel in which the dying, materialistic worldview can be redeemed with meaning and divine purpose.

Like the mythical Grail, we all want to open ourselves to purpose, to create a capacity through which the mystery may express itself in our lives. Yet even for those of us who follow this vocational call, the perpetual allure of the external world, with its promises of success, wealth, and status, is powerful and can cause a gradual but critical shift in the emphasis of our service—away from the holy, towards growth for growth's sake.

The way to meet this difficult guest is actually embedded in the word itself, with *rest* at the secret heart of restlessness. But it's not as simple as taking a nap or binge-watching your favourite TV show. Rest, in this sense, is about relaxing what Don Juan (via Carlos Castaneda) called the "first attention."[39] First attention is our ordinary consciousness that helps us meet the demands of the daily, physical world. 'Second attention' is the non-ordinary awareness that we call the dreaming body. It is the subtle, non-physical part of us which perceives and moves energy. Rest is about dropping into that second attention so we can perceive which way the energy wants to go. You may know the second attention as those infrequent gap-times in your day when an idea comes to you out of nowhere: when relaxing in a bath, or in those final moments before sleep when you reflect on the day's events. But with practice, you can engage the second attention throughout your day. It is through the dreaming body that we receive a sense of meaningful direction.

Often, it is only when our well runs dry that we realize how thirsty we've been, and we finally become aware of having lost our ability to be present in life. We may find ourselves asking: what happened to those magic eyes that saw poetry in ordinary things? Where went the wondrous self whose very countenance is invitational? Put quite simply, restlessness is when our emptiness has become full.

For a long time, I thought the practice of 'emptiness' went against my philosophy of affirming the totality of life. I believed it was something detached and cold that pushed life away instead of embracing it. It wasn't until I considered the image of the Holy Grail, with its most luscious emptiness, that I began to understand what it means to *rest* the first attention, so our dreaming body can lead the way.

Listening to the dreaming is what puts us into right rhythm with the world. The rushed and busy heart is too closed to make a true encounter with life, but when we engage the dreaming in our quiet moments, or in relationship with others, we have beckoning power. We have the ability to perceive and shift the order of events, calling on the support that is already trying to reach us. This could be as simple as taking an afternoon away from work with the intention of being open to synchronicity, or lying your body down in the outdoors so you can feel the earth's support.

Rest is the dropping of effort and allowing of ease. Like an airplane that sails into cruising altitude, we can push with great initial force into a direction— but then, if we can open our receptors to notice it, we can also be lifted. It is the moment we let ourselves be undefended that grace can move through us. Like the lone bird singing the sun's rise, her breast full with the tender song of now, a melody of yes, rest takes us into communion with the holy moment which, like a cadenza, is always playing through us, living to be heard.

Impatience

Impatience is that irritable guest who shows up before we've established a sense of belonging, when we're shy and awkward and prone to self-doubt. It can stay a good, long while. Impatience is our urge to bypass this awkward phase, when things aren't yet comfortable or settled, and rush to redemption. Paradoxically, it is essential to really inhabit this awkwardness if we want to find our particular way of belonging.

It is before familiarity sets in that we are most alive and porous to our environment, our relationships, and even ourselves. If you've ever gone travelling with just a backpack, you're familiar with this magic. Travelling where we don't know anyone, or how to get about, we are forced into complete unfamiliarity. Though part of us is impatient to have community and other anchors in place, this clumsy period is full of potential. We could reinvent ourselves or meet different kinds of people outside our habitual type. Now imagine that we could be symbolic travellers every day of our lives by becoming friendly with the awkwardness of all that is unresolved in our hearts.

It is a complete reversal of the way we traditionally think about belonging. Rather than striving to be inside knowing, we recognize the privilege of being outside, where our eyes can look freshly upon a thing, before familiarity works its soporific influence on us. In these awkward periods, *we* are also not the same person we are familiar with. Impatience calls us deeper into that awkwardness, perchance to meet ourselves anew.

In our bottomless craving to reveal what's unknown, we deprive ourselves of the sensual encounter, the anticipation, and the potential to rejig reality. To be baffled and obstructed is what engages creativity. This is the practice of poets, dreamers, and artists alike: to show up at the frontiers of uncertainty where we are met by ten thousand things. We practice there, on the verge, amateur and unprepared, at being friendly—or at least willing—towards the discomforts of our confusions. As Rumi says, "Sell your cleverness and buy bewilderment!"[40]

About seven years ago, my partner Craig and I pulled up our roots in search of a new home. We were longing to live rurally, in a community aligned with our values, but we weren't sure where that was. We finished out our lease, put everything we owned into storage, and with truly meagre savings began to follow the breadcrumbs.

After three months of bouncing around, from house-sit to temporary rental, we were exhausted and impatient. I asked an intuitive friend for some advice and she laughed and said, "Do not lose the faith. Sometimes we are being tested. Give thanks." The next day, packing up our things to move one more time, I found a mysterious stone in the bottom of our food basket, with the word Faith painted on it. I have no idea where it came from, but feeling uprooted and skeptical given the length of our search, I wasn't convinced it was a synchronicity. Still, I kept the mysterious stone in a prominent place while we made yet another transition.

Two days after arriving at our next location, Craig and I went exploring down a path into a nearby forest. A few minutes later, we came upon a magical gate surrounded by trees. The sign on the gate said "Public Sculpture Garden," so without hesitation we went in, only to find the very first installation was a giant boulder, suspended invisibly from a tall cedar branch. It was quite a sight, all that weight strangely suspended like that. I crouched down to read the title of the piece: Faith.

The next installation, just in case I needed some contrast, was another boulder suspended in the trees, only this time it was bound by many complicated, twisted ropes and anchored from four corners, called Lack of Faith. With my synchronicity now in triplicate, I was convinced. Though I was still suspended in the land of not-knowing, I could draw upon these healing images and remember that this place of suspension between things is a kind of freedom. It was an opportunity to engage my dreaming body, to trust that something aligned with our vision was ripening on its own timeline. And rather than indulging in impatience, it was an opportunity to beckon it towards me.

It was another two months before our perfect home appeared. As it turned out, the house had been occupied by another tenant who needed that time to give her notice to vacate. It has now been seven years living in our lovely home, perched in the trees, in a vibrant rural community.

The awkwardness of unfamiliarity is also an essential phase in new relationships. Occasionally you meet someone with whom you can dive right in, but in general it's better to move slowly into closeness with others, because it is a worse thing to call someone *home* and leave them, than to not call them home at all. It is better to love slowly, even cautiously, while your tenacity for commitment is still growing.

117

These shallow loves, taken and given too quickly, are like animating archetypes or gods. They play out in tragedies beyond their own deserving. They are just temporary dwellings, already furnished with the keepsakes of our combined pasts. Never a place to live for long, but a way to pretend at living, to play house.

Some people are just meant to pass through your life, taking or leaving comfort, bringing catharsis, or serving as a catalyst. Love will burn hot and cold, but neither extreme can be withstood for too long. Let love take its time with you. Let it surprise you when it comes back even though you thought it was lost. Let it circle around you, let it seek to understand what you love. Let it deepen in endurance, as only history can guarantee.

To make a real home with another is to start with an emptiness, a 'next to nothing' space into which you can contribute. Dare to step together into an 'usness' that has no guarantees but the shared vision of belonging, whose embers you continuously agree to tend. History provides the furnishings that are slowly and discriminatingly added to your insides, in the form of moments shared in grief and celebration, language and images that surprise you, stories revealed at the rate of trust, and the responses you receive to the calls you've only made silently.

Like the mother who is careful about those she brings home to meet her child because she wants to create stable attachments, we must be similarly cautious with our hearts. The path from heart to heart must be walked often before it becomes well-trodden. If it's neglected too long, it will become overgrown and impassable. Or if a love stops giving of itself, the path can veer somewhere unsafe. The invitation into community with others should be careful and reverent, because the betrayal of friendship takes a toll on the heart that may never recover.

Invariably there will be times when inferior forces prevail in our lives. In these moments, all attempts to force a solution or gain advantage just worsen the condition of our dilemma, like the bound-up boulder that couldn't move if it tried. In times of suspension, we have to ask ourselves if we are sticking firmly to our vision—and if we are, then we must trust that it is quietly coalescing itself. Far from 'doing nothing,' this practice of non-action takes real perseverance, a quiet modesty which invites the grace of The Creative to come to our aid. It is said that only through acceptance great change is made possible, "like a vast school of fish instantly reversing its direction."[41]

I offer you the following poem in praise of patience, the practice which is also an invitation to The Creative, to show us the way:

118

Waiting

There is a good kind of waiting
which trusts the agents of fermentation.
There is a waiting
which knows that in pulling away
one can more wholly return.
There is the waiting
which prepares oneself,
which anoints and adorns
and makes oneself plump
with readiness for love's return.
There is a good kind of waiting
which doesn't put oneself on hold
but rather adds layers to the grandness
of one's being worthy.
This sweet waiting
for one's fruits to ripen
doesn't stumble over itself
to be the first to give
but waits for the giving
to issue at its own graceful pace.

Shame

Shame is perhaps one of the most insidious of the dark visitors, because it is rarely specific enough to be rooted out. It colours everything we say and do with an overall feeling of being wrong, inadequate or worthless. It is at the root of many other difficult emotions, like feeling insignificant, invisible, left out, misunderstood, unimportant, and unsupported. It is the belief that we should remain quiet, remove our contributions, spare others our very presence.

The origin of the word 'shame' means 'to cover.' However misguided, some of us hold the secret and painful conviction that certain parts of ourselves are so ugly and unworthy that unless we mask or hide those pieces away, we will never be loved or accepted. And so begins the sham of shame. We cover the very things that make us who we are. Dreams, however, will go straight for those things and throw off the covers. They work tirelessly to retrieve our forgotten, neglected and rejected soul-parts. Dreams can be threatening to the ego, whose whole existence depends on keeping those things hidden, but the greater Self lives to be seen.

When we dream of our places of shame, it might look like being naked in public. Or trying to sing when nobody is listening, or giving a talk and everyone leaves the room. It might look like others gathering for a meal where there's no seat for us. Or it may even be the humiliation of being abandoned for a more attractive lover. These dreams are not to make us feel bad about ourselves, but rather to show us in excruciating detail what shame looks like as an inner dynamic.

When I was in my early twenties, I had my first serious relationship with a man who I felt inferior to in many ways. He and all his friends were ten years older than me and already accomplished in their careers. I was still fresh out of System life, with little more than a few songs of survival to show for my life's accomplishment. Every night I would dream he had another lover, who was prettier and more talented than I was. And he wouldn't just abandon me, he'd flaunt his attraction for her, making me feel like a loser. I woke up devastated by these dreams, tearful and needing reassurance from my boyfriend who was actually devoted to me.

It took years for me to understand that these dreams were not foretelling of any actuality that was present in my relationship, but about my own shame. If we look at all the characters in the dream as aspects of the self, we can see that it is we who are abandoning our commitment to ourselves every time we compare ourselves unfavourably to another. Every time we stop listening to our heart's song. Every time we give away too much admiration and leave ourselves with a deficit.

Naturally, the antidote to shame is to risk showing up as fully as we're able. The discipline needed for shame is to practice revealing yourself. It is bringing into the open the full brightness of your spirit, despite your fear of failure. It is to brave your secret gifts into the open. It is revealing your fears to trusted others, allowing them to be assuaged. It is reaching out when you'd rather hide. It's asking for help when you feel abandoned.

Though it's terrifying to do what scares you, the dangers of not confronting your shame are far more numerous. Depression, addiction, eating disorders, and the judgment we project onto others in an attempt to feel superior are all common symptoms of toxic shame. Though these strategies may temporarily relieve the acuteness of the wound, real healing happens every time you drop your self-judgments and be vulnerable enough to engage with the world.

For those who suffer with toxic, unnecessary shame, there is a distorted view of yourself which, at least for a time, will need to be reassured. It's important to surround yourself with people who inspire you to open, and who never shun you for doing so.

Take for example Amy, who suffers from such debilitating shame that she can barely walk into a room without feeling like an imposition. One time she slunk into her singing circle, sure that she was unwanted there, when the leader of the circle, a woman named Allison, sang out her name in front of everyone, "Amy! I'm so glad you're here today!"

This moment was a blow to Amy's shame monster, who by contrast was trying to convince her she was a nuisance. Amy had forgotten that she'd revealed to Allison in a previous conversation how she'd struggled with feeling unworthy in the circle. So when Allison saw her looking so glum that day, she made a point of making Amy feel welcome. And it worked! In that moment, Amy could see the distortion between her inner dialogue and outer reality in which she was loved and celebrated. The experience helped her see that she needed to keep practicing transparency—naming those moments when she felt herself shame spiralling to trusted friends—so that she could put them to the inner-outer reality check. Shame can't survive in the open light of day.

Imagine the size of your fear, revulsion, and shame embraced and you will have successfully estimated the power of your wholeness.

Grief

Grief is the response to a broken bond of belonging. Whether through the loss of a loved one, a way of life, or a cherished community, grief is the reaction to being torn from what you love. As Martín Prechtel teaches, the words for *grief* and *praise* are the same in the Tz'utujil language because you can only grieve what you have dearly loved.[42]

We grieve the loves we've lost. We grieve our abilities vanishing through illness or age. We grieve the loss of faith in our religion. We grieve our children leaving home. We grieve the paths we didn't walk. We grieve the family we never had. We grieve the suffering of the planet. But while grief may look like an expression of pain that serves no purpose, it is actually the soul's acknowledgment of what we value. Grief is the honour we pay to that which is dear to us. And it is only through the connection to what we cherish that we can know how to move forward. In this way, grief is motion.

Yet in our culture, we are deeply unskilled with grief. We hold it at a distance as best we can, both in ourselves and in each other, treating it as, Joanna Macy says, like "an enemy of cheerfulness."[43] There is unspoken shame associated with grief. It is sanctioned in very few places, in small doses, for exceptional occasions such as death and tragedy. Beyond that, it can feel dangerous and weak. Perhaps because we fear we'll drown in our despair, or because it means falling apart in a world which values 'holding it together' above all else. But grief plays an essential role in our coming undone from previous attachments. It is the necessary current we need to carry us into our next becoming. Without it, we may remain stuck in that area of our life, which can limit the whole spectrum of our feeling alive.

Developing your feeling takes time, especially if it has been systematically discouraged in you. There may be an initial layer of shock, numbness, or anger you have to move through before you can touch that backlog of grief. Sometimes if a person sees right into the heart of who you are, it can release the grief you've been unable to acknowledge yourself. It is like a pinprick in your heart that releases a flood of tears, because you know that what's been reflected is true—and that you have been waiting to hear this truth for a long time.

Grief is the expression of healing in motion. As you make the seemingly bottomless descent, it helps to remember that grief is the downpour your soul has been thirsting for. Because what remains hidden for too long doesn't change. It is calcified in place, often sealed by shame, left untouched and forgotten by time. But when it can finally come into the open to be seen, it is exposed to new conditions and it begins to move. It rises on a salty geyser of tears, sometimes sung to the surface by a terrific moan, streaming down our cheeks until it moistens the soil where we stand, preparing us for new growth.

Have you ever noticed how beautiful a person is after they've wept? It's as if they are made new again by the baptism of tears. Indeed, when something stuck can be released through grief, we are freeing up a greater capacity to love. Conversely, when left ungrieved, stagnation can turn into resentment, cynicism, and even violence.

These days, the media is so full of cataclysmic news that we are barely able to process our grief about one thing before another surfaces. Forest fires rage in drought conditions, tsunamis sweep entire cities into oblivion, animals are becoming extinct at unprecedented rates, oil spills are devastating vast ecosystems, refugees are drowning in desperate attempts to escape persecution, people of colour are being murdered in the streets, and it is too much to conceivably grieve without slipping into despair. So many of us have grown accustomed to living with a level of numbness to this compassion fatigue. Denial serves a purpose in that it helps us to compartmentalize so that we can continue to function. But just as numbing our personal grief results in a stuckness which keeps us from truly belonging to our lives, disconnecting from the great grief of our planet puts us out of touch with the feeling of kinship we need to inspire us to act.

We are the product of several generations of ungrieved wounds. Focused on survival, our ancestors had little choice but to retaliate or repress the wrongs that had been done to them, so that they could persevere. But with so few elders in our midst who teach about the importance of grieving, or who create culture and ritual around honouring grief, we feel alone with our private suffering. We rarely witness the grief of others because of its cultural taboo, causing us to believe our own grief is shameful or weird.

In the old ways, when a person was struck with loss and grief, we would keen as one village, letting our own grief be joined with theirs, elevating it with our combined capacity, declaring it a public act. We would lean in towards one person's suffering because we knew we would all be there sooner or later, and it cannot be done alone. In some traditions, there are women whose job it is to grieve on behalf of those who are stuck with inability to touch their own grief.[44] In the Dagara tradition, an actual physical space is created at death rituals for those who might need to fall apart, and designated helpers are chosen to comfort them if they need it.[45]

Learning to grieve well must begin with the self. There are ruins in each of us. A place where 'what once was' lives on like an echo, haunting the landscape of our lives with its weathered foundations. Abandoned, scavenged, and dismantled by time, the ruin is the holiest place in our heart. It is the ways in which we have been broken that have earned us a place to stand. It is in our life's absences that a wild longing is born. This ruined place is a temple in which to worship, to throw down our grief and our forgetting, and praise what remains. After all, these remains are the evidence of how greatly we have loved and they should be venerated as the legacy of survival that they are.

Welcoming your own grief may take some practice because everything we are taught runs counter to this approach. Certainly, it would be lovely to see more community spaces dedicated to grieving in the open, so we could explore the depths of our grief knowing we are being held by a larger, supportive structure. But until then, we must learn to trust each other. We must learn to share our sacred ruins with one another, giving each other a chance to confirm that we are not alone.

The events of your loss, the discrepancies in your upbringing, the deficits in your making, are what shape you uniquely. Your limitations are what give rise to the imagination, and your regrets are what put you into right relationship with your future. So you must bless every grief you've encountered on your exquisite and treacherous courtship of Self, for they've made you the slow diamond that you are.

Like rain, the more excellently and prodigiously you grieve, the more growth and fertility you can expect. There is a future beyond the aridity and meaninglessness in our times that is teeming with life. If each of us has the tenacity to retrieve the elixirs of our discomforts, our combined medicine can heal the collective wound.

The House Becomes a Home

In the end, so much of the conflict we feel in our hearts is because we've split ourselves off from the very life we are living. We partition ourselves from the things with which we are at odds, treating them as unbelonging even as we live them. We vaguely imagine some other place, some better job, some other lover—but the irony is that so much of what makes us unhappy is our own rejection of the life we have made. Eventually we must take our life into our arms and call it our own. We must look at it squarely, with all its unbecoming qualities, and find a way to love it anyway. Only from that complete embrace can a life begin to grow into what it is meant to become.

In this chapter we've met a few of the unwelcomed guests that, when respectfully welcomed, reveal a concealed wisdom. With enough practice at this, we develop resilience. Resilience is our ability to meet with difficult feelings and setbacks, and not only trust in our capacity to adapt and recover from them, but to find something redemptive hidden within adversity. It takes a lot of energy to distance ourselves from pain; not only do we become more vital by entering into relationship with our feelings, but that resilience grows into a place of refuge for others.

There is a special quality of stillness in a person who encounters their shadow wholeheartedly. Your body may relax in their company because it understands, in the subtle communications of their presence, that nothing is excluded in themselves, or you, from belonging. Such a person, who has given up guarding against the shadow, who has come to wear their scars with dignity, no longer squirms from discomfort or bristles at suffering. They no longer brace in avoidance of conflict. They carry a deep willingness to dance with the inconstancy of life. They've given up distancing as a strategy, and made vulnerability their ally.

Because we often think of vulnerability as a negative trait which leaves us exposed to harm, I thought we could do with a new word which acknowledges its power: *vulnerabravery*. Instead of putting up our defences when we meet with conflict, vulnerabravery is the conscious choice to keep our heart open so that we might discover what's hidden within it. It is a great paradox that when we let ourselves be undefended we find our true strength.

124

Many of us can relate to feeling vulnerable a lot of the time. We may be afraid to leave the house some days because we worry so much what others think; we may be afraid to say something out loud in case we have an unpopular viewpoint; we may wait for others to approach us because we're afraid of being rejected. But while these things may look like vulnerability, they are actually the opposite. As dreams show us, when we allow our fears to dominate us, it is a kind of internal tyranny against vulnerability.

Often we are unaware of how dismissive or violent we're being to ourselves because these habits operate unconsciously. If we've internalized a critical, dismissive, or patronizing inner voice, then we will consider it normal to discourage ourselves at every turn. This is where dreams can be helpful, in that they'll show us in vivid detail how we are treating ourselves. In their unflinching honesty, dreams show us how the psyche experiences an event from both sides.

In my early twenties, I remember getting stuck at an outdoor jazz festival on an evening I was supposed to meet a friend. Though I'd left in plenty of time to meet her, all the roads were jammed with traffic and the few streetcars that could get through were filled by the time they reached me. Wracked with anxiety about abandoning my friend and the failure of my promise, I walked for miles trying to find a bus that could take me home. By the time I finally made it, it was close to midnight and I collapsed into bed with a blistering migraine.

Through the Wringer, Toko-pa's dream
I dream I have a little girl trapped in a dryer as punishment for something she's done. It's not clear what that is, but when the spin cycle stops, she pushes the door open, desperate to get out, but I shove her back in for another round.

I woke up from this dream horrified with myself. What perverted trenches of my psyche had turned up this place of cruelty within? How could I behave with such meanness to a small and innocent being?

After many hours of trembling with the shame of this dream, I finally connected it to the events of the previous day. Indeed, I had been behaving with unreasonable cruelty—but the little girl was also me. She was the vulnerable part of me that was being punished for some vague wrongdoing.

Though I consciously identified with the blaming part of my personality, I never would have touched how abusive that inner-admonishing was without the empathy generated by my dream's decision to punish a little girl at my own hand. This 'putting myself through the wringer' felt like violence to my psyche, and it led me to my first awareness of the unconscious guilt I'd been carrying since I was the same age as the girl in the dream.

The great task ahead of me was to learn how to become kinder and more cherishing to my little inner-orphan. In practical terms, this meant changing my inner dialogue to be more forgiving to those places of hardship and vulnerability. I also learned how to encourage myself in times of failure or defeat. And perhaps most challenging of all, it was about nurturing my physical needs for rest, food, and connection with nature. All of these attributes are essential to creating resilience.

Like any creature who has known abandonment, bonding does not come easily to the orphaned life. It may at times seem that your neglected self fights you and wrestles away from your love, holding itself out of reach. Learning how to be loved, even by yourself, can be exhausting and sometimes even feel fake. You may succumb to the urge to hide, or eat junk, or do things you know are bad for you. But this is always a call for love.

It is in these fallow times, when our efforts feel forced and there's no momentum with our progress, that we must aspire to love ourselves more generously. It is up to you to name your orphan's secret beauty and lure it out of hiding. Shame, when it is welcomed, allows dignity to emerge; betrayal's hidden medicine is true loyalty; isolation hides a longing for intimacy, and so on. If we take the foundational idea that there's a redemptive quality behind the darker, edgy, difficult emotions and experiences, then we are well on our way to making our house into a home.

After working with a dream like the one I shared above, people often ask me, "But what should I do?" as if there were some special formula or action we could take to fix ourselves. But the truth is that simply seeing a pattern is often enough to make it change. Once something is brought to consciousness, it can no longer operate covertly. It may not disappear altogether at first, but you'll catch it sooner next time. The important thing is not to rush the redemption, but devote yourself more deeply to what's being revealed in present time.

I have a dear friend and mentor named Rita who, for the last five years, gets up with first light and begins chipping away with a small axe at a giant root in the centre of her garden. Her vision is to make room for a bench to enjoy the company of the many perennials she has planted around that spot. Even though she could rent a machine that would dig the root out in one fell swoop, instead she makes this humble progress her daily ritual. Healing is like this. Relinquishing the race to arrive for a tender devotion to being present with what is.

You always have the choice to turn away or to look for redemption in the shadows. Sometimes turning away is exactly what you need in the moment, especially if you're tired from toiling down in there. Trust that whatever you decide is the right decision. Also know that if the issue being presented has roots, it will still be there when you're ready to look at it. But you can give thanks for the terrors which shake you from sleep with ferocity because their dawning in your awareness is already the promise, the beginning of their retreat.

Call on life to fill and overwhelm you, to excite, terrify, capture, and spill through you—like the warm breeze from the whirling skirts of a dervish, which carries the pain of too much tenderness. Find the fertile path between good and bad things and walk on it. Oh, this mournful triumph of dismantling, battering through our cherished losses, preparing the cold ground for new allowing. Oh! This is why we break our hearts! To open them.

Ten

Pain as Sacred Ally

*O*f all the dark visitors who arrive unbidden on our doorstep, pain is perhaps the least welcome. It can show up suddenly, debilitating us physically as well as energetically, sapping our ability to attend to anything else—and it can be dogged in its determination to never leave. For the person in pain, there is nothing more immediate. Pain can feel malevolent as it holds you hostage. In extreme cases, like the biblical suffering of Job, a person can even feel tortured by some punishing upper hand.

Many will counsel you that there is a reason for your pain and that if you could only heal your underlying emotional wounds, pain would leave you alone. But the body is not an abstraction, and pain laughs at the over-simplicity of this way of thinking. As Harvard Professor and author Elaine Scarry describes, unlike interior pain, physical pain "has no referential content. It is not of or for anything."[46]

This isn't to say that pain won't put you on a path of psychological growth, but as Job discovered, the ripping, destructive agony of an illness doesn't have inherent value. And this can, as it did for Job, bring the entirety of your relationship with god into question. But I believe this meaninglessness is, in and of itself, a confirmation of our duty to *create* meaning from adversity.

There are some cultures that actually seek out pain because its totality and immediacy can act as a portal to an altered state of consciousness. For example, the Sioux Sun Dance ceremony involves many days of fasting and strenuous dancing, followed sometimes by putting hooks into the skin that are then ripped from the flesh. There are thousands of cultural rituals in which intentional pain, like self-flagellation, fire-walking, piercing, and body modification, is viewed as an act of purification to the soul.

When we are in extreme states of pain, we sometimes separate from our body, travelling into an etheric or altered state of consciousness. In some cases pain can, through the release of endogenous opioids, even bring on a state of ecstasy. As the author of *Sacred Pain*, Ariel Glucklich writes that in the mystical context, intentional pain "unmakes the profane world with its corporeal attachments and leads the mystics away from the body to self transcendence."[47]

Paradoxically, as much as pain takes us out of the body, it can also be the tethering which brings us inescapably back into belonging with our body and the body of the world.

The body is the first gate of belonging. And though so many people struggle to feel at home in their own bodies, I am amazed at how rarely it is mentioned in the many conversations I have on belonging with others. Its absence in our consideration speaks volumes. As we've explored, there are many contributing factors to humanity's body-soul disconnection, but the Western medical model is a huge proponent of detachment in that pain and discomfort are considered unacceptable and ubiquitously controlled with medication.

If we can lessen the suffering of those who need it, then of course it must be a good thing. But modern medicine has been so consummately estranged from its sacred origins that it no longer sees how pain can be viewed as meaningful or even beneficial. This paradigm makes us not only intolerant of our own pain, but intolerant of those who suffer with chronic pain. Though times are slowly changing to be inclusive of people with different abilities, for most of recent history they have been pushed to the margins and treated as a drain on society. As Glucklich writes, "We have lost our capacity to understand why and how pain would be valuable for mystics, members of religious communities, and perhaps humanity as a whole. The role of pain, before it was displaced, was rich and nuanced, and ultimately situated persons within broader social and religious contexts."[48]

In *Sick Woman Theory*, Johanna Hedva tells her own story of living with chronic pain and illness, and how challenging it is for a sick person to find relevance in a world that aggrandizes wellness.[49] Hedva articulates how 'wellness' and 'sickness' are treated as a binary of opposites in our culture. And those who fall on the wrong side of those tracks are considered unproductive and therefore excluded from the collective conversation. We are so fixated on curing illness and eradicating pain that we're unable to consider people living in pain as leading intact lives. But perhaps more insidious is how this estranges us from our own pain and wretched illness. We are so driven to 'get well' that we rarely show any welcoming kindness to this unexpected guest in our lives.

A few years ago, not long after my fateful exile from that spiritual community, I woke up one day with sharp, stabbing pains in both of my feet. Every step I took was like walking on shards of glass. Other than some minor discomforts, I'd never before had any problems with my feet. Alarmed and bewildered, I kept trying to walk it off, thinking whatever it was would just go away. But rather than dissipating, the pain got increasingly severe.

Before I knew what was happening to me, I was critically disabled. Days and weeks passed and the pain only got worse. I was barely able to walk a few feet to the bathroom. It hurt even when I wasn't moving, with sharp jolts of electrical pains coming out of nowhere, followed by radiating aches through my feet and toes. Even the slightest brush with a sheet would feel like being stabbed. Every morning I expected the pain to be gone, but instead I would wake up, if I'd slept at all, and find myself in the same body that was beginning to feel like a prison.

It would take a full five minutes to descend our flight of stairs and, by the time I finally reached the bottom, I would be in tears. The pain was excruciating. But it was more than that; I may have wanted to make coffee or wash the dishes or go for a walk, but I was entirely unable. Though I'd never given my feet any credit before, I was now acutely aware of how I needed them for everything.

The doctors had no idea what was wrong with me. They did blood tests and physical examinations and said I was in perfect health. These visits were usually patronizing and humiliating, because they would tell me to *just lose some weight*, and *exercise more*. I would try to explain that there was very little exercise a person could do without feet, which is how I gained thirty pounds. I tried to explain how, before this, I was a yogi—extremely active, practicing at least five days a week. But since getting ill, I had such extreme fatigue that I couldn't do more than one activity a day, and I had to conserve the tiny spoonfuls of energy I had for things like bathing or seeing clients. I was usually bed-ridden by early afternoon and would remain so until the next morning, when I'd have a small window of energy. The doctors made me feel like I was wasting their time and treated my growing list of symptoms as the complaints of a hypochondriac just looking for attention.

For the next six months I lived with constant pain and, since we didn't have a car at the time, I barely left the house. I'd never been so stopped in my tracks. My desire to power through the difficulty was so great and habitual within me that whenever I'd feel a little better, I'd do far too much and set my healing back again. I even undertook my healing protocols, which were varied and numerous, with tremendous ambition. And if my body didn't respond, I would be angry at my feet! "What do you want!?" I asked them—and heard nothing back.

The body is the home we never leave, though some of us may try. It is the place where our soul has taken root for a lifetime and it is only through the body's senses that we come to know the world in which we live. It is with our hands that we offer tenderness, our voices that speak truths, our ears that differentiate noise from music, and our feet that take a stand. It is in the souring of our bellies that we know the wrong way, the rising of our temperature that expresses our longing, and our hearts that flutter at the anticipation of newness.

The body is also the first place of separation from belonging, where we leave our mother's body to become our own person. It is the terrible-wonderful learning ground upon which we come to know where we end and where otherness begins.

For those whose mother was absent or lacking in kindness, there is a much harder road ahead in recognizing and navigating pain. If you never knew the comfort and safety of a mother's presence, you will have grown up, as I did, unaware of the value in attending with presence to your body's needs and feelings.

When I was in my early twenties, I had a terrible bicycle accident. I was knocked unconscious by the impact and awoke to a stranger asking me if I was okay. I lifted my hands up to my face to see they were covered in blood, and I discovered that so was the rest of me, from sliding some ten or so feet along the gravel. "I'm fine," I replied, and tried to get myself upright. I don't remember much of what happened after that, except at a certain point in my attempt to hobble home, I realized I was seriously injured and knocked on a stranger's door to ask for help. He drove me to the rooming house where I was living at the time, where I got into bed and hid in my room, slipping in and out of consciousness for the next three weeks.

It fills me with the grief of compassion to remember this young girl who didn't know how to ask for help or take care of her body. It didn't even occur to me to go to a hospital or ask a roommate for some support. I felt, as I'd been taught, that if something bad happened to me that it was my own fault, so I was ashamed of being hurt, and terrified of being an imposition.

Ironically, it is this fear itself that so often keeps us outside of belonging. We live our lives in avoidance of those places and risks which might lead to our rejection, pre-emptively excluding ourselves, then suffering the same loneliness as if the rejection had come from the outside.

Unconsciously, I believed my acceptance in the world was somehow tenuous and dependent on my being a contributing member of the family, the household, the community. To ask for help would burden others with my pain, which I feared might mean my rejection from belonging. So my instinct was to hide away, to absent myself until I was better.

Some weeks later, I began having grand mal seizures. I would come to consciousness on the floor of my vestibule, my legs jerking and, still, I never asked for help. Though my story is extreme, perhaps there's some part of you that can relate to treating your body poorly, as if in breaking down it were an inconvenience to you and to others.

Collectively speaking, the prevailing relationship we have with our body is much like the one we have with cars: we treat them like mechanical robots to drive on automatic and expect them to always be at our service, no matter how little we attend to their needs. We use them as a garbage dump and push them beyond their limits, then are mystified and frustrated when they mysteriously break down. Sometimes injury or discomfort is the only thing that will bring us back into relationship with our bodies.

Marion Woodman tells a story about a pianist who had such terrible stage fright that for thirty years she refused to play in front of a single person.[50] So she entered analysis with the wholehearted desire to overcome that fear and, after some years, mustered up the courage to connect with a local chamber quartet. The other musicians were so astonished by her gift—they couldn't imagine how she managed to hide it for so long. But just as she began to play with others for the first time, she developed a mysterious and excruciating illness that caused paralysis in both her hands.

For anyone who has overcome great obstacles only to have the rug pulled out from under them, the temptation to believe we are being punished is deeply embedded in our cultural dogma. As Christ called out in the ninth hour of being nailed to the cross, we might find ourselves crying out, "My God, My God, why hast thou forsaken me?"

But as Woodman explains, consciousness must be enlightened at the cellular level of the body. It isn't enough to know something with the mind, or even the spirit. It's as if every cell of her body needed to remember. As Edward Edinger wrote, this apocalypse of the body is necessary for "the coming of the Self into conscious realization...The shattering of the world as it has been, followed by its reconstitution."[51]

Indeed, six months into my mysterious foot pain, my life was feeling shattered. Images of being in a wheelchair haunted me, and I wasn't convinced I'd ever be able to walk again. Overnight, I became utterly dependent. Unlike going it alone in my twenties, now I was in a long-term, loving relationship with my partner Craig. Living together, there was nowhere I could hide. And even when I tried, he wouldn't let me. Instead he came after me every time and, like the Runaway Bunny, coaxed me back into the world. He took such compassionate care of me, which was astonishingly difficult for me to receive. I could see in his eyes that he felt my pain as if it were his own, and I wanted to spare him. But any time I tried to take matters into my own hands, pushing harder than I should, Craig was there, reminding me to surrender.

Ancestral Wounds

About six months into my inability to walk, still in a state of total resistance, I was given a dream that shook me from sleep.

Barefoot in Refugee Ghetto, Toko-pa's dream

I am living in a curfew state. There are large ghettos of refugees living in exile from their homes. I am one of them, but am with my boyfriend walking in the street when the hour of curfew tolls. I am told that the law requires me to remove my boots. My boyfriend tells me to follow him, because he knows the safe way to walk in bare feet. But I am too independent and don't like to follow anyone, so I take my own way. As soon as I do, I step into glass which pierces me in the exact spot of my waking life injury.

This was the dream that began the writing of this book. Even now, several years later, it continues to teach me down through its many layers. But the first thing that struck me was the context of living in a curfew state. Certainly, we can interpret this symbolically as the loss of my freedom, which was being detained in injury. But there is also an ancestral echo here of my maternal grandparents who survived the Holocaust.

Though my grandmother was Polish, she wasn't Jewish and spoke perfect German, both of which helped her 'pass' and survive much of the war. My grandfather, on the other hand, was a Polish Jew who was a prisoner in the Warsaw Ghetto for three years before the Nazis put him on a train to Auschwitz, where he would have met his death in the gas chambers. But while it was still moving, my grandfather jumped off that train and, in the fall, broke his leg. He went on to survive with the help of the underground resistance by hiding in the woods until the war was over.

I knew without a doubt when I received this dream that there was a psychic vestige of my grandfather's pain living through the generations into my life, and into my feet.

When an individual can't (or won't) do the inner work to heal their pain, the wounds get passed through the generations, metastasizing through our family tree in the form of mental afflictions, patterns of fear, and even physical injury. Until someone in the younger branches has enough support and awareness to face and grieve that ancient grief, it continues to find expression in all of the following generations.

Survivors of the Holocaust mostly use one of two ways to cope with the horror they lived through: one is to speak at length about their experiences and the other is to never speak of it at all. My grandfather was a never-speaker. In fact, it wasn't until my mother was in her fifties that we even found out he was Jewish. I can only imagine how it must have unconsciously affected my mother to live with that hiddenness. As Jung says, "Nothing influences children more than these silent facts in the background."[52]

"The child is so much a part of the psychological atmosphere of the parents," he goes on to write, "that secret and unsolved problems between them can influence its health profoundly...causes the child to feel the conflicts of the parents and to suffer from them as if they were its own. It is hardly ever the open conflict or the manifest difficulty that has such a poisonous effect, but almost always parental problems that have been kept hidden or allowed to become unconscious."[53]

After this dream, I was overwhelmed with feelings of kindness toward my pain. It was a complete reversal of my attitude, where I felt victimized, as if I were being punished for something I did wrong. But with the growing awareness that there was something bigger than, and inclusive of, my personal history that was trying to express itself, I felt the very first measure of affection towards my pain.

The resistance I'd mounted was against my own helplessness, yet helplessness was the very thing I needed to feel. In its infinite intelligence, my body only broke down when the conditions of my life were supportive enough to withstand that level of collapse. I began to think of my injury as an ally, who could only emerge at a time when my life was hospitable enough to welcome it.

My feet were tired of finding their own way. I'd been running all my life. I remembered how my mother hid all my shoes and boots so I couldn't run away. But like my dream, I ran anyway, into the night with bare feet. Motivated by my unconscious yearning to be recognized by the family who'd rejected me, I'd developed a fierce independence and never trusted another's lead or ability to protect me. But underneath that show of invulnerability was this collapsing waiting to happen: exhaustion, grief, and the deep longing to receive support.

It was time, the pain said, to stop. To come to know this beautiful essential nature that had always been at the core of me. My loving, kind and radiant self, through criticism and neglect, had grown to believe she needed to prove herself worthy of being alive. To earn her standing in the world. There I was, celebrating my fourth year in true love with my partner, living out my vocation as a writer and dreamworker in a veritable paradise on earth, within an incredible community of like-minded folks, and it was time to let go of these old notions of being outcast and unworthy of love.

But my story was also an iteration of the greater ancestral pattern of trauma that my grandparents experienced. The Jews were made into scapegoats for the unacknowledged shadow in the collective, abandoned by the world, and sent into exile or to their deaths. My personal story echoed that of my ancestors who were sent running in the night, made to believe they didn't belong, treated as if they were expendable.

I felt that I was being given the privilege and responsibility to heal these ancestral wounds through their manifestation in my life. As Paul Levy so beautifully puts it, "we have the precious opportunity to liberate these ancestral, rhizomic strands of trauma which extend far back in time and equally far into the future, but which also converge and are spread throughout the present in the form of the society and culture in which we live. We can be the ones to break the link in the chain and dissolve these insidious, mycelium-like threads, which are literally the warp and weft upon which the tapestry of the past, present, and future history of our species is woven."[54]

In an unconscious bid to gain or retain belonging, so much of our lives are constructed around how to be useful and impressive. But when you're no longer entertaining or can be of service, what of you is left? As anyone who has been in long-term pain or illness knows, there is a deep humbling that takes place in injury. All the anglings of the personality to 'get going' or 'push through' are made useless and you are brought down into the very essentials of your beingness.

In my injury, I spent the better part of a year housebound. It was a period of intense isolation and attrition. There were many invitations I had to refuse, endeavours I had to give up on and friendships that fell away. People I thought were great friends distanced themselves from me, while others appeared with surprising consistency and kindness. The acuteness of my pain and fatigue was so primary that it became very clear who I could trust.

Every day I tended to my feet with love, gratitude and acknowledgment. And every day I grieved new depths of my pain, both personal and ancestral. I depended on my beloved partner for most things and had to ask more of my friends than ever before. And all of it softened me.

Rumi says that to cry out in weakness is what invites healing to pour in towards it. He writes, "All medicine wants is pain to cure."[55] How strong one must be to allow themselves to be seen in their weakness. And how brave the other to be unwaveringly helpless. Pain took me into the practice of showing up empty-handed and still being loveable. Pain and injury and illness ask us to consider that our lives are worthy without justification.

True healing is an unglamorous process of living into the long lengths of pain. Forging forward in the darkness. Holding the tension between hoping to get well and the acceptance of what is happening. Tendering a devotion to the impossible task of recovery, while being willing to live with the permanence of a wound; befriending it with an earnest tenacity to meet it where it lives without pushing our agenda upon it. But here's the paradox: you must accept what is happening while also keeping the heart pulsing towards your becoming, however slow and whispering it may be.

For all the times someone has asked you how you are, and you felt pressured to say "I am well" when *well* wasn't your whole truth, I offer you this wish: that this finds you not just well, but all the things that being human asks of us. And to remind you that your being alive, in all its magnificent and complicated colours, is more than enough for love. Rather than endlessly seeking to get well, or yearning for 'how things used to be' or 'may be one day again,' we must be willing to walk with our pain. Or at least be *willing to be willing* to say, "This too is welcome. This too belongs."

Eleven

Holy Longing

*O*ccasionally you meet someone who knew their great-great-grandmother, who wears the handmade, ceremonial clothes of her people, who still stewards the land and sings the songs of her ancestors. But most of us are not so rich. Most of us have been orphaned from our ancestral land, and with it, our people's history, including the songs, teaching stories and wisdom ways of our lineage. And we may find ourselves looking in on families who are more intact than our own with a kind of unassuageable grief. This ache for something deeply familiar, yet entirely unknown, is our longing for a home we've always-never known.

Distant now from the generations before us who spent their lives escaping and willfully forgetting, it is like we have lost the context for our longing. It blinks in and out of our quiet moments like a faint but constant signal, muffled by the fog of modernity. Author and soul activist Francis Weller says there is a part of us that expected, when we emerged from our mother's womb, to find forty pairs of eyes anticipating our arrival. Indeed, we keep missing those forty pairs of eyes throughout our lives. It isn't so much that something important is missing from us, but that we are missing from something important.

There is an intactness we intuitively feel in an unbroken lineage, whose structure or set of traditions not only guides its members in the ways of the world but confers upon them a responsibility and position inside belonging. We imagine, and sometimes witness, the pride a person feels in carrying an ancestral heritage. It is as if they are made richer, stronger and more dignified by their inheritance of a long-standing tradition. Maybe in hearing our ancestral songs or language, or seeing a dance in ceremonial clothes, or even tasting a meal that's been prepared the same way since anyone can remember, we are suddenly transported into the depth of our longing to be woven into an older story that ennobles our own life as the fruiting from an ancient tree of kin.

Instead, many of us have a broken story. It starts when our parents or grandparents landed in the West either by choice, or because they were escaping persecution, or were brought to the Americas, Europe, and Asia against their will in the African diaspora of the slave trade. In North America, we have a horrifying history of colonialism, in which the Indigenous children of this land were stolen from their families, put into residential schools, abused, and forced to assimilate with the Eurocentric culture.

For many of us, our ancestral culture is either deeply damaged or on the brink of extinction. While many have fought to keep their traditions, language, recipes, and art forms alive, globalization is a powerfully homogenizing force. While this process of integration has provided many with opportunities and freedoms they might not have had otherwise, culture loss is a devastating consequence of surviving the demands and pace of the New World. Many of our predecessors had to focus on adjusting to modernization, rather than upholding ancient ways. In some cases, the previous generation might have even rejected the old culture or language, under the pressure or threat to fit in. But I think many of the younger generations are now feeling the longing for what's gone missing.

Without being entirely aware of it, we are perpetually driven by that longing for reunion with those eyes we're missing. But while that longing is for a complex mixture of kin, land, purpose, and mythos, we often project it onto temporary forms. In an attempt to quell that ache, we may join established groups, or we may give ourselves to other forms of union which reveal themselves eventually as places of conditional or false belonging. So when we come up disappointed or unrequited in our search, we begin to distrust longing itself, which feels like a hungry ghost who will never be satisfied.

Mostly in vain, we try to fill the hollowness of longing with pleasure, busyness and distraction. But it always returns. In a quiet moment, an upwelling so great it feels like it could swallow your life whole. Like the tidal wave in a dream which races for your windows, longing can be fierce and unapologetic, threatening to dismantle everything we've built. But what if our attempts to subdue it are actually growing its size? What if we are depriving ourselves of what could be a cathartic encounter? What if that tsunami wants to pick us up on its crest and carry us into new ranges of being alive?

Many spiritual traditions put an emphasis on detachment from our desire-nature that causes 'endless suffering,' but this is often misinterpreted to mean that we should bury, suppress, or rise above longing. Different from desire, which is the projection of our longing onto form and is always interested in being satisfied, longing is not something to be quelled.

In the Sufi way of seeing it, longing is a divine inclination, drawing us towards the Beloved. Just as lover and beloved long to be in each other's arms, so too is it between us and the life which is meant for us. Like a plant growing towards the sun, longing is nature inclining us towards the light we need in order to be fruitful. But also, as Rumi writes, "that which you seek is seeking you." So longing is not only the quality of seeking reunion, but the sound of something in search of us: the calling homeward.

When the longing we have for our lives has been neglected over time, even across generations, it may appear threatening, distant, or twisted in its expression. And yet, to attempt to detach from it is to put ourselves in jeopardy. Attachments are the arteries across which we give and receive love. These arteries of attachment to one another, to god, to the beauty and suffering of the earth, are essential to our vitality. We risk becoming isolated and dead inside when we detach ourselves from the things we love, the things that can break our hearts. Because when we armour ourselves from pain, we also seal off aliveness in other areas of our life.

The mystical path is to return to our longing even when the pain of separation is excruciating. This is why longing is in the root of belonging. To be longing for what the soul hungers after, even when that hunger can not be satisfied, is to be truly alive; paradoxically, it is in our deepest presence with those absences in our lives that we are returned to coherence.

Leaving the Reedbed

Using a lyrical metaphor, Rumi writes of our original separation in his poem "The Reedbed."[56] He tells of the paradox of being human: like the reed who is harvested from the reedbed, we are separated from the divine to take part in incarnation. Only in that tearing away from the Beloved can the reed become a flute, making the beautiful music of longing, aching for the return to the bed from which it was plucked. "The reed is hurt and salve combining. Intimacy and longing for intimacy, one song. A disastrous surrender and a fine love together."[57]

There is an essential paradox in this rhythm of separation and attachment. We can only ever come to intimacy through the longing which arises from our distance. In the same way that a fish might never notice the water it swims in until it is beached, we must be separated from that which is familiar in order to develop the longing for the unknown. This longing is what stirs curiosity in our hearts, drawing us further into our encounter with life.

> Listen to the story told by the reed,
> of being separated.
> "Since I was cut from the reedbed,
> I have made this crying sound.

Anyone apart from someone he loves
understands what I say.
Anyone pulled from a source
longs to go back.
At any gathering I am there,
mingling in the laughing and grieving,
a friend to each, but few
will hear the secrets hidden
within the notes. No ears for that.
Body flowing out of spirit,
spirit up from body: no concealing
that mixing. But it's not given us
to see the soul. The reed flute
is fire, not wind. Be that empty."
Hear the love fire tangled
in the reed notes, as bewilderment
melts into wine. The reed is a friend
to all who want the fabric torn
and drawn away. The reed is hurt
and salve combining. Intimacy
and longing for intimacy, one
song. A disastrous surrender
and a fine love, together.

Lovers are drawn together through their longing, sometimes creating life itself in their coupling. Eventually the time comes for the child to leave his mother's womb, and a longing is born to keep returning to her breast, that sweet comfort of safety and nourishment. But one day the child must separate from his mother, becoming his own person. Until one day, he grows a longing for the tenderness of a lover and the cycle begins again. This is the rhythm of life itself. The togetherness is what breeds apartness, and in that separation, a longing for togetherness is born.

Longing is the dynamic element of belonging which, if we're clever enough to follow, will bring us into reunion with the life we're meant to be living.

Practiced well, longing is the act of honouring separation. It is the impulse of the soul calling us deeper into life. It says, "It's time to go home." It is a piercing ache in the heart that knows there is more than this and pulls us, like a magnet, in orientation towards it. And yet we must respect how distant we may remain from it. Longing is not satisfied by worldly forms, because it knows there is a home that can only be reached through the portal of our vulnerability to the living moment. Like the reed plucked from its bed, there is something exquisite in being torn from what we love, which allows us to make the terrible-wonderful music of being human.

James Hillman writes quite jarringly about innocence, calling it "the addiction to not knowing life's darkness. Not wanting to know."[58] In other words, in order to come to consciousness, innocence must be broken. While I know this is a controversial statement, it has helped me a great deal in coming to terms with my own trauma. Instead of being fixated on the wrong that had been done to me—the obsession to return to innocence—I began to see my own heartbreaks as necessary. Without them, I would never have known true belonging, which is inclusive of exile, not in spite of it.

Loving again would mean doing so from a broader and more complex understanding of life itself, including the ambiguous partners of betrayal with trust, exile with belonging, separation with attachment. In the same way that Adam and Eve were cast out of Eden for eating from the Tree of Knowledge, there is a price to pay for consciousness—but the gift of consciousness is a more mature and nuanced relationship to life. I think this is the true meaning of forgiveness: not to forget what has happened to you, but to stop wishing it had been different. To choose it after the fact.

Longing is the call to this reconciliation with the events of our lives. Instead of trying to curate reality so that it is only filled with pleasure and peace, longing asks us to make a mingling of laughter with grief, a combining of hurt and salve, a willingness to enter into our lostness so that we may be found.

Just a few days after my mentor Annie's death, I dreamed of meeting her in a sunny garden. I was overjoyed to see her and she took me lovingly into her arms. But I must have lingered there too long, clinging to the comfort of her soft body, because she began to growl like a mama wolf who was teaching her young to brave out on her own.

Startled by the fierceness of this dream, I began to take journeys into nature which felt like the only place big enough to hold my grief. I remember sitting on a remote beach, weeping in the sun on a rounded rock, the ache for my beloved motherfriend pouring from my heart, when I looked up and spotted the shell of a cicada left entirely intact on a nearby log, a single split clean up its back.

In a moment that rushed in at me, I suddenly understood how, like the cicada, Annie must have sprouted wings and left the limitations of her human encasement behind. I was flooded with an ecstatic joy which, mingled with my grief, brought me to a sudden awareness that death wasn't an end at all, but a beginning. I felt as if there was an opening created by my longing, through which nature, who was also Annie, could communicate with me. I understood that I was the cicada too. Annie's death split my heart clean open, and out of it came the wings of my longing for a broader life.

Though it took big bravery to leave the comforts of familiarity and answer the call of my longing, I started connecting more intimately to life itself. Like dropping the oars on an upstream course, I let my little canoe be turned around by an undercurrent, offering up a deeper trust in the unknown. Death made me more courageous; not in the outward sense, but in a way that I could live with a greater porousness to my surroundings after grief grew my capacity to show up. Even my creativity took on deeper proportions of honesty because I'd become more vulnerable to life, and it to me.

Embodied living is to involve ourselves not only with goodness, but with the ache of longing and absence, including them in our way of going. Can I *be* with my *longing*? Can I allow the emptiness of what is missing from me remain without trying to fill it with stand-ins and facsimiles? Can I be longing without expectation that it be soothed? Can I, in living with absence, become the presence it is so hungry for?

Our longing lives in the unapproached regions of our lives. Because we are always trying to placate or outrun it, we rarely listen to what longing has to say. But if we can learn to treat that absence with reverence, as a place that is fully dilated, readying to receive the very things it is missing, longing then becomes a call to the edge of the question we have for our lives. Am I in alignment with the great nature of things? Am I in service to that which I love, and which loves me? In showing us what is missing, longing is a siren calling us towards our true home.

One of the greatest stories of longing followed is the one told of Rumi who, when his beloved teacher Shams of Tabrizi was murdered, began to circle a pillar in his courtyard. Struck with grief and longing for reunion with Shams, who had introduced Rumi to music and poetry, he turned and turned, grieved and longed. As he did, a holy portal opened up and poetry started tumbling out of him. All of the poems you now read today are poems not written by Rumi but by his followers, who were the scribes for what was being channeled through his longing. There are some who say this is also the origin story for the whirling dervishes who practice turning as a way of opening that portal to the divine.

Rumi's poems went on to be one of the greatest contributions to human culture in the last 700 years. In his willingness to dance with his longing, Rumi created such exquisite beauty that it became places of shelter for wanderers and outcasts, romantics and dreamers worldwide. Poetry became Rumi's belonging to the world, and in turn created a place of belonging for others to recognize themselves in.

There's a quality of encounter that we can make with life that is directly proportionate to our willingness to be penetrated by its influence. As we explored in the Inner Marriage, this kind of *active receptivity* is a wonderful undertaking which has no end to its apprenticeship. We are learning in every moment how to fully belong to a choice, an idea, a place, our body, a relationship, a regret, a loss, our story. All of this can be contained within a single embodied moment.

There are moments which feel too harsh to embody, and the temptation to absent yourself from the encounter is great. You may not yet have the competency to show up completely (or at all) for the event. But these are the moments that have the greatest poetry concealed within them. Though your body may be trembling with the terror of being that close to your edge, it won't always be this way. You will eventually become able to belong yourself to it. The time will one day come when you shake less and laugh sooner.

This is the living vow: to show up with increasing presence for the moment. To make an honest encounter with your longing at every turn. To listen to it, learning which way the energy of your life wants to go. Paradoxically, it is in our emptiness—another way of saying willingness—that we become full. It is in our being fully where we are that we are put in touch with our next becoming. This grows you. You begin to understand that your life belongs to more than yourself alone. It belongs to a momentum which, like Shams continued on in Rumi, is set in motion towards its destiny through longing.

You may dream of a wolf that wants to bite your hand, but instead of being afraid of pain, instead of feeling subject to the aggressions and demands of the other, you know you are partners. You are a wolf whisperer and you recognize its bite as a veiled desire to know you and be known by you. You make the encounter with a quiet power, a willingness to engage with that which previously frightened you. And when he lunges to take your hand in his teeth, it doesn't hurt at all, but becomes tender and full of telepathic mystery. You belong to one another, the wolf and you; you have been initiated into one another's belonging.

When we are open to our longing, which is to say not refusing or silencing it, it puts us in touch with a place where we can be accepted in our wholeness. No part of us should be split-off, but rather embraced and strengthened in our inner multiplicity.

You are Also the Drop

Many people misquote Rumi to say, "You are not a drop in the ocean but the ocean in the drop," which is comforting to us when we forget that the infinite depths reside within. But the true stanza, "Let the drop of water that is you become a hundred mighty seas. But do not think that the drop alone becomes the Ocean—the Ocean, too, becomes the drop!"[59] is more complex and asks us to wrestle with the paradox of being both part of that greater oneness and entirely separate, unique expressions of being.

The awareness of our separateness is what often brings on despondency and despair. We begin to think of our small human lives as inconsequential, even unnecessary, to the great diversity of things. If we let this awareness unconsciously drive us, our lives can become endless treadmills of desperation. Wishing to create a legacy, to make a mark, to create evidence of our specialness, we build from the lowly perspective of the drop. Forgetting our belonging to the greater ocean body, we become trapped in this cult of individualism, where nothing we achieve can ever be enough.

But purpose, in its purest sense, is not that different from being an organ in a body. By themselves organs are useless—unless they work together, in their wholly individualized ways, to serve the greater body. So Rumi asks us to hold both: we are not separate, but also we are. We are these completely unique individuals who are capable of infinite configurations of innovation and beauty, but we are embedded within and entirely dependent upon the larger ocean of allness.

In the mystical way of understanding it, longing is a memory of belonging to god. As we follow our personal longing, we are coming back into that original coherence. Though we need to learn how to live with the grief of having lost the traditions of our ancestry, we can reconnect through our longing to the origins from which those traditions were birthed.

Ancestral Longing

It's a fundamental mistake to believe that unbelonging begins with the self, because although we are stewards of this perpetual missing, it did not begin with us. Our first experience of unbelonging is like a pattern in our substrate which, like rocks in the soil, causes everything to grow awkwardly around it. Tracing our longing back to its origins, reconciling it to its history, is an important step to healing belonging forward.

This missing has been passed on, gaining in momentum through the generations, starting with an actual exile of your people's people. Perhaps when your village was made to flee from the humble patch of land to which they

147

were promised, separated from the faces that looked like their own, distanced from the secret ways in which they attuned to and praised beauty. Maybe they were once a people made proud by their numbers and shared identity, a compendium of songs and myth and an unrequited debt—the cherished kind—which kept them bound to the holy, which showed them how to walk on the earth knowing their magnificence.

Perhaps your people were broken apart by the betrayal of your own brothers and sisters, your elegant compendium suddenly and irreparably scattered into anonymity, forced away from the wealth of togetherness, given a nameless, placeless status: slave, immigrant, refugee. Of course there is a triumph in surviving, and new stories to be made of how a new home is hard-won, how a family can be made of strangers. But like any great grief that never goes away, we must learn instead to live with it, often for many generations.

The convergence of ancestral momentum into a single body can be both confounding and liberating. On one hand, if we trace our history, we may find a sense of purpose in reuniting with what our ancestors loved and were longing for. On the other hand, we may also carry vestiges of their trauma and embittered hopes in our bloodstream and mistake it as only our own.

An inherited alienation may live in us like an invisible condition, haunting us with feelings of unbelonging, causing us to absent ourselves from life in various ways, but never showing its true face. Sometimes we glimpse the origin of these patterns in our parents or grandparents who never evolved out of their identification with the Outcast archetype, assuming their own rejection before they ever ventured to participate in community. We may also recognize our own tendency to distance ourselves, dwell in alienation, believe that we are unwanted wherever we go. But consider that these strategies have deeper origins than your life alone.

During that awful period when I was unable to walk, I was taken deeply into the heart of my own isolation. Forced to give up my work and too fatigued to participate in most events, I was overcome with my longing for community, for the family I never had. But when I received that dream of stepping on broken glass in what seemed to be an echo of the Holocaust, I felt a powerful connection between my own injury and my grandfather's broken leg from when he leapt from the train to Auschwitz. The roots of my longing felt older than my life alone, and I was compelled to connect the chapters between my grandparents' story and my own.

Searching the internet, I found my grandfather's name listed as a survivor in the Warsaw Ghetto database. It was the first time in my years of searching that I found evidence of him online. I contacted The Jewish Genealogy Center and within twenty-four hours I heard back from the director who, in a single email, blessed me with fifteen names of family members from my grandfather's Jewish line. Overnight that ominously empty branch of our family tree flowered with fifteen gorgeous Hebrew names which, though I'd never heard them before, felt familiar on my tongue.

With the help of various organizations dedicated to Jewish memorial, I spent the next year of my illness piecing together some of what had been lost during the Holocaust: internment papers, newspaper articles, phonebook listings, even a few photographs. Some weeks into this project, I had the shock of a lifetime when I found a historian in rural France who had collected the memorial stories of the local townspeople during the war. Told they would be spared from the round-ups taking place in Paris, Jewish refugees were sent to live in rural workhouses for the short year and half before they were deported in 1945, on Convoy 66, to their deaths. Among those refugees was a small family of three, ancestors from our Konbrat line. We were immediately in touch with the historian, Christine Dollard-Leplomb, who informed us that one of the members of the René family, a friend of our ancestors, was still alive in his nineties now, and wanted to meet me!

A few short weeks later I flew to Paris to meet my brother, who travelled from London, and we ventured into the countryside of Ardennes to follow the path of our brave cousins. The great hope was that in tracing some of these small fragments we might come upon other living relatives who would help us remember all that had been forgotten. It was about a year into my illness and I was just beginning to walk again, for short trips to the end of the drive, or around the block on a good day, so travelling to Europe felt like a daunting but urgent odyssey that I couldn't refuse.

One of the first stops I made in Paris was to the Mémorial de la Shoah where I found my ancestors' names carved among the 70,000 Jews killed in France on the great stone Wall of Names. There aren't sufficient words to describe the haunting quality of the exhibits at the Holocaust museum. The air seemed to turn crisp just for our visit. The photographs were at times poetic—our beautiful people, dignified even in squalor—then of course horrific, depicting unimaginable acts done by people with hearts of stone.

The images which moved me in particular were of the women whose feet were so mangled and full of sores from their enslaved work in the fields that they had to go about life barefoot in all seasons. Shoes made of more holes than they were leather. With tears streaming down my cheeks, I understood that living in my feet was an ancient pain longing to be remembered.

I am struck by the difference between remembering and not forgetting. The latter requires a great deal more of us. It is the putting of our attention in these places where we would sooner look away, to spare ourselves an ever-renewing heartbreak. There was one exhibit in the museum where, after photographing a dying man writing the word "vengeance" in blood on the wall near where he lay, the photographer wrote that real revenge is to keep our records and memories alive. I think what he meant was that the greater vindication is not in reciprocating hatred, but in bringing to cultural consciousness the horrors humans are capable of. Not forgetting is the act of conscious recalling, retelling, and memorializing of what has been done, so that its impacts can be felt and shared by those who weren't there, so that it may never be done again.

Next, we set out on a train in the direction our cousins would have fled when deportation began in Paris in 1942, seeking refuge in the countryside. We spent an unforgettable day with Christine, who was responsible for not only erecting a commemorative statue in the name of our family and the many other Jews deported from the region of Ardennes, but who single-handedly resurfaced the long buried records of the province's involvement in the Nazi occupation.

These records, ranging from deportation papers to records of the confiscation of belongings and sealing of apartments, were sitting in some government basement collecting dust for decades. So much time had passed that the villagers now denied that Jews were ever interned and enslaved in this province. Against great resistance, Christine surfaced it all and began to collect the personal stories of those old and brave enough to remember, and published them in a book.[60] Since then, this heroine has reunited many families with surviving relatives. I've never met anyone so selflessly impassioned and driven by purpose. She is fond of saying, "*Cité c'est reussité*," a proverb meaning, 'To cite is to succeed.' Indeed, the work she has undertaken with her life, to create a record of our ancestral story, has given us back so much.

The next day we met the farmer who, in his nineties, remembered our family well. The moment we set eyes on one another, the tears began to fall. M. René had been carrying this grief since the day he said goodbye to his dear friend, our cousin Ginette, who was only seventeen the day the Nazis rounded up all the Jews in Champigneul. His family wanted to hide Ginette in their house, but she didn't want to leave her aging parents Frydel and Rajzla alone, even though she knew they were heading to extermination camps.

I understood too little of what M. René said in his old, regional dialect, but he kept looking at me with a mixture of awe and loss, saying that something in my mannerisms reminded him of Ginette. It's hard to put into words what it felt to walk on those same cobblestones, to gaze out upon the rolling fields where they worked, to turn the same corners of the golden stone village where they lived out the last of their lives. It was a numinous encounter, whose healing effects were felt by us all and for the first time in months, my feet didn't hurt at all.

At the heart of exile, we must finally encounter the longing we have hidden in our own hearts. Longing is an impulse, born out of what is missing from us which we ache to return to, even if we've never known it directly. It aches too, for our homecoming.

The great, albeit faint hope that started me on this genealogical work was that I might discover a living relative from the Jewish branch of our family line. Until just a few years ago we believed, as we'd been taught, that everyone perished in the Holocaust and all records were lost.

Though Ginette's story ended tragically, a small but meaningful detail on her mother Rajzla's document kept that hope alive in me. The letters in the bottom left corner "M3E" meant that there were three children, two from Frydel's previous marriage, who were left behind in Paris when Ginette and her parents were sent to the Ardennes to work in the fields. The day before we left Paris, we learned that we could request the birth records with our family name from any town hall. And just like that, in the final hour of my voyage, I found Sabine, the half-sister of Ginette who was separated from her father at the age of ten.

After taking a week to summon up the courage and the French, I finally spoke with my dear, kind cousin Sabine in Versailles for the first time! What a startling joy it was for us to hear each other's voices. We were, of course, sad that our connection came too late for us to visit in person, but we've already begun to set another trip to France in motion. "*Dépêche-toi*," she said, "*j'ai 87 ans!*"

As it turns out, her family line is strong with two children, grandchildren and great grandchildren. Amazingly, she knew nothing of her father's fate, so it was my privilege to send her these photographs and stories and help her to visit the Konbrat monument in M. René's village.

I do not know what hungered in me to connect these chapters, to collect these disparate names; what in me was longing for a coming together, a cohesion, both a beginning and a proper burial. It is like the effort of the spider who lets the wind sway her as it will, but then, in the brevity of its pauses, works with all her upwards might at the invisible structure to create a new plane between things. I do not know what kept me in search of the familiar, but perhaps it is the same thing that swims salmon, or murmurs starlings. Maybe it is the earth upon which I'd not yet tread but which my body remembers from before the before, whose landscape is always pulling me home.

We can't know what is attempting to come unbound in crisis. We only know the narrow parameters before pain breaks us apart. Now, what is hidden within us wants to be met. It wants you to know it. And nothing holds you closer than this wanting to be known.

Perhaps it was my feeling of insufficient belonging, in my life and in the world, that drew me not forward but into history, where the momentum was weakened, where the stories and poems were burned from memory. Maybe it was the search for those mentors and parents and great elders who had done this all before, who could laugh, put a cool hand on my brow, quiet my questions and remember me into belonging.

But it was this ache in my feet, this longing in my heart for the stories that were never told to me, which drew me into my history and, as it turned out, my future work in the world. A rabbi once told me that, though every physical remnant of my Jewish history was burned in the Holocaust, the lost stories lived in my bones. I have dedicated my life to listening to my bones so that I might, in some windfall bestowal of grace, catch the faintest wisp of a song that I've always-never known. A way spoken, a likeness recognized, a familiar rhythm to carry me into the sway.

We are the expression and extension of a long line of survivors. Our lives are but a continuation of all those who came before. And though many perished, your people didn't. They saw and lived and endured and their resilience is your true inheritance. In this way, their wounds are our own, in that it is always up to us to turn the salt of bitterness into the salt of wisdom. It is liberating to consider that when we heal an ancestral pattern, we are healing backwards through time, liberating all those souls who were left unresolved, unforgiven and misunderstood.

In the beginning of the world, there was longing. Only in this state of missing, of absence, can life be drawn into itself. Like the womb which is an empty vessel waiting for the seed of life, longing is the force that pulls potential towards it. Rather than a thing to be tolerated or gotten rid of, longing should be venerated as the elemental gravity that attracts towards us the life and world we want for ourselves.

May all those who are being re-membered in your personal journey of belonging feel the great relief of love come alive in your reunion with longing. May their dignity be preserved in our care of one another, and may all our relations be fortified in our not forgetting.

Twelve

Competencies of Belonging

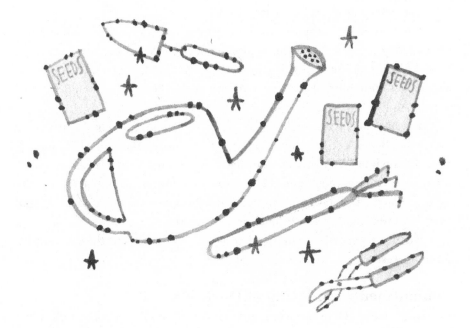

aving walked a great distance from our initial estrangement into the orphaned depths of exile, we have learned the difference between fitting in and belonging. We now know belonging is a dynamic process, requiring alternating periods of togetherness and aloneness to remain vital. We are making friends with the often terrifying Otherness within, learning to make allies of even our most loathsome guests. And we have begun to follow our longing, which reaches to us through our ancestral lines, right from the soul of the world. We are coming into the great secret that belonging is really a skill, a set of competencies at which we must practice if we are to rise to the call of an aching heart and a fractured world.

Over the next few chapters, we'll investigate some of the core competencies of belonging. In many ways this is just the beginning of a larger conversation to which other disciplines could contribute a great deal, but I hope to offer you a variety of both internal and external tools with which to begin your practice of belonging.

Like any practice worth undertaking, belonging cannot be mastered overnight. Because it is a disappearing art, we might find ourselves going it alone for a while. We may find ourselves disappointed with a lack of response when we try to reach out, and the temptation to lose hope will be strong. But we must keep a vision of how we want our lives and the world to look, and work towards weaving those first threads together. Even when the garment of belonging seems flimsy and inadequate we must keep to the task until it substantiates.

Commitment: Tendering of Devotion

Earlier we spoke of the word 'endurance,' which has its root in the Latin *durus*, meaning 'hard.' To endure is to make your way through something hard. But we might also interpret that hardness as the inner firmness of resolve. This 'staying put' or committing to something, even as it changes its shape, is a fundamental capacity of belonging. How can we belong ourselves to a place, a community, or even a craft unless we stay put long enough to become bonded with it? Similarly, how can others belong themselves to us unless we prove the fabric of our friendship sturdy enough to be the warp to the other's weft? Staying put requires commitment and accountability, qualities which make the nomadic heart shiver with dread.

When we hear the word 'commitment,' most of us think of obligation and restriction. On one hand, modern life is already so heavily structured that many of us ache to live in a more fluid and spontaneous way. But on the other hand, we have become casualties of a culture that emphasizes efficiency and convenience, which teaches a cursory mindset, never lingering for long on any one thing. So we may avoid making commitments. Or if we do make them, we keep them 'soft,' in the event that something more glamorous comes along.

As a sampling of how uncommitted we have become as a culture, consider how we change careers an average of seven times in adulthood; half or more of all marriages end in divorce; we communicate in the undemanding ways of text messages and emoticons; and we are infinitely scrolling on our devices, rarely giving the fullness of our presence to any one thing. By extension, we are growing to expect that life should be immediate and convenient.

While convenience proposes to make your life easier, and there are obvious benefits, there are often hidden tolls being taken elsewhere. *Easy* puts work into robotic hands, undermining our own necessity. *Easy* destroys the mentoring-apprenticing relationship. *Easy* robs us of the privilege of courtship, the very thing which bonds us to a place and its resources, or a craft and the persons who have made a slow mastery of their lives.

Consider the ancient alchemists who, despite very little success, were convinced they could transmute lead into gold. Through painstaking experimentation, they pioneered an art form which, though it contributed little to science, was later discovered by Carl Jung to be the historical counterpart of the work he'd been doing to map the psyche. It was as if the alchemists were unconsciously projecting their inner processes onto the matter of their experiments. Jung later worked with the dream cycle of a patient who knew nothing of alchemy to discover a parallel set of images and archetypal processes unfolding in his psychic development.

Taken symbolically, alchemy is about turning the lower, primitive aspects of the self into a purified state; to illuminate the darkness with a sense of value or meaning, making conscious what is unconscious. This becoming whole is the process Jung called individuation, which is what we're doing with dreamwork and belonging.

One of the key conditions necessary for alchemical transformation was a hermetically sealed vessel that could withstand the pressure necessary to synthesize base elements, that *prima materia*, into gold. I'd like to propose that commitment is that container. Like the alchemical crucible, commitment is the vessel in which something raw and undisciplined can be transformed into something valuable. Commitment is like a womb in which a new life can grow.

It is hermetically sealed so that nothing extraneous can enter into the process. No projections can be made upon it, no introduced doubt or criticism can reach it during its critical formative stages. But it's also sealed for our own good, so that we don't have an easy out. In times of exhaustion and suffering, fear and frustration, we must hold the tension of wanting to give up while remaining committed long enough for the process to complete itself.

No Strap Guitar, Geoffrey's dream
I am playing my electric guitar, trying to strum a few chords, but without a strap it is nearly impossible to support the weight of the instrument, and my song is awkward and fumbling.

Marriage is the vow we make that, through hardship and doubt, keeps us bound to one another; so too must we create a tethering to our own creativity. This commitment ensures that in times of doubt and inadequacy, we keep returning to it to deepen our craft. In this dream, Geoffrey's guitar strap is symbolic of his commitment, his belonging to music as it belongs to him. It's the vow that has been broken somewhere along the way, and now the weight of his vocation feels too burdensome.

When we place limitations and boundaries around something we care about, it isn't meant to be a prison that keeps us stuck or stagnant. It is to create a paradoxical freedom which allows us, through restraint, to fully explore the relationship, the craft, or the experience in all its subtle dimensions. Commitment in these terms is not an obligation but a deep devotion to that which we love. In our devotion to it, the very thing we are committed to is set free. Our constancy is what allows our beloved to pull back and contract, or expand into their fullest essence, while we hold the steadfast container of commitment.

Waiting for providence to step in and show us the way is a little like keeping one foot out the door, in case it never comes, so we can still make a break for it. But really, providence is quietly waiting for our dedication. Commitments that go unmade, or have a lack of intent, can destroy even the noblest of dreams.

To make a commitment, of course, is one thing, but to keep that commitment is harder and must be renewed in a continual, active practice. Whether you wear a symbolic object, get a tattoo, repeat a special mantra, or sit at an altar adorned with sacred items, these things act as a steadying staff to secure us in times of doubt. It becomes an outer firmness, a third presence we can rely on in periods of difficulty. And so it must be tended to, visited, and replenished in some meaningful way to ensure the commitment is still alive for you, as you are for it.

This is the unexpected truth of commitment. To the casual glance, it might look boring, like something is taking too long, like you're missing out or unwilling to adventure and change. But to the discerning eye, endurance is the great friend of passion. It is slow to burn, but lasting in warmth. It sees beyond the temporary trends and swells into the unchanging depth of things. If you've ever stood next to a person who won't be moved, then you know what freedom taking a stand can inspire. There, in the anchoring itself, is the invitation to soar.

What is needed to bring about the new world you yearn for but devotion to its course? The calling is in your blood, like a vow that was made for you. Everything your dream requires is within the provisions of your being. If nature didn't intend you to succeed, why would you have been given the urge to? All a dream asks is for your vow to be made back, through every small contraction and expansion, renewed in a continuous tendering of devotion.

Thirteen

Handmaking a Life

The longing to handmake things overtook me some years ago when I was gifted a deerskin medicine pouch by a friend in ceremony. She had learned to skin and tan the hide herself, working it until the tassels hung gently and the slipknot moved gracefully along its braided path. Instantly, I felt a longing in me to know things with my hands as she did, since music, writing, and dreamwork are all intangible arts.

At the time, I wasn't able to articulate why handmaking was such a powerful calling, but after learning a few important crafts such as basketry, lightsculpture, and needlework, I began to understand that in the act of creating something with my hands I was, as Alice Walker puts it, "reliv[ing] the thrill of [my] own conception."[61] This is why so many creative people dream of pregnancy, labour, and birth. Handmaking is an act of conceiving, labouring for, and contributing to culture.

Consider the word 'heirloom,' a compound word with its roots in both heredity and looming, suggesting that history is woven into the things we make. Certainly you have felt this in older objects or garments you've inherited, that they carry energy from the places and people who made them. And if they come from your own family, perhaps you can feel their stories, which are the prequels to your own story, living between their fibres. Indeed, this is why handmaking and singing our stories into the things we make is a way of keeping belonging alive.

In my grandmother's time in pre-war Poland, girls were made to do needlework as a matter of course. It was believed that "idle hands were the devil's playthings," so from the time my grandmother was a young girl she was taught to design, sew, and embroider. She made all of her own clothes and took great pride in the way she dressed; this artfulness was also a means of survival for her during the Nazi occupation, because her beauty (and perfect German) allowed her to pass as 'Aryan.'

Later in my genealogical research, I found out that some of my other relatives were also seamstresses, tailors, and clothing designers—a detail that suddenly explained my desire to handmake things. As a friend recently said, heritage is not just stored in things but in our hands. And my hands were hungry to be of use, as my ancestors' hands had been.

My granny managed to save some of her intricate embroidery from the war and kept them folded neatly in her dresser drawer. On occasion, she would pull them out to show me and, as if the stories were embedded in the threads, smooth out the wrinkles of the garments as she told me what life was like for her during the war.

To find stories embedded in handwork is not surprising, considering everything a person experiences is transmitted into what they create. The materials and tools they use also contain the traces of the place they are from, so the work can't help but be storied, fathoms deep. In some cultures, this *storying* of objects is done consciously. The Shipibo, one of the many indigenous tribes in Peru, have recorded their songs (*icaros*) into elaborate embroidery, geometric designs that correlate directly with nature. The Aborigines of Australia create songlines that are also maps of their landscape. If even one generation is denied that inheritance, in cultures such as these, the way home will be lost.

While those of us who are the children of refugees and settlers, or the descendants of prisoners, may no longer have this symbiotic relationship with the land upon which we live, our history is still embedded in the things we make with our hands, which is why I consider handmaking to be a great competency of belonging. The materials we chose, the teachers who imparted the craft to us, the necessity or beauty which called the creation forth, the style of music contained within its curves and lines—all of these elements live quietly in an object made by a person's hands. And wearing, using, or living with handmade things allows the essence of a place or a lineage to be kept alive through us.

For centuries, the only tools and objects people used were made by hand, usually by someone from their own village, creating a reciprocal economy. In other words, by engaging a baker to make your daily bread, or a blacksmith to forge your knives, you are receiving an original creation—but you are also giving the makers a purpose in your village. With the advent of plastics and factory production, many of the traditional hand trades like shoemaking, forging, basketry, textile-weaving, and boat-making were suddenly facing extinction.

Though this means we have access to buying cheaper, more colourful products, it comes at an unseen cost. The disappearance of both human mastery and other-than-human resources happened very quickly over the last seventy years. We are seeing the extinction of innumerable hand trades from the absence of apprentices, who were unable to see a future in the dying ways and moved into urban centres to work for business instead. Contained within these losses are the cultural legacies of those places and its people.

But another important shift happened simultaneously: things were no longer created with individual needs in mind but rather for profit. This forced us to adapt ourselves to the uniformity of things. And this is a harder, more subtle thing to discuss because most of us have never known anything different. But when we adapt ourselves to the tools and clothes and objects made by machines, we are in a sense threatening our own uniqueness. As the originality of objects dies, so too does our relationship with *indigeneity*, both within and without.

Anything that is designed for maximum 'efficiency' casts a profound shadow that we rarely take into account: the abdication of human accountability. If you contextualize the time it takes an individual to gather raw materials, which are often living organisms, the honour and grief that is felt in their losses to our ecosystems, the lifetime courtship of a material's ways, the craftsperson's relationship with their instruments and land, then you have a life which is interwoven with art. You have a person who is beholden to their place in the world and you can trace a path across their wounds and wrinkles to their love of a thing, which they will protect, and which will feed you with its long history, beauty, and richness. A person like this thinks twice about 'developing' an unblemished piece of land.

Consider, for example, a knife you use every day. Like most people, you probably bought yours in a group with others just like it, at a large store in your neighbourhood. It was likely made by a machine that was created expressly for the purpose of making things efficiently and homogeneously. The knife performs a kind of slavery for you in its endless cutting of things that you consume. Because that is the extent of your relationship with the instrument, it is reflected in the way you use it.

But imagine for a moment that your knife wasn't like any others. Imagine you sought out a bladesmith, who procured the metal from a miner whose lifetime has been spent collecting iron from the earth, and who knows the ancient alchemy of alloying elements. Then imagine your bladesmith shapes it in a fire he always keeps alive at a forging heat. Notice its handle is carved in bone, only one of the precious elements of a fully esteemed deer who was killed in a night-long hunt that bestowed its hunter the honour of its death. Then imagine your bladesmith is allied with a leatherworker who has cleaned, tanned and tailored the deerskin into a sheath that protects your blade which also sits snugly at your hip.

A knife like this would humble you with its beauty. Every time you felt its weight in your hand, you would remember the earth that gave of its bones to become your blade. You would think of the man who lives in the dark to find your metals. You would remember the fire, fuelled by so many trees that gave their lives for the heat. You would be astonished at the artfulness your bladesmith has mastered with his life, as well as your indebtedness to his skills. Every time you sheath your knife, you'd think of the deer who ran through the dark forest by the strength of its brave heart, and the hunter who left a generous offering to the deer's spirit, whose body would feed his family for a half a year.

When you learn to make things with your hands, you begin to awaken an awareness of the beauty and value of things in your life. Handmaking teaches us about slowness: the antidote to brevity and efficiency. It shows us, through the patience and skillfulness of our own hands, what goes into a thing.

When we put those long efforts into bringing beauty into the world, we are honouring that which made us by creating as we have been created. We are taught to respect the slow, attentive piecing together of the life we yearn for. Stitch by stitch, we apprentice the craft. We work in tandem with mystery, feeling its rhythms awaken in our bone-memory. As the hands work, the mind is stilled and a greater listening is engaged as we drop down into the deep rhythm of devotion, where the whole world is in communion. The ferns unfurl, the daffodils trumpet, the rosebuds fatten, and the song of creation can be heard.

Handwork also teaches us the patience required to make a life materialize. There are no shortcuts, and it can't be done cheaply or en masse. The work is small, the work is slow, and all we can do is stay with it. As Dr. Clarissa Pinkola Estés says, "the shortcut, the easy way, always falls apart. Then one returns to the handmade life. One has to pick it up painfully, and piece it back together, holding the overall pattern in one's mind, but working patiently, piece by piece."[62]

As we head into unknown times, where resources are disappearing proportional to the scale of demand and centralized systems are crumbling under their top-heavy models, the value of handmaking skills will be enormously prized. Already we see a growing emphasis being placed on local food for sustainability, which has the great side benefit of also strengthening community ties. The natural extension of this idea is that we also begin to source our tools, clothes, and other objects from as close to home as possible.

With this in mind, consider apprenticing yourself to an elder in your community to learn the craft they have mastered. Allow yourself to become a living record of the lineage carried in that craft, perhaps one day growing skilled enough to teach the younger ones what you know. You may find the process exhilarating and enlightening in ways you weren't expecting, as I have with basketry. My teacher Joan Carrigan transmits the stories of the places she's gone to learn certain traditional basket techniques. Sometimes she'll take me out onto the land to show me where the willow is growing, or in a rowboat to pluck reed sheaths from the muck. One day I hope to get an invitation with her from the Tsawout First Nation to harvest cedar bark when the sap is running in the spring.

Rather than feeling the insufficiency of your skills, or stopping at the unapproachability of an art form, a teacher can help you begin to penetrate its mystery. Any master in their field will admit that skills are not inherent, but learned. Once you've got some momentum with a craft, you may crave to learn another. I've found this for myself: after I discovered I could belong to basketry, I could belong myself to any number of crafts which attracted me, like lightsculpture. This spellbinding art form, invented by a man named Stephen White from Eugene, Oregon uses paper, basket reeds, and electrical wiring to make an unearthly, shell-like lamp. After that, I took up knot-work and crochet, and have even started dabbling in watercolour.

To be in a constant state of learning is to be receptive to life itself. It puts you in what the Zen Buddhists call *shoshin*, or 'beginner's mind.' *Shoshin* is a state of eagerness and openness when studying a subject, even at an advanced level. When we approach a craft without preconceptions, we are open to what a friend of mine calls our 'possibility space.' Our possibility space is that field beyond our expectations in which anything can happen. Though our possibility space may feel cramped and crowd in on us sometimes, it can be expanded by pushing into the spirit of inquiry.

When we are focused on our questions instead of answers, the whole of our energy goes to discovery—the only state in which failures are encouraged—and we are caught by surprise. Incidentally, *shoshin* is essential to dreamwork. Though it's valuable to have knowledge of symbols and archetypes, the greater skill is curiosity. When you have a refined curiosity you can draw meaning from the dreamer herself, who is the only expert of her dream. As Zen teacher Shunryu Suzuki says, "In the beginner's mind there are many possibilities, in the expert's mind there are few."[63]

By taking up the competency of handmaking, we are becoming the future ancestors we wished we'd had. Paradoxically, in this reversal, we are relieving the longing to be connected to a legacy. But, like all of belonging's requirements of us, it can feel mountainous to approach these heights from nothing; with such slow rewards, it can often feel as if no progress is being made.

One of the great practices that Martín Prechtel teaches to alleviate this anxiety is to create what he calls a Place of Origin in your home.[64] This can be even a small corner of your house which is dedicated to knowing the origins of everything in it. By origins, I don't just mean where a thing came from, but who made it, with what skills, and at what cost to its roots. For instance, I might put my grandmother's embroidery there, knowing as I do its embedded stories. I might even attempt to learn her craft so that I know the process in my bones. I might put one of my cedar baskets there, made with materials I harvested myself. I might also learn more about the ecosystem in which those cedar trees grow and the First Nations people in whose traditional territory they grow. I might also create a string of cloth prayer flags, crafted from the hand-me-downs of my ancestors, learning more about my genealogy as I sew them.

Your Place of Origin may be small and sparse at first, but you can add to it over time and, when young ones come up around you, you can tell the stories that you've collected there in the hopes that one day, this corner you attended to becomes a place of belonging for them.

Making Beauty Medicine

There is really only one way to restore a world that is dying and in disrepair: to make beauty where ugliness has set in. By beauty, I don't mean a superficial attractiveness, though the word is commonly used in this way. Beauty is a loveliness admired in its entirety, not just at face value. The beauty I'm referring to is metabolized grief. It includes brokenness and fallibility, and in so doing, conveys for us something deliciously real. Like *kintsukuroi*, the Japanese art of repairing broken pottery with powdered gold, what is normally seen as a fatal flaw is distinguished with value. When we come into contact with this kind of beauty, it serves as a medicine for the brokenness in ourselves, which then gives us the courage to live in greater intimacy with the world's wounds.

To become a fully fledged member of the ecosphere, each of us must find a way to make a contribution of beauty medicine to the world. Most of us don't think of our gifts as contributions, though they are clearly called 'gifts' for a reason, but this may be because they've never been properly received.

I've heard it said that home is the place where your gifts are received. Indeed, for those who have never had their gifts acknowledged, a true sense of belonging is rarely felt. After all, how can you belong if you are but partially

165

appreciated? If we are honest with ourselves, most of us will also admit that we are stingy with our gifts because we underestimate their worth.

As we apprentice ourselves to the way of nature, we begin to understand that all of life is in a continuous cycle of giving and receiving. It is the honouring of this cycle that makes us feel at home in ourselves and in relation to the rest of nature. In order to experience true belonging, we must not only acknowledge the gifts we are receiving, but also give our beauty away, no matter how it may be received by others.

When I first opened the Dream School, I spent years in relative obscurity and always had to work at part-time jobs to make ends meet. Though my column "Dreamspeak" appeared in magazines and newspapers all over North America, I was rarely sought out professionally. A friend of mine invited me to host a Dream Tent in her import shop downtown, to offer my services as a dreamworker to anyone needing support. I sat in that silk tent twice a week, several hours at a time, for months, and never received a single client. It was so dispiriting that I slipped into indulging thoughts of giving up on my vocation many times. But no matter how I tried to abandon it, it followed at my heels like a devoted hound.

When you walk a path you love, there is something deeper calling you forward on it, like a beautiful question that can never be answered. In hard times you may turn away from it, but a part of you knows you'll always turn back—because you can't give up on what you love, even if you try.

It is the way of all nature to be of service to something greater than one's life alone. Real worth can only be achieved in relation to the greater whole. The apple tree, for instance, is generous with its fruits, offering those gifts to anyone who wants to be fed by them. But it also serves itself in that the apple-eater becomes a carrier for the tree's seeds to proliferate. When we tune into our belonging with all things, there is a similarly combined urge to both succeed in life and to make our life an offering unto the commons.

When one sees the true value that goes into a thing, be it from nature's ingenuity or our own, we can't help but feel responsible for it. When we appreciate beauty in something, we instinctively want to protect it.

Let's say there is a particular sugar maple near your home that you decide you'd like to know better. You watch it for a few seasons, because courtship always takes time, and begin to notice how, as the nights get longer, the tips of its first leaves turn yellow and gold. Some years, when the days are sunny and the nights are crisp but not freezing, the tree turns the most spectacular crimson and reds. When its leaves finally fall and decompose, you notice how they nourish the soil and many invisible organisms with their nutrients.

You decide to scoop up a pile for your own garden, where it will hold the rainfall in its spongy layer of humus, protecting your young seeds from the cold. You watch as the tree grows out its slender budded twigs in the winter, an early promise of more yet to come. Sure enough, those buds begin to swell in the spring, birthing new leaves in just a few weeks. It flowers soon after and the bees come to pollinate, making you wonder what all the fuss is about. So you pop a maple flower in your mouth one day and decide it tastes a lot like broccoli and becomes a regular feature of your salads. As September rolls around, the tree begins to fruit its double-winged seeds, which you learn are called samaras, and which you remember clipping to the end of your nose when you were a kid. When they helicopter down to find new soil, you notice that some of the squirrels and birds eat the ripened seeds, helping the tree find new life elsewhere.

So when the city authorities roll up in their big felling truck to cut the tree down one year, because it's showing signs of age and is an inconvenience to keep pruning back from the power lines, you are as startled as if its pain is your own. You and the tree have a relationship now, and its cycles help to locate you in time and in place. But you are also aware of everything else that is dependent upon the tree. The birds and squirrels and other tiny organisms who call it home, the bees who pollinate its flowers, the soil that depends on its humus, and the regeneration of future life in its seeds—all of which would end. But it is more even than all of this, because the maple has enriched your life with its beauty-making and its graceful tenacity.

This isn't to say we should never cut down trees, but if we did so from this engaged and embodied perspective, we would feel the impact of our taking. The grief of all that is lost would weigh against what is to be gained. Though this may seem like a harder way to live, it preserves our sensitivity, the porousness necessary for true belonging.

As we heal our disconnection from the distanced parts of ourselves and from Otherness in general, including that of the natural world, we become inseparable from it. Rather than practicing at detachment, we are rapturously attaching! When we weave our threads together, we become *response-able* for each other. Which is to say, we now have the ability to respond to the other's experience as if it was, in some way, our own.

You might say grief is the price you pay for loving something or someone, but it is also a privilege, because *it* is what allows authentic beauty—which isn't always pretty, but is always truthful—to find its way through you. And this beauty medicine is what the world needs most to heal.

Stepping into Being Seen

Beauty must be shared in order to complete its natural cycle; but for many, putting our gifts into the world is a daunting step to take. No longer looking in on the lit-up warmth of belonging from the shadows outside, we must step into being seen. Like the flowering bush that gives its fragrance to anyone willing to appreciate it, there is a reciprocity intrinsic to all life that wants to give away what it has been given. Belonging begins when we give our gifts away in order to be filled again, and again. So long as we are only offering ourselves partially, from behind the protections of our persona, our true kin will never recognize us.

It should be said, however, that sharing your beauty in an unsympathetic world isn't a path for the weak-hearted. As you step into being seen, you'll come face-to-face with your fears of being judged, criticized, dismissed, and derided. In fairy tales, there is often a character whose sole purpose is to introduce doubt into your mission, like Jack's mother, who forbids him from climbing the beanstalk. Or Bluebeard, who threatens wrath upon his wife should she enter the locked door of her destiny. Like a strong tide, there are some people in our lives whose influence can pull us away from the shores of our truth, tempting us to renounce our mission altogether. These characters are not always unsympathetic—they may even be folks you admire. But when you are subtly attuned to your nature, you'll notice yourself wilting in their presence or taking on their diminishing view of your abilities. Like eating something that doesn't agree with you, this will give you a sour feeling in your belly, which can grow into a rejection of life itself. In the worst of times, it can stretch into an ocean of lostness in every direction.

When you find yourself in such an untethered place, there is a secret to anchoring yourself back into intimacy with your vow: the recognition that you are only susceptible to an invalidation that matches an area of ambivalence or doubt in your own stance. In other words, an invalidation or dismissal from the outside won't unsteady you if you are in a committed relationship with the beauty you are making. So when you are triggered, it's a good reminder to check that place of susceptibility and ask yourself, "Where am I at odds with myself on this issue?" This isn't to say that the other is not being an empirical jerk, but that in their *jerkness*, they've brought to light a place within that requires fortification.

Unchecked places of doubt within can keep us in relationship with those who think too little of us, and they can also hold us back from fully emerging with our gifts. You may even recognize your reaction to certain triggers as an almost comfortable self-abandonment, where you expect your losses before they happen.

A good example of how indulging in doubt can lead to self-sabotage is the story of Marlon, a first time author who'd been invited onto a prominent radio show to promote his upcoming book release. When the interviewer asked Marlon to prepare his own questions for the interview, Marlon felt insulted, as if the interviewer didn't respect him enough to do his research. In the end, he declined the interview and lost a potentially great ally for his work. What Marlon didn't realize is that it's common practice for radio hosts to ask the author to direct the conversation to their key points. As we worked on this humbling experience together, Marlon connected to an early childhood pattern of not being respected by his critical father. Having internalized his father's doubt of his own abilities, he was now unconsciously projecting that onto the outside world.

"Doubts are traitors," Shakespeare once wrote, that "make us lose the good we oft might win, by fearing to attempt."[65] When we doubt that our friends really love us, we will expect them to abandon us. When they cancel plans, or show up late, we feel like we saw it coming. When we doubt our value in the workplace, harmless interactions can feel like petty exclusions, causing us to become cynical and avoid connection. Then when we don't get the promotion or the raise, it can cement our belief that we're not valued. Even when we do have good fortune, as Marlon did, we may see it as a fluke and retract our contribution before it can be rejected.

Doubt has an insidious nature that will undermine our life unless we learn to pull back its projections and take responsibility for creating disappointing outcomes. As the Abraham Maslow adage says, "If all you have is a hammer, everything looks like a nail."[66] Once we understand that we experience what we expect, we can begin to play with fresh ways of thinking to get different results.

One of the first ways to recognize a pattern of doubt is by its automatic, serial quality. Anywhere you find yourself thinking, "I'm cursed in this area," or, "This is what always happens," or, "I'll never succeed," you can be sure you're in a doubt-loop. But the hidden truth about doubt-loops is that they're actually defences against our being rejected or criticized. In other words, doubt is a sneaky way of avoiding a challenge. Underneath Marlon's defensiveness was the fear that he wasn't equal to the level at which he was invited. However humbling, this realization helped him to think of doubt as a place where he was being called to bravely move through his fears. When doubts come up, we can acknowledge them as the scar tissue they are, carrying the memory of our wounds. But in order to heal, we have to suspend our habitual contraction from fear and treat opportunities as innocent of harbouring any ill towards us.

Doubt is an invitation to make boundaries against those sour-belly influences, tightening your circle of intimacy to those who would sooner support than discourage you, and choosing fresh ways of thinking that do the same. Marlon used his experience to notice when he was becoming defensive with doubt, and took up a new inner mantra instead: "Something amazing is about to happen." Doubt asks us to step towards that which frightens us, reassuring ourselves that if we have the courage to make a true encounter with it, a favourable outcome lies beyond fear.

Destiny is not to be mistaken with fate, where one has no influence upon its outcome. Destiny requires us to take steps towards it, to parent its growth, especially in times of doubt and weakness. And if we find the courage to move in its direction despite the absence of grand signs, we are often graced by the small miracles of confirmation and synchronicity that we'd been hoping for all along.

That being said, it's important to forgive ourselves when we aren't feeling brave. Until we are ready to give our hidden stories expression through beauty-making, we'll have these stopgaps, or what I call Guardians of Vulnerability, which may take the form of paralyzing inadequacy, anxiety, fear, and depression. But here's the paradox: the moment we honour those guardians, acknowledging the value of their protections, their rigidity begins to soften.

The Guardianship

Do not be ready before your time.
There's no knowing what symmetry
is marshalling itself below this confusion.
First the long attentiveness of listening
must be paid. Don't brave your way
out of this husk while it serves
to protect your impressionability.
Let yourself be kept a while longer
in these origins
where you are mine alone
and I am only yours.
Let something sweet be made of our secret.
Put not your offering into the world too soon.
Let it ripen in the guardianship

of your trepidation.
Let this fallow time be stretched.
For it is in this unreadiness
that beauty takes its form.
Live a season longer in this holy refuge.
Because soon what nectar
is made of our union
will be for all the world to drink,
or not drink.
And you will need to remember what grace
was allowed only
by your long staying hidden.

Life as an Offering

Make of your life an offering to the debt that can never be repaid. Know the joy of this indebtedness, because so long as you are beholden to it, beauty will run through you like a river gathering momentum. So long as there is something to repay, you are receiving far more than you can ever give back. What an assignment: to find ever more eloquent and myriad ways to say thank you. To be forever in conversation with the sacred well within which never runs dry. To dwell in the act of giving.

Make beauty that gives more than it takes. In recognition of the energy behind all creation, make that which requires little of the world and contributes a great deal. Write poems on paper you've stained with watercolour, and give them away to strangers! Be glad never to see them again, because your gladness affirms your affluence. Make art in barren places using discarded things. Make bouquets of fragrant herbs from your garden and give them to folks who seem lonely. Teach someone in a city how to grow tomatoes. Dance, sing, and orate your prayers. Disarm unexpecting others with your gifts, helping to grow their own receiving muscle. Create a holy refuge of your life that others may seek solace there, feeling the strength and dedication in the medicine of your beauty, and upon it rest and be encouraged to their own summoning.

Don't just give your gifts to people. Give relevance to the invisible by leaving offerings at rivers, or sewing prayer flags for the forest. Build cairns on mountain tops, plant wildflowers in parking lots, and live your life as it were an endless offering of beauty. Any small crumb of thanks we give to the holies makes them come alive with delight. The more we remember our invisible helpers, the more they remember us. Our days get progressively plumper with significance: the woodpecker drumming on the roof like a winged shaman reminds us how thin the veil between worlds is; the warm breeze through the sugar maple is whispering a secret for our ears; and the friend we bump into was sent by our own longing.

Place your roughly hewn piece into the world in the faith that, wherever you are, another is elsewhere doing the same. If they aren't, it is because they don't yet know their worth. And if you don't, it's because you don't yet know how gravely you are missed. Your small disappearances, your holding back, your choosing to forget, is what breaks the momentum of our belonging together.

Take your attention down into the tiny, miraculous stitching of the life you are creating from nothing, and trust that each small thread is connecting you to the greater body of belonging. One day, maybe today, you will look back on everything that came after your decision to attend to your life like an artwork, and you will see a great number of years symbolized in moons and stained with blood, stretching across a great landscape behind you, and you'll know you have come a great distance. Here, with your great cape of wound-moons, a piercing presence in your eyes, a living history on your skin, you will know you have always belonged.

Fourteen

Bearing the Pleasure

*E*mergence never happens all at once. It is a slow stepping into the expanded capacity of your next self. When the time to remain hidden comes to its natural end, you must begin to inhabit your new dimensionality. We've spoken a good deal about bearing suffering in the body and heart, but as much as we may be challenged by our darker nature, sometimes learning to emerge from pain into pleasure is the greater work. By pleasure I don't just mean the sensual kind, though the comfort of a good meal and a hot bath are important. I mean pleasure as a state of being at home in your own skin, of feeling *well* where, when, and with whom you find yourself.

Our capacity for embodied pleasure depends on our ability to receive, which is like a muscle that can atrophy if it's been habitually contracted. A learned sense of unworthiness can act as a barrier against our well-being, keeping us from opening to the beauty that's all around us. Whether it's our ability to receive positive feedback and support, or to expect things to work out in our favour, we may be distrustful of goodness even when it stands on our doorstep. But this doesn't have to be a permanent condition. With practice, we can learn how to welcome beauty and receive pleasure wholeheartedly.

In the mythic Hero's journey cycle, the Return is the final stage. After you've been through the hell of initiation, and though you may still feel ragged from its challenges, you know the worst is over. You've earned yourself a place to stand. You know what you value. You have a story to tell. And it's time to return to the world with your beauty medicine. Though much has been written about what you had to go through to get here, the Return is often treated as a footnote, as if walking into the world with the elixir of your journey was easy. Sometimes you can't quite believe the turning of the tide. You're still expecting the worst. Unable to trust your own feet to support you again, this is when you're tempted to curl back into your cave and refuse to emerge.

The world is different than when you left it and you are different than when it left you. Traces of the ways you compensated for pain still live on in your body's memory. Like moving into a more spacious home, you may still brace for the narrow passageways and tight corners you used to live in. You may need to practice at expanding into your new size. After all, that which restrains you, like a tight swaddle, can be comforting in its limitation.

If you were someone who survived on scraps of affection, you may have a lifelong habit of contraction that is only obvious when you are showered in appreciation. In those moments, your heart is challenged to receive at a greater capacity than it has ever known. And while there is enormous relief that floods your unbelonging heart, it can also be painful in its pleasure.

Though I lived in urban centres most of my life, in my secret heart I was a country girl. It wasn't until the death of my mentor Annie, the woman with whom I entrusted my dreams, that I began to realize it. Annie's death yanked my anchor from its comfort zone like a tidal wave. The very foundation of my beliefs began to quake apart; old things flying out from the centre, new things entering there. The city became intolerable to me and flooding through the portal of my grief was an urgency to live a truer life.

At first I just took weekend trips into the country. But the more time I spent in wilderness, the less I wanted to return to the city. The dissonance of traffic and conflict was getting louder. All I could hear was the collective moan of survival. I was becoming allergic to the pavement. I was growing appalled by the edges and lines and corners of convenience. I was awakening.

Heedless of how long we've neglected it, the soul rushes back in an instant under the stars. One night in the forest, one meal cooked by fire, one naked plunge into a lake is all it takes. How bizarre the city seems then, with its strange values plastered on billboards in place of trees. How maudlin we seem then, grabbing onto the banks for security while the sea of plenty flows by.

My nature was growing, poetry started flowing, and I just kept going. Armed with a tent and a backpack, I positioned my home differently every night: down in the soft needles and roots with my door pointed eastward for the sunrise show, up in a clearing of woodchips to best see the stars through netted skylights, on a grassy bank of wildflowers where I took care not to crush too many violets in my sleep.

Annie's death was a precipice which fell me deeply in love with life. Paradoxically, her separation from me was bringing me into a deeper connection with everyone and everything. I was overcome with knowing that if I followed my longing, I would find the life I was meant to be living. Two months later, I hitched across the country to the Rocky Mountains of British Columbia. Not knowing where I'd stay or how I'd manage, I followed the simple yearning of my heart to be where the eagles lived. In a week's time, I found myself in an unimaginably beautiful place called the Kootenays.

Though it took some time, and it wasn't without bumps in the road, eventually I moved my life there and my heart began to expand in a way it never could in the city. I found love, created community, drank wild water, and grew my first garden. I made music about praising beauty. I became the artist Annie always told me I was meant to become.

After a year of living in this land of like-heartedness, my dear friend Sage organized a birthday party for me. It was so joyful to share the day with these wonderful new friends, but after dinner Sage gathered us in circle for an unexpected ritual. She asked me to stand in the middle, which was hard enough, but then she asked everyone to share what they loved most about me!

One by one, each of these lovely people offered their gift of reflection to me, and by the fourth or fifth person, I was in tears. The unexpected quality of it, and the forced position of receiving, was too much to bear. Somehow I managed to listen to twenty-five people's validations of my goodness—but when it was all over, I ran away into my bedroom and sobbed uncontrollably with the grief I'd carried since my eighth birthday. There was so much of it that my friend had to come fetch me and clean me up so I could cut the cake.

With the expanded capacity to receive comes the awareness of how long one has lived constricted. How long one has felt unseen. How long one has hidden their tender parts away from hostility and invalidation. Imagine the enormity of grief and gratitude that flow in simultaneously, stretching the receiving muscle. As the poet Nikki Giovanni says, "We must learn to bear the pleasures as we have borne the pains."[67]

Bearing the pleasure means beginning to invite a gentle exploration of love into those jumpy places that anticipate pain, expect abandonment, and brace for danger when it's no longer there. Instead of dismissing or armouring our vulnerability, we must begin allowing life into those areas that have been cordoned off in self-preservation. We must acclimate, often through grief, to the life-giving nature of love.

For the person with a lifelong habit of contraction from receiving, a skillfully-landed generosity can break the husk on the heart and release the grief of how long they have survived without their needs feeling seen. But know that this grief is the sign of healing, the opening of those places which for too long have been declining love. There is a deadening that can set into the heart that has borne too much pain. When a situation becomes too shocking or painful to bear, we may develop a chronic sarcasm or minimizing attitude that says, "Oh yeah, that's nothing new." But over time, this protected way of being can have a sterilizing effect on the entirety of one's feeling alive.

Coming out of numbness and back into feeling can be initially painful and jarring, like blood returning to a sleepy limb—but those pins and needles are a sign of life returning. The undamming of tears in your unfelt places are what Gibran calls "the pain of too much tenderness," but this is a healing grief that restores fertility to your soil.[68]

But don't bow your head too long in the river of despair. Its undercurrents are strong and may pull you into always travelling downstream. Make a choice against its worship. Thank it in earnest for the softening it makes of the hard ground in you, for the vitality it ushers into the stale riverbed of unfeeling, bracing, and holding. But know the true altar of your worship is with the love that broke you open.

Worship at the altar of your being supported. After all, you are the receiver of too many generosities to count. Count them anyway. As Wordsworth wrote, pleasure "is an acknowledgment of the beauty of the universe...a homage paid to the native and naked dignity of man..."[69] Even thinking about pleasure brings pleasure. At any given moment we can attune ourselves to well-being, which is a tributary of belonging. It is that place in our hearts where we are grateful for all that we're receiving and, for a moment, want nothing more.

The Receiving Muscle

More than just a physical act, receptivity is the capacity that allows us to accept divine support, as well as the gifts of others and of nature. Like a plant drawing nutrients from the earth, we are equipped with the ability to receive guidance and well-being from a field greater than ourselves. But if we've been conditioned by scarcity, or the culture's pronounced bias towards *doing*, we may have atrophied the receiving muscle. Once we understand the value of receiving, we can begin to draw on the support that so many of us crave.

As we learned about in the Inner Marriage, receptivity is associated with the strengths of yin: waiting, listening, accepting, and magnetizing to us the things that reverberate with our well-being. In times of scarcity and doubt, we are taught to get organized, launch plans, plot directions, and build agendas. There is nothing wrong with these actions—in fact, they are essential in any creative process. But if we don't first come into the sincerity of solitude, these are just defensive postures against the course of events.

To receive well is to know the wisdom of surrender. Yin chooses to yield even when everyone else is getting ahead. Like an inner earth, yin is the soil in which we gestate our dreams, refine our intuition, listen to our bodies, and come into the stillness of our centre. When actions arise from the receptive still point they have real meaning. Ideas that emerge from this level of imagination serve more than the individual: they serve the great ecosystem from which our well-being is drawn.

Active receptivity is the cessation of all striving, even for an hour a day. It might look like putting your bare feet in the grass, or letting the sun caress your skin, floating on your back in the lake, or wandering in the forest without purpose. It might look like pulling out your yoga mat or tinkering with art supplies, playing with your tarot cards, or hunkering down in your sit-spot. All of these acts put you into relationship with pleasure.

When we're not observing yin, we might have dreams that we're driving out of control. In waking life, this might look like busyness or a constancy of ambition to get somewhere with your endeavours. Dreams like this are asking us to put the brakes on. To come into quietude and well-being before we make ourselves sick, or burn out completely.

A similar dream is the inability to find a bathroom or find privacy to use the toilet. Since the bathroom is the one true place of solitude in the house, it is the symbolic out-breath; the place where we check in with our feeling body and release what we've been holding. If you have one of these frustrated bathroom dreams, you will likely notice a corresponding lack of pleasure and well-being in waking life.

Though it may seem counter-intuitive, pulling back our energy is like drawing the bow to find the aim before releasing an arrow with precision. Yin knows that sometimes we have to withdraw to enter. We are just like the earth, from whom we take so much and give back too little: our energy body has so much to give, but it needs to be harnessed sustainably. It requires pleasure, contentment, and periods of grace. If we are to come into right relationship with the earth, we need to practice at yielding to the rhythms of our own bodies.

One of the reasons we avoid the receptive state is because it's scary. We've all heard the old adage, "It's better to give than to receive." But giving and receiving happen simultaneously: they are interdependent acts. And underneath the phrase is the unspoken suggestion that to receive is to be the weak one, the needy one, the poor one. Of course, from this perspective most of us would rather be the 'giver' than the 'taker.' The giver is rich and secure and doesn't need anyone's help. But taken to its extreme, giving becomes pathological.

We may give and give and give so much that we run ourselves ragged. In reaching out to others, we give our own arms away. We are under the spell of a misguided belief that if we aren't always offering, providing, and holding space for others, that we will lose what little love and security we have. But even deeper is the fear of being vulnerable enough to show our weakness, to ask for help. By indulging in this fear, we are unconsciously closing every receptor to pleasure.

There is no such thing as one-sided generosity. Giving and receiving are necessary to one another. There is a symbiosis in the relationship which benefits both parties. Receiving something fully not only allows pleasure to penetrate the receiver, but it lets the giver know that they've made an impact with their offering. When a gift or compliment is truly received, the giver feels recognized for the authenticity and energy that went into making their offering.

The same is true with that larger field we might call divinity. To have a reciprocal relationship with the unseen holy in nature, we must not only create beauty in petition of its grace, we must also receive its response! I've heard it said that the soul doesn't live inside our body but that it is more like a womb in which we are contained. With some practice, you can drop the perceived boundaries of your 'self' and tune into the larger womb that stretches far beyond your own body. Imagine that it extends several feet beyond your body, then several metres, and see how far you can extend your perception. Feel how you can then draw on the nutrients and support of that womb so your 'small self' doesn't have to do it all alone.

When we fear that we aren't good enough to receive, pleasure can't reach us through those defences, and it translates into the belief that we are alone in the world. To receive well is to make yourself vulnerable enough for a generosity to penetrate and enhance your sense of worthiness.

Worthiness

Unworthiness is often the greatest barrier to receiving love and pleasure. Even when someone gives us a genuine compliment, it can be hard to receive if we don't feel equal to what's being said. Imagine how difficult it is then to receive divine support when we don't feel equal to the generosity of life. Most of us think that worthiness is something we either have or don't; I'd like to propose that worthiness is our intrinsic state when we dismantle those barriers.

Worthiness is the value, importance, and goodness that we ascribe to ourselves and to the world. But so much of what we value was inherited from our families and our culture. On the path to belonging, we must untangle our true values from our inherited, collective ideas of worth—and lack of worth— that have been woven into our beliefs.

To know what you truly value, you have to follow what makes you feel alive, what gives you enthusiasm, what raises goosebumps on your skin, what sends your imagination running wild. It springs tears to your eyes and gives your soul a feeling of relief. It makes you laugh with delight or weep with poignancy. It's not always pretty, but it is wholly alive! And this aliveness will grow your sense of worth in the world and, by extension, your capacity for pleasure.

One of the great, unexpected places to find what you value is in envy. Those people you admire, who are doing what you wish you were doing, are actually lighthouses on a dark sea. They seem so far ahead and tempt you to fall into the despair of comparison. But if you're clever, you'll see them as showing you the way to sail towards what you love. Often in envy you will find which of your gifts have been sent behind the barrier of unworthiness because they were rejected, or worse, humiliated. And while that barrier may have offered them protection for a spell, envy is a signal that they want to come back in to belonging with you.

Along the same lines, too much admiration for another can signal a deficit of esteem for ourselves. Marielle was a dreamer who'd been working for a number of years to heal a deep creative wound that often left her feeling unworthy and unable to move ahead in her projects. As a girl, her natural gifts for dancing and language were a source of great solace for her. But they were frequently and harshly shamed as being useless, indulgent, and even embarrassing to her mother. She learned to hide her gifts over the years, focusing instead on the development of her analytical and administrative skills, until her own gifts became strangers to her.

As we worked together, Marielle had many dreams that took place in old world castles. In these dreams there was always a hidden garden, a valuable object to be unearthed, or a deep pond to swim across. As we explored the symbolism of these old castles, Marielle associated to them as places of tradition, history, and academia. Marielle had great admiration for the old world; she loved these mansions full of books and antiques. But the dreams seemed to say that there was something wilder, wetter, and more valuable that was calling her towards it.

We began to see how Marielle was pulled between the pressure to write with precision and objectivity, as academics do, and the wild feminine voice which was arising from her dreams. As she risked letting her inner knowing guide her pen, she began finding joy and pleasure in the creative process again.

But given the right triggers, especially reading essays by an analytical person in her field, Marielle would slip into periods of depression when she felt paralyzed and unable to write at all. One day she had the following dream:

One-Way Admiration, Marielle's dream
I am sitting in a beautiful boutique full of handmade clothing and toys for children. Across from me is a man who is my husband, and

he has our baby sleeping on his chest in a carrier. I look at him with
such love and admiration, but when he looks back at me, I can tell
he doesn't feel the same way.

As we engaged this dream, Marielle explained that her husband in the dream was the lead character from a television show she liked. She described him as an exceptionally observant profiler who could read people's body language to discern clues to solve crimes for the police. Marielle described this fellow as someone she really liked. But as we got deeper into an exploration of his character, it turned out he was also sorely lacking in empathy and skeptical of anything that wasn't factual. His catchphrase was, "There is no such thing as a psychic."

Suddenly it became quite clear to Marielle that her own psychic or intuitive feeling was under invalidation from that Logos archetype within—a pattern which mirrored her early childhood experiences. A good inner marriage, we have learned, is a mutual admiration between the opposites. Certainly there is a place for Marielle's love for the refinement of language, the objectivity of the editor, but it was admired at the expense of her intuitive voice. These feelings wanted to roam free again in the garden of expression.

We found the medicine of this dream in the newborn baby, which Marielle understood was the life she'd been raising in her feminine voice. Just as the dream took place in a handmade boutique, she was beginning to know the true environment of her creativity, which was not mechanical and tedious, but inclined to play and wrought with artistic beauty.

The work ahead for Marielle, as for so many of us, is about slowly, sometimes imperceptibly, reclaiming her vitality from behind the wall of rejection until a sense of worthiness emerges. Just as we miss those who aren't with us, we are missed by our wholeness. It works with diligence to provide images of our essential nature in dreams. But it also generates images of the invalidations that inhibit our becoming so we can face them in the open light of day.

Under our scrutiny, the barrier of unworthiness can't help but crumble. Rather than absenting ourselves from our creativity, from relationships, from the call of the world, believing that we are undeserving of a place at the table, this inner work substantiates us. We become more present to others and more grounded in our lives. Worthiness is like an open door through which pleasure can enter and be received.

Often in the second half of life we realize we can't judge our worth by impossible standards of beauty, strength or success any more than we can judge life's worthiness with a one-sided measure. We don't expect the earth to remain in a prolonged springtime, but rather appreciate each of the seasons, from harvest to dormancy, for its particular gifts to us. Worthiness is not some state of attainment, but the ongoing willingness to meet life squarely. Worthiness is the ability to say *I am up for this. I am equal to life.*

Gratefulness

In the cultivation of belonging to your pleasure and well-being, gratefulness is the sun around which all other practices revolve. When you are genuinely attentive to life, gratefulness is the inevitable reply to all the things conspiring to endow you with their beauty and intricate genius. By showing up for the generosity of life, even in its left-handed forms, we are declaring our worthiness to it. When we allow the privilege of being alive to really penetrate us, we are participating in the holy moment of life's becoming. Gratefulness is the recognition of our belonging to that dance.

For those who have learned to see the world through lack and fear, gratitude is a practice. It's a way of gentling the eyes to see life, and ourselves, with kindness, causing generosity to multiply as we seek it out. There is an incredible view from my treehouse perch that looks out on the Gulf Islands for miles. When friends see it for the first time it often brings them to tears. But after many years of living here, we get accustomed to it, and sometimes forget to praise its magnificence. On days when I am busily rushing off to work, I have to pause and actively drink in the beauty. In just a few minutes, my well-being is full again and my heart is open. Gratitude resensitizes those places we have armoured over until they become palpable to the atmosphere of beauty rushing in from all sides to reach us.

Even when we hold back our gratitude because we are lonely or defeated, life keeps bestowing us with the melody of songbirds, the steadfast rising of the sun on a new day, the unexpected warmth of a friend's smile, the twinkling of stars in the Milky Way.

As we become aware of the invalidations and scarcity patterns we've inherited through the generations, or developed in response to our upbringing, we have to establish new habits. The old fathoms of scarcity are deep and darkly inviting for their familiarity. Gratefulness can feel like a stretch when we are so confronted with our suffering, but it is precisely then that we should be engaging it.

One of the most romantic things I've ever heard was the story of a woman named Astarte, whose husband knew how much she loved playing music—and how terrified she was of performing in front of others. So he bought her a beautiful, leather-bound book carved with a flamboyant peacock to record all of the positive feedback she received about her music. Whenever she was slipping into self-doubt and fear, she would then flip through the pages and fill herself up with gratitude.

With this in mind, I highly recommend taking a moment at the end of every day to write a list of five to ten things you are grateful for. At first, a gratitude practice may feel forced—and making a daily list, arduous and pointless. You may find yourself only grateful for a piece of chocolate, or a cuddle with an animal friend, and it's tempting to weigh these small luxuries against the many other hours in which you found no gratitude. But if you keep a discipline to the writing of these lists, your attention throughout the day will gravitate towards beauty as you search for things worthy of mention. Your lists will grow longer—but more importantly, it is the subtle shift in your way of seeing that will transform your life.

Gratefulness brings our awareness not only to what is beautiful, but to what we are excluding from our concept of beauty. In this way, gratitude is a great mentor in the practice of belonging.

There will of course be clear highlights in a day, moments in which the fullness of our gratitude naturally gathers, but through the practice we come to see that poetry lives in ordinary places. We may suddenly realize the service our teapot has so cheerfully provided for us, offering its loyalty to the steeping and good keeping of our tea without question. We may be struck then with the lack of tenderness with which we have washed it. Or perhaps we notice for the first time the subtle music fish roe makes when it snaps in our teeth and we can't believe all the senseless conversation we've made over sushi, missing it completely. Or maybe there is a brief month in spring when the cottonwoods release their intoxicating perfume and it's not until winter that we miss the weeks we neglected to climb the hill to breathe it in.

The act of gratitude is one of the great acts of remembership. Whether through prayer, ritual, poetry, or song, gratitude solidifies our relationship with the living mystery. It rejoins us to the intangible wholeness from which we feel disconnected. As we remember ourselves to the holy in nature, we are forging our own belonging.

Gratitude is also a form of forgiveness. Things must be respectfully thanked before they will release us. After years of keeping a gratitude list I call Beautiful Things, I would find oddly difficult things like pain, loss, and even conflict making their way onto my top ten. In my practice of *yesness*, which is the funny little word I use to describe the discipline of affirming whatever arises, the lines began to blur between beauty and pain, between crisis and opportunity. The more curious I became about those troublemakers, the more I began to see them as Rumi did in "The Guest House," as "guides from beyond" who were "clearing [me] out for some new delight."[70] As long as I was resisting them, they hung around and became more threatening. But the moment I treated them honourably, even moving into appreciation for them, they would open the door to unexpected pleasure.

We reclaim our membership in the divine family of things by remembering that the language of appreciation is our mother-tongue. To sink down into the fullness of even a single moment is to become aware of all the helpful conditions that are enabling our well-being in every given moment. Joseph Campbell's famous saying, "Follow your bliss," is not an irresponsible phrase that ignores the pain of life, but a reminder to also receive pleasure and contentment, even in the depths of suffering.

As we pay respectful gratitude for the jewels of beauty strewn throughout a day, pleasure begins to reach and flow through us. We become more generous of spirit. Not simply in the sense of giving things away to others, but as a demeanour. Like an open door to the divine, pleasure is an invitation to joy, that it may live more fully in our lives. Breathe into the fullness of your expanded self and consider that what presents itself as fear may actually be exhilaration. As your future approaches you, worry less how it may receive you and say a prayer instead for your becoming approachable.

Recognize the invisible hands that guide you, the breath that breathes you, the walls and roof that keep cold from chilling you, the water that magically springs from your taps, the long line of ancestors whose every step made your incarnation possible. You belong to these holy helpers. You have undisputed membership. In your recognition of this wealth, your own life cannot help but become an offering back to that which feeds you.

Fifteen

The Invitational Presence

*W*e spend so much time worrying about how to approach our future that we rarely consider how approachable *we* might be. We armour ourselves with savvy, strength, and certification so that when our moment arrives we feel sufficiently prepared. But with our shoulder always to the wheel of life, we can miss the very encounter we've been preparing for. To be approachable to life, to each other, and to mystery, we have to cultivate an inner hospitality. Like the host who prepares an extra helping of food, a fire in the hearth, and a seat at the table even when guests aren't expected, belonging always begins with an invitation.

When a person extends an invitation to us, we immediately feel welcomed into their world. In fact, much of the loneliness people feel is the result of *not* being invited. It seems our culture has lost the skillfulness of hospitality. My grandmother used to tell me how, when she was a young woman living in Poland, it was customary to have one day a week when the community was given a blanket invitation to visit your family home. The hosts would prepare a generosity of tea and refreshments and open their doors to their friends and acquaintances. For those few hours a week, the community would share their lives and weave into belonging with each other.

By contrast, in modern times we have become increasingly distrustful of our neighbours and protective of our privacy. But the price we pay for that independence is a sense of exclusion on all sides. One of the reasons I had to leave the city was because it was too painful to smile and say hello to passers-by and be continually ignored or even scowled at. At the time, I took it personally, but I think it's more that folks live in a state of overwhelm, and isolationism is a way of protecting themselves. If we want to create belonging in our lives, we have to relearn how to extend our hospitality to others, both physically and energetically.

Whether we are looking to create closeness with others, with nature, or with the living mystery, an invitational presence is the prerequisite to any form of intimacy. Like the physical flinging open of our doors to guests, we can cultivate a quality of hospitality in our presence which signals to the other that they are welcome in our company just as they are. This quality naturally emerges when we put down our own manoeuvrings long enough to be truly interested in who someone is, what they need, and what they love. Simply put, it is to clear an opening in our hearts for the other to take shelter.

When your presence is hospitable, the other can become their essential self in your company, even if just for a holy moment. One of the greatest contributions we can make to our communities is to hold this welcoming presence for others, without any presumption that they give something in return or conform to our expectations, without giving into the temptation to change, fix, or solve their questions for them. This presence silently communicates that it believes in the part of them that knows which way to go. And they can feel that. With their inner knowing reflected, they begin to move in the right direction.

If you've ever had the experience of someone listening to you not just with their ears, but with their heart, then you'll know how contributive this practice is to belonging. When they listen to your secret pieces at this level, they begin to carry them as their own. And at some future point, they may even hand you back those pieces in a better order and say, "I remember this," and the tenderness between you grows. This kind of exchange is a silent vow to our inseparability.

It is this attentiveness, which alchemizes distance into intimacy, that we'll call presence. It's a place outside of ordinary time, full of ambiguity and risk, where the chance for something amazing can happen. Like a form of lucidity, presence is wakefulness. We are no longer acting automatically but involving ourselves in the unfolding of reality. This kind of attentiveness to life is one of the greatest spiritual practices. As our capacity for it grows, presence can lift us into an exalted or ecstatic state.

If you're doing it right, presence sensitizes you to your environment. It puts you smack-dab in the discomfort, the disagreeability, the pain, the awkwardness, and the contradiction—this is where you can grow more skilled at meeting life where it's at, rather than how you'd prefer it to be. In other words, allow the full spectrum of events to be included in your experience rather than mounting resistance to them.

By extension, presence also makes us more porous to life's mystery. When we think of presence in these terms, as an opening to what is, we immediately feel a spaciousness stretching around the word. It is this capacity for presence that awakens a sense of accountability towards, and authentic engagement with, our relationships, communities, and the natural world.

Sometimes when I am working with someone over a course of time, I begin to feel as if I am having a conversation directly with their dreaming. Though the dreamer might not be conscious of feeling validated, given the gift of presence, the dream will blossom images where it feels seen.

A retired engineer named Tom came to me with a series of dreams of being lost. In his dreams he was left behind, somewhere unfamiliar, without a wallet, trying desperately to find a way home. Night after night, he would have to navigate obstacle courses full of machines and narrow passageways, and he always woke up in a state of unresolved panic. Tom worked hard all his life to succeed in his career and provide for his family, and now he suffered with feeling a loss of purpose in retirement.

For many, the second half of life requires us to drop our worldly ambitions and turn towards inner development. When I suggested this to Tom, he dismissed it as something he was already aware of. But in our next session, he brought up a dream which contained an interesting detail we'd never seen before. In his effort to find his way home, he briefly came upon a pond filled with colourful fish. For a moment, Tom admired their beauty and even jumped into the water with them before continuing his search. I took this as a sign that the dreamwork we'd been doing was bringing some life into his otherwise parched and busy psychic landscape.

Like the warming sun, a bit of admiration and encouragement to a neglected area of the soul will coax the prettiest flowers from its soil. This quality of listening opens an aperture into the other's secret mythology, which becomes a path home to their belonging. What's more, the invitational presence exemplifies for the other how to listen to themselves. If we begin to do this with our children when they are still young, they will much sooner come into their true belonging.

Unfortunately, in Western culture we rarely give ourselves the briefest 'downtime' anymore, because we are checking our devices while standing in line with strangers, at the park with our children, or even at the dinner table with our beloveds. But downtimes are like invitations to the unconscious. They invite the question on your heart to form, they entice originality to emerge, they create a welcoming space for an unexpected encounter.

Often the first question we ask a stranger is, "What do you do?" as if that were the sum of a person. Rather than sizing each other up like this, which is a covert measuring of status, we need to revive the art of courtship. Courtship is when you sit near the other and try gently, patiently, and respectfully to discover what they love. As in the ancient Celtic tradition, when you meet someone new, you ask, "To whom do you belong?"[71]

This old tradition can be found in many other cultures too, where a person introduces themselves not solely with their given name but with their designation in their lineage and the place from which their people come. For instance, in the Ojibwe language, you would introduce yourself by your spiritual name first, which is your role within your tribe; followed by the name of your clan, which describes the larger identity of your tribe; and then finally the place from which you originate, which governs all of the above.[72]

In the Navajo culture, every person has four clans, all of which must be introduced in a specific order: the mother's first clan, then the father's, the maternal grandfather's, and the paternal grandfather's, followed by the place from which you all come.[73] Not only does this acknowledge your roots, it is also an act of respect to the other, serving to humble you in their eyes should you not know the customs and cultural boundaries of the place you are visiting.

You can feel how belonging is tended when we recognize ourselves as the fruit grown on our ancestors' tree. We are weaving into those roots every time we name them. Even if we no longer know the names of our ancestors, or where they came from—even if their stories have been lost and their songs forgotten—still we can be re-membered into our *indigeneity* by remembering, inviting, and courting our dreams. As Martín Prechtel explains, every human being, "tribal or modern, primal or domesticated, has a soul that is original, natural, and, above all, indigenous in one way or another. The indigenous soul of the modern person, though, either has been banished to the far reaches of the dream world or is under direct attack by the modern mind. The more you consciously remember your indigenous soul, the more you physically remember it."

When we ask someone, "To whom or what do you belong?" we are bringing presence to the larger whole of their life. The question itself is an acknowledgment of what's important to them and what they are destined for. And when we ask the question of our own dreams, it puts us onto the path of our purpose. Just as you might take an acorn and plant it on another continent, given a welcoming presence it will still grow into what it's meant to become.

While presence is essential, we must also come to recognize the impact of our absence in the lives of others, something that is often proportionate to the leave we take from our own. This absence is more than just not showing up physically, it is the 'absent presence' we give when we're divided, distracted or avoidant. Listening to someone with only cursory attention can do more harm than good. It unconsciously communicates your disinterest in their secret story, so you can't be surprised when a distance, a forgetting, develops between you.

Believing the unworthiness of life and ourselves to be true, we go about a lifelong practice of not receiving, not speaking, not joining, not noticing, not creating. We become a ghost in our own lives and then, when others don't invite or acknowledge us, we think, "Why can't you see me?" With this question, we push them, and ourselves, further away. The problem of absent presence also plays out in our relationship to the divine impulse which wants to express itself through us.

Unless we learn how to become hospitable to it, the holy can never enter our lives. There are many ways to invite the holy into our lives, but none so immediate as prayer and ritual. I once asked a master musician I know named Scott Sheerin why his albums always have such a spontaneous, living quality to them. He explained that before entering the studio he always makes a sacred fire to burn his offerings of gratitude and remembering before ever playing a note. Indeed, a kind of grace reveals itself in his recordings, as if the music thrives in his invitational presence.

Call upon the holy, who you may be unfamiliar with, but who knows everything about you. Stay in that listening moment where you may at first hear nothing, but where something always begins. As you listen, know that the quality of your listening is also being heard. The invitational presence dilates the heart and it is through this aperture that the holy travels. As you remember, you are being remembered by that which belongs with you.

Soul is not a thing, but a perspective. It's the slow courtship of an event that turns it into a meaningful experience. It's the practice of trusting that if we sit silently and long enough with the *absence* of magic, the miraculous will reveal itself. Nothing is sacred until we make it so with the eloquence of our attention, the poetry of our patience, the parenting warmth of our hospitality.

For many of us, this kind of sacred presence—when we feel total belonging to a moment—is a fleeting experience. It may be brought about by an overwhelm of beauty, a psychoactive drug, a transporting piece of music, or an unexpected generosity, but it never lasts long enough and is often followed by a crash or disenchantment. How did I get there? How can I find my way back? Was it even real?

While it may not be realistic to think that we could maintain this kind of presence permanently, we can grow our capacity for sustaining it. Like lucid dreaming, there are techniques which can help us stay awake longer in the dream. Inevitably, we fall back 'asleep,' allowing ourselves to be consumed with automatic thoughts and fears. But as we learn to intentionally surrender our preferences for how reality unfolds, we begin to see how well we're being guided. Our trust in the ordering intelligence of nature grows stronger than our need to control outcomes.

There was a wonderful book I read as a young person called *The Way of a Pilgrim*, a 19th-century Russian novel about a mendicant who, after coming across a passage in the book of Paul referring to "prayer without ceasing," goes in search of someone who can teach the technique to him.[74] He travels from monastery to church, village to village, resting only when invited into the homes of those charitable to his mission. It isn't an easy journey, and it isn't without suffering and doubt. But with each stranger's invitation, he learns to trust life increasingly because every encounter brings him an essential piece of his spiritual development.

What affected me most about this book was the devotion the pilgrim had, not only in his quest for communion with that 'something greater' he called God, but his trust in life itself to support and carry him on that quest. There is something very powerful about intentionally giving ourselves over to the trust that magic will happen: and so it does.

Making an invitation for the holy to enter your endeavours needn't be anything extravagant (though that can be fun too.) It can be as simple as my musician friend lighting a fire, clearing off your desk to make room for poetry, or setting your device in another room while you sleep so dreams are your first consideration when you wake. It could be a daily visit to hear the river, or to leave an offering with a tree that knows your name. Whatever your ritual of invitation might be, it is any act that opens up your living conversation to receive a response.

Another word for the invitational presence is wonder. When we are comfortable with not having answers, we remain curious. And this curiosity is what draws life closer into belonging with us. One of the great places to cultivate your sense of wonder is, of course, in nature. Simply by listening for what the land loves, by how it communicates and how it moves, we accumulate a slow intimacy with our place.

After a few years living on our little island in British Columbia, I began to fall in love with this one summer bird who sings at dusk in a mesmerizing melody of upward spirals. I came to know it not by sight, but by its song, which praises the setting sun, signalling the end of a long day. In our house, we call it the 'goodnight bird.' The goodnight bird revealed itself in stages, through the courtship of our attention to it. We may one day come to know what it looks like, when we've made ourselves trustworthy. Maybe it will land nearby on an evening when we're still and welcoming enough. Until then, we dream up stories about how the sun cannot begin its descent without the goodnight bird's blessing. Maybe the moon would never enter the sky without it, and we would forget to dream our dreams.

Our simultaneous familiarity and not-knowing of this bird, whose song is such an important part of our day, has aroused such affection in our hearts. Sometimes when we are beginning a ceremony around the sacred fire, it graces us with its threshold song. A hush falls over us as we listen to its ventriloquist call, which seems to travel from far to near in a single phrase. And if your ears are keen, you can hear another distant brother of the same family singing the spiral song to its part of the forest. It's as if they are each responsible for singing their own circumference to sleep with gratitude.

As we listen, we wonder at its true name. In our longing to belong with it, the aperture of our attention grows. We notice that it disappears in September, with the geese and the tourists. Its absence signals the changing of the light when everything is bathed in golds and the moon appears in the sun's place in the west. Our feet begin to ask for socks and moccasins and the first apples ready themselves for plucking.

All of this intimacy with the place where we live came from wondering, which is the invitation to mystery to reveal itself on its own time. In contrast, if I told you this bird was a Swainson's thrush, which is extremely common in the Pacific Northwest and migrates in autumn, what of the poetic choreography of life would be enlivened in you?

By honouring what is out of reach, we preserve our own wonder. And it is this wonder that keeps us responsible to the things under our stewardship. This slow kind of learning requires us to stay put, to live many seasons in relationship with a place so that we may come to know its fragrances and particularities, preferences, and gifts. In this way, knowledge is earned by the depth of our commitment. We can approach the other slowly, respectful of what is essentially mysterious at the centre of us all.

Embodying Ambiguity

Dreams teach us how to be wondrous by offering us endless ambiguity. Though it is our habit to always look for a bottom line so we can have certainty, dreams operate on many levels at once, forcing us to diversify our viewpoints. People often ask me something along the lines of, "Is this dream about having a conflict with my partner, or is the character in my dream an aspect of myself?" But ambiguity and the lack of taking sides answers the either/or question with a strange, unchoosing "Yes."

Ambiguity, or the willingness to hold many perspectives at once, is a core competency of dreamwork. It teaches us that there are many sides to a story, and as we grow more adept with it, we can hold an increasingly diverse number of perspectives at once. In the above example, it may be that the dream was triggered by a waking life interaction with our partner, but it may also be true that they represent an aspect of ourselves that we are in conflict with. When we consider that we only see each other through the lens of our own perception, then the distinction somewhat falls away.

The initiated adult is one who learns to withstand uncertainty, embody ambiguity, and straddle paradox. In dreamwork, the ability to hold the tension of the opposites is essential. We let contradictions have out their mythical argument until paradox can be held—until harmony can be struck. Until a creative third solution has a chance at appearing.

But modernity is infatuated with binary thinking: we erect and uphold opposition in politics, religion, race, gender, and perhaps most insidiously, in education itself. We begin to educate our young people in the ways of exclusion from the outset, by teaching subjects as separate from each other with an emphasis on categorization. This is a quiet, insidious form of Othering that breeds in our mental processes. We teach that whatever category we are inside, it is different, and often superior, to those outside of us. Our entire socio-economic system of power relies on this kind of factional thinking.

Imagine an education system that does not treat subjects as separate but as belonging to each other. Contextualizing a topic within the greater whole creates a 'point of entry' for every type of learner. For example, in the reading of a children's story, we also learn about and practice the illustration of images; the physical binding of the book; we learn about how a tree must be harvested to make the paper upon which the story is written; and study the impact the tree's removal has on the rest of the forest; we learn then what it takes to grow a tree, planting one ourselves; and we make up a song to help our saplings take root.

A whole year of lessons and activities could revolve around this one cycle of learning. It would require us to be present through them all, lest we miss a link in the story. During this long-form learning, we'd be intimately engaged with the environment around us, to which we are naturally indebted. We would be more inclined to preserve, replenish, and express our gratitude. In this gratitude we would better understand our own belonging. We would see more clearly the particular ways in which we might be useful to our place and people, and we would share our own gifts with a humbled sense of where they merged with the larger dance of life. We'd aim to give more than we take from that which gives to us so unconditionally.

The work of undermining the barriers between things moves us from alienation to intimacy. We begin to see the partisanship in our own ideologies, the mechanisms we employ to keep others at any distance from our lives. Rather than waving our flags of belief and superiority over others through what the poet Leonard Cohen calls "emotional patriotism," we are growing our capacity for ambiguity.[75] Naturally, this inner diversity translates into outer inclusivity.

In the practice of belonging, we are not seeking prowess or dominion over anyone else, but the ability to live into the conversation between things. This is a deepening movement into relationship with self and otherness. As we make ourselves keepers of each other and the world around us, so too are we kept. When we invite others into the landscape of our lives, giving them influence with our secret pieces, we are better held in our own becoming.

The No-Time is Now

There is a music that is always being played by nature, whose channel we occasionally dial into when our hearts are at rest. It is an improvisational music which, like the pilgrim, trusts where it may be led. Like an unceasing prayer, the invitational heart allows itself to be played as an instrument would.

Yet so much of modern life is structured with angles and plans, perhaps because we secretly believe that if we aren't constantly steering our lives, we might lose our way. We might end up living under a bridge, outcast from the human choreography we call society. And it's true that, in consensus culture, there is a balance that must be struck between charting a path and meandering, but I'm sure you'll agree that the time we spend contriving eclipses the spontaneous.

Left to our own devices, we would be constantly driven. Even when we stop, we are still thinking of what must be done next. Especially now, in this age of devastating environmental and social collapse, there are those of us who feel an unrelenting urgency to attend to the world before it's too late. But the great paradox is that it's this condition of rushing anxiously ahead that got us into trouble in the first place.

While ancient Egypt was already measuring time by observing stars and the interplay of sun with shadows, it wasn't until the 14th century that mechanical clocks were invented[76] and nature stopped being our gauge. Before that, people measured time with sundials—so at night, when the sun was no longer in the sky, we stopped measuring. We moved instead into a timeless time, the dark hour of the moon and tides and the rhythm of dreaming.

It was the Catholic church who standardized time, divvying up day and night into equal parts. Morning prayer bells rang to signal the beginning of the work day. There was a significant shift at end of the 16th century when we began to count the minutes within an hour to measure the productivity of labourers.[77] Hence, the concept of 'wasting time' was born into cultural consciousness. The Industrial Age established a tremendous pressure to be productive with time; it became culturally ensconced that 'time is money.' It wasn't until the 19th century that a standardized, uniform concept of time even existed.[78]

Rather than understanding time's passage in relationship with the natural world, the artificial measuring of time shifted our cultural allegiance to the disciplines and expectations of capitalism. Clock time was also mixed up with religious doctrine, and clocks were often decorated with reminders of death like *ultima forsan* ('perhaps the last' [hour]) or *vulnerant omnes, ultima necat* ('they all wound, and the last kills'). Even today, many clocks are inscribed with the motto *tempus fugit*, 'time flies.' Though these axioms were originally meant to invite a person to contemplate the nature of death, once they were paired with the economic and religious doctrines of the time, they devolved into threatening reminders.

But as many aboriginal cultures view it, time is more circular in pattern; not like the Western linear comprehension of time as past-present-future, but flexible to the individual at the centre of that "time-circle."[79] In the Australian Aboriginal Dreaming, the past and future are embedded in the present. One's embodiment is the ground into which all continuity flows, so the past can be just as influenced as the future by one's way of going in the here and now.

If we are going to come back into the rhythm of nature, we have to slow down. If we imagine the world as our own body, speaking to us in loud, desperate pleas, the first thing we have to do is listen. We must acknowledge the limitations that have brought us to this terrifying precipice. We don't know what we don't know, and instead of pushing through our injury and confusion, we need to surrender the rush and show up instead with our heartbreak to encounter what is becoming. As they say in Taoism, "let your toes be still," for they are always twitching into action. Be hospitable to what stillness has to offer. Cherish the opportunity to sink into the eternal, which is available to be bathed in at any given moment.

There are times when the mind and body must be made to stop. The unruly is made to feel safe by limits. Limits to our productivity, limits to our activity, and limits to our directedness are what allow the imagination to wander, to perceive greater goals, to invite rather than lead.

We all have those dreams of being late for something. Though we rarely know where we are going, we are anxious to catch the train or plane that will get us there. Taken symbolically, these dreams often have nothing to do with linear time so much as they express our feeling of being out of sync. Consider those moments in your life when you were in 'just the right place at the right time,' and I'm certain you got there not through careful planning, but by being swept along by an unknown fate, maybe even through a series of blunders. It is this meandering openness, unyoked from the demands of solar time, that allows unexpected magic to reach us.

For those whose lives are relentlessly structured, there can be a deep exhaustion in the body which is barely satisfied by a full night's sleep. That exhaustion is less of a need for rest than it is the bone-deep dispiritedness that comes from our slavery to schedules and directedness. In such cases, it's best to follow the exhaustion, despite how much has yet to be done, and give yourself wholly to it. It's only when you get off the treadmill that you can see how it is not actually getting you anywhere meaningful.

Unexpected Detour, Sheila's dream

I dream I am late to catch a ferry, driving down an unfamiliar country road. Somehow my attention is not really on the road, but sideways, as if half-steering, and the car is driving itself miraculously without having an accident. I don't have any time to spare, so I'm worried when I make a turn in the wrong direction. I drive to the top of a crest to get my bearing and the most beautiful vista opens up before me. It is a range of snow-capped mountains as far as the eye can see. There are some lambs just napping in the meadow.

Exhausted from her demanding career, Sheila let herself have the day before this dream to just collapse. That afternoon, she and her hard-working husband spontaneously decided to drive to the ocean. They discovered a lovely spot they'd never been before where they walked in bare feet along the sandstone shore, discovering jellyfish and hermit crabs in the tide pools. She even dove naked into the cold sea and napped in the sun to dry. Sheila described her afternoon by saying, "I was tingling with aliveness. It was as if we had time to just be in love."

This sideways attention, when we take our eyes off the symbolic road, when we seem to be going in the complete opposite direction of our goals, is when we can get ourselves in the *good kind of trouble*. Our lateness might be an ally, trying to open us up to a different quality of living. The deeper tides of nature are pulsing through our body's inclinations. If we can dissuade our plan even for an afternoon, we have a chance at opening to that grander perspective. Trusting, as the lambs do, that all is well right here where you are.

There is a story wanting to come through every life, a story that connects backwards through time to our ancestors, our chthonic place, down to our bones, which are the bones of the earth itself. If we can, through our invitational presence, draw that story into the open for others and for ourselves, there is a chance that we can begin to live in alignment with our deepest contributive nature.

Sixteen
Storywells and Songlines

We are literally made of story. Every night, something in our biology compulsively spins out dream-stories in order to keep us healthy. As essential as breathing, these stories have layers of usefulness that are part self-regulatory, part transmission of wisdom, and part connective tissue to a networked intelligence unconstrained by time and space.

The biological necessity of storying is mysterious, but we know a few things for certain. Regardless of religion, race, or identity, everyone dreams. Whether we remember them or not, something in us requires the forming of a narrative in order to survive. Dreams serve as an integrative bridge between our psyche and physiology. We see this clearly in small children who require huge amounts of dreaming time in order to integrate information from their rapid rate of learning. When deprived of REM sleep, people become increasingly unable to complete simple tasks. In some studies conducted, dream deprivation resulted in a battery of symptoms including mental breakdown with hallucinations and memory loss, a rise in stress hormones and blood pressure, and an increased risk of physical disease.[80]

But beyond the physiological necessity of dreaming, there is something more mysterious that generates symbols and stitches them together in a narrative order. Though often seeming like nonsense to the rational mind, when approached symbolically, these dream-stories often follow the classical arc: from exposition to rising action, into a crux or climax, followed by the falling action, which resolves in the dream's denouement. It is the same literary plot upon which most plays, films, and stories have been modelled.

The story also acts as a conduit of information, wisdom, and values around which people can unite. In this sense, a story creates coherence. It takes disparate and confusing elements and integrates them into a meaningful plot. It turns a problem into a mission and moves us through a series of events towards redemption. The story guarantees a kind of wholeness. As writer Barry Lopez said, "We are pattern makers, and if our patterns are beautiful and full of grace they will be able to bring a person for whom the world has become broken and disorganized up off his knees and back to life."[81]

While almost every known religion has a creation story, nobody knows the origin of these sacred myths because they come from a time before language was recorded. But it's possible to imagine that early people received these transmissions from a visionary or dream state and passed them down the generations through the oral tradition. What's astounding is that all the world's creation stories can be roughly categorized into five central motifs: creation from chaos, life out of nothing, birth through a world parent(s), emergence from another form, and the earth-diver who finds the first grains of earth deep in primeval waters.[82] As discussed in the Origins of Estrangement chapter, if we strip even the most seemingly unrelated stories down to their essence, we find the same archetypal patterns or motifs around the world, throughout time.

Myths, fairy tales, and archetypal stories give us a sense of cohesion because we recognize the patterns, even unconsciously, as bone-deeply familiar. Stories serve to remind us that whatever difficulties we might be experiencing have been encountered many times before. We are not alone; we are connected to an ancestral storehouse of experience, and embedded within those tales are the solutions and instructions for how to navigate difficulty with grace and wisdom.

This is why one of the great competencies of belonging is the cultivation of a mythic imagination. So long as we are disconnected or unaware of our ancestral inheritance embedded in myth and story, we will think of ourselves as alone. But when we reunite with that accumulation of wisdom living in dreams, mythology, and stories, we are drawing from the same original well that our ancestors' stories came from.

It's important to understand that language is much more than a means of communication. It is a vehicle in which values, cultural heritage, eco-biological knowledge, and even cognitive perception of reality is carried. For instance, in Hawaiian and many other Polynesian languages, there is no verb for 'to have' or 'to be'—so with the disappearance of traditional language, this non-possessive worldview could also disappear. In Tahiti, the hooks for catching tuna are made from many different varieties of shells that are found on specific coastal stretches around the region. A good fisherman knows the names of every shell on every beach, because people on these small islands still depend on the sea for their food.[83] For the Western Apache, the names of places are not only descriptive of their landscape, but are embedded with stories in which are contained codes of wisdom and morals.[84]

Perhaps you have witnessed how an ancestral language has been lost in your own family line as the generations were exiled from their place of origin. As each generation was assimilated into the dominant culture of their region, they may even have internalized a rejection of their 'foreign' tongue in order to blend into the place they have landed.

There is an Indigenous tribe from the Daly River region in Northern Australia called the Ngangikurungkurr, whose name translates as 'Deep Water Sounds' or 'Sounds of the Deep.' For the Ngangikurungkurr, it is understood that there is a deep spring of story within that calls on each of us. In order for us to live in harmony with the soul, we must listen for the call of that story so that we may know where we are, in mythic terms, and which way to go next. This sense of soul location is not just for our own well-being, but a responsibility to our tribe which depends, in a cascade of influence, upon us being our true self.

The Ngangikurungkurr practice what they call *dadirri*, a form of deep listening for these sacred stories. As Aboriginal elder Miriam-Rose Ungunmerr puts it, "Through the years, we have listened to our stories. They are told and sung, over and over, as the seasons go by. Today we still gather around the campfires and together we hear the sacred stories. As we grow older, we ourselves become the storytellers. We pass on to the young ones all they must know. The stories and songs sink quietly into our minds and we hold them deep inside. In the ceremonies we celebrate the awareness of our lives as sacred."[85]

For the Aborigines of Australia, storytelling and song are considered a cultural necessity. Passed down through the generations, they carry the history and wisdom of the ancestors, and explain their own creation and relationship to the elements and the landscape.

As we explored in Handmaking, the songs of the Aborigines can also be painted because they are actually maps of the landscape. An elder who has never been to a place can navigate their way there if they know the shape of the song. Each word and rhythm represents a tree, stone, or curve in the earth, making a 'songline' which they can follow to their destination. This living archive is made up of 270 distinct languages and about 600 dialects, but language differences between tribes are not a barrier because the "melodic contour of the song describes the nature of the land over which the song passes."[86]

These storied songlines originated in the 'time before time' that is also known as the Dreamtime. We can imagine how, many moons ago, the ancestors had very little impediment to their dreaming and received clear transmissions explaining their origin and the way creation required them to walk in the world, each with a special totemic purpose, like Crocodile Dreaming, Uluru Dreaming, and so on.

Though the songlines can be traced back at least 40,000 years, they are being lost at the alarming rate of the indigenous languages in which they are sung, which is about two a year. As Yanyuwa professor John Bradley writes, "You have to understand that where I work, the ultimate form of knowledge is the ability to sing songlines. These are the professors. The ultimate way of knowing is being able to dance your country."[87]

This death of indigenous languages is a worldwide epidemic as the dominant culture subordinates the speakers of minority languages. Roughly 50% of known languages have disappeared in the last 500 years alone.[88] And along with mass language extinction, many of the oral traditions, including song and story, are also being lost.

The loss of ancestral language not only means the extinction of cultural heritage, it is directly linked to our worldwide ecological collapse. Polar Inughuit have more than twenty words for different kinds of ice, but as the ice melts, those words disappear with it.[89] Research also shows striking correlations between regions that are rich in biodiversity and areas of the highest linguistic diversity.[90] But as we lose languages, that loss is reflected in plant and animal extinctions.

As we create an increasingly homogenous human culture, we are rapidly losing the broad diversity of knowledge necessary to our tending of the land upon which we are dependent, as well as the ability to commune with and protect the other beings who call it home.

Language, song, and story reflect life as we experience it—in return, life emulates the stories we carry. In the old way, you'd be expected to listen to your elders telling about the epic odysseys of the ancestors and you'd never get anywhere fast. Your food would always go cold for the long prayers that are owed to your people's endurance that allowed you to come into being. And eventually you'd come to know the stories by heart because they'd wiggle down into your bones and take life in the landscape, in the fire and the lakes and the mountains your people have named because they've earned the right by crossing them.

And when your time comes to be cooked by the flames of life, as it does for all of us, you'd know that you aren't the first to be chosen by the fire; it will hurt for as long as it takes, and there is a way through if you follow the songlines, the archetypes, and the energy of the dreams.

Without the timeless wisdom of myth and dreaming, we are mirroring an increasingly shallow storying of our life-worlds. Television, the most popular form of storytelling in Western culture, is increasingly focused on violence, ruthlessness, and explicit sexuality. While it may feel entertaining to watch these images, they are lacking in archetypal nutrition and take an enormous psychic toll. The reinforcement of hollow narratives narrows the bandwidth of our mythic imagination and flattens the complexity of the human experience. By paying them with our attention we further emphasize those psychological and cultural stories. Like a question that goes unanswered, we recreate conflict and objectifying violence in our communities as if on an endless loop.

Because television broadcasts into the privacy of our homes, the participatory element of storying—the ability of listeners to contribute to cultural storying—is truncated. The result is a deluge of exclusionary narratives, featuring the images of mostly male, caucasian, heterosexual heroes, effectively erasing queer, female, differently-abled, and people of colour from the storying process.

As Nigerian novelist Chimamanda Ngozi Adichie explains, there is a danger in this narrow form of storytelling. "The consequence of the single story is this: it robs people of dignity. It makes our recognition of our equal humanity difficult. It emphasizes how we are different rather than how we are similar."[91] Indeed, when we don't see ourselves represented in the language and images of a story, we don't feel a sense of belonging to that culture. And for those of us who do have the privilege to be represented in those stories, we may be unconscious of the Othering effect it has on our own psyches and in the culture to which we contribute.

Nowadays, we sensationalize stories that have no redemptive quality at all. For instance, I recently saw a film in which, through his own ignorance and neglect, a man causes his family great harm. The movie takes us through a long unfolding of his story and provides him with opportunities to express his terrible grief, and even to love again. But the film ends with him walking away from love, declaring recovery impossible. The critics loved it! People praise this kind of anti-storytelling because, "it's more like real life." But I believe this is a reflection of a culture impoverished in mythic imagination. It's a mistake to think of stories with a redemptive quality as unrealistic, because their function is not to reflect 'real life,' but rather to rescue the events of our lives from randomness, restoring them to meaning.

While it may not be possible to 'go back' to living as our ancestors did, we can each practice at *dadirri*, drawing from the same ancient spring of stories. By listening to our dreams, and the stories of our bones, by hearing the manifold voices of the land, we can repair the bridge of our belonging to the great unfolding story of creation.

Restorying your Life

Whether we know it or not, we are constantly storying our lives. In conversation with others, or taking stock of our own experiences, we have a deeply instinctual, even biological imperative to turn our experiences into stories. They might begin more obviously with, "You'll never believe what happened to me…" or, "That reminds me of the time…"

But more subtly, we are always involved with an inner storying. This process is largely unconscious and heavily influenced by the authority figures in our lives, whose definition of us may have become internalized as our own story. This ventriloquizing, where someone else's voice behaves as our own, might sound like, "I'm doomed to fail," or, "I am irresponsible," or, "I'm not very smart." As my friend and fairy tale expert Michelle Tocher explains, we are often, like characters in fairy tales, under the dark spells or enchantments of those more powerful than us.[92] Whether it was a teacher or a parent who once told us 'how life is' or what we are like, we ate that poisoned apple and it put us into a deep sleep of inherited belief.

To break these spells, we must first become aware of them. With the help of dreams and myth, we can expose the narratives that are operating compulsively in our lives and begin to restory ourselves out of the places where we feel trapped or stuck. As Tocher frames it, Rapunzel may believe she is forever stuck in her tower with no stairs and no door—but her captor, the witch, comes and goes through a window, so there must be a way out. We too are provided with windows of opportunity to escape our outdated myths. These windows of opportunity are the moments when we feel the dissonance between who we are and who we appear to be.

To give you an example, when I was nine years old, I saw my father for the first time since my parents' divorce five years earlier. The very first thing he did when I got off the plane in England was give me an IQ test. He was an intellectual who literally wrote textbooks on intelligence. I remember feeling terrified that I would fail and waited for him to tabulate my results. As it turned out, I waited for twenty years. For most of my life, I thought I must be stupid because he never gave me my results. And what's more, I was pretty sure that my being stupid was the reason he was absent from my life. This inner storying ran deep and affected many of the decisions I made, including hanging back from certain challenges and comparing myself negatively to those with intellectual accomplishments. Finally, when I was twenty-eight years old, I had the courage to confront my father and ask him why he never gave me my results. Without any kind of explanation, he pulled out my IQ test sheets from his files and showed me that I'd scored in the highest percentile!

That moment for me was the sudden opening of a window in my awareness. It was the first crack in the spell I'd been under. I wasn't who I thought I was at all! Carrying that new awareness changed the way I moved in the world.

Awakenings can also be those simple moments when we are engaged in an activity or relationship where we feel entirely ourselves. For instance, you may take a vacation by yourself or remember a time in your life when you devoted your energy and space to your creativity, but then realize you have to return to a busy and demanding life. These awakenings can be painful because we are never more aware of our predicament than when we're briefly outside of it.

Whether we are working with nocturnal dreams or with our own stories, we must look for the mythical thread that tells us where in the story arc we are. From there, we can follow the archetypal patterns which, by their nature, never remain in stasis, but always move us towards redemption. In the act of connecting to archetypes we feel the spark of vitality, a hint of life, a tiny becoming. We begin to remember who we were before we fell under the enchantment. We trace back to our root purpose, when we were engaged and alive, when we were our best selves.

Though it is our habit to focus on the more threatening or victimizing elements in a dream, the greater art is to find the way the energy wants to go. As soon as we find that small flame of longing, we begin to recognize the other elements in the dream as attempts to call it forward. Though recurring dreams may all feel the same, when we attend to its details we find a tiny moment, a small shift, or a supportive element that wants to take the story forward. Even in a dream's antagonism, it is attempting to return us to wholeness.

A person with PTSD who has recurring dreams of their trauma is actually showing signs of positive adaptation to the original trauma through those images. In a sense, they are being called to defragment the memory so that it can be wholly integrated. It is best, of course, to work with a professional who can help carry the difficult images until the individual can witness the trauma in its entirety. From there, they can find a way to live with what's happened to them.

With the help of myths and stories, we can begin to reconstruct the past through what the author Toni Morrison calls *rememory*.[93] This is a process of re-authoring our experiences, taking ownership of those narratives through which we've been ventriloquized, by bending or reframing our story to better represent us.

A woman named Lisa came to me some years ago with chronic dreams of intruders coming into her home at night. Inevitably, these dreams always turned violent with either the intruder or the dream-self getting badly hurt.

As we worked gently with Lisa's associations to the dreams, we discovered that she had a very hard time saying *no* to her friends and family. As a result, she often felt intruded upon by others' needs over her own, and it was making her increasingly antisocial. We explored the intruder, then, as an aspect of herself that 'left the door open' on her own boundaries. It was a revelation for Lisa to realize *she* was the intruder, invading her own needs by prioritizing others. As Lisa explained, "[the dreams] taught me to really listen to the most vulnerable part of myself, and to respond in the most caring way I could."

Over the next six months, she practiced honouring her own boundaries and had fewer and fewer of these dreams. Instead, she began to dream of living with others in community. She was able to stop all the medications she'd been using for years to get her through the nights and, as she put it, "I began to make new friends, and to trust the world for the first time in my life."

Restorying is the work of welcoming and aggrandizing the small voice that emerges when we unhinder ourselves from the spells others have cast on us. We watch for those new images to appear in our dreams, following them until a way out the secret window is found.

For many years, I was a struggling writer and musician working as a waitress to make ends meet. In my late twenties, I was offered a highly coveted position as an artist scout for a well-known record company. I went from living in a cockroach-infested flat in a rough part of town to flying around the world signing other artists to record deals, eating in fancy restaurants and staying in high-end hotels.

For my ego, this was a thrilling time in my life: I finally had a respectable answer to the "What do you do?" question. But the things that were of deeper consequence to my soul—my own music, my relationships, and my spiritual life—fell into a state of disrepair. I might never have left that career if the label hadn't gone bankrupt. Overnight, I went from being a gold-card-carrying executive to being unemployed with no direction. To my amazement, the same people who had praised me for the position I'd landed began to bombard me with judgments for 'doing nothing.'

But it was within my own psyche that the real wrestle took place. For months I dreamed about being shoeless in the city, barefoot in horrible alleys where all kinds of needles and diseases were festering, desperately trying to find my shoes. I would wake up in a sweat, haunted by these recurring dreams. You see, I had lost my 'standing' in society. My identity had been so wrapped up with my position, and the workaholism it demanded, that I was now terrified of all the unstructured time stretching out before me.

Night after night I tried to regain my footing. Sometimes I'd find one shoe and not the other. Other times I'd find a pair that was beautiful but impractical, sewn out of purple cabbage, or covered in rhinestones. I'd go shopping at the dream-mall and find a sensible pair, but they were always too small. In waking life, I was looking for what to do with my life.

Frustrated, I told my recurring dream problem to my friend. She took one look at me and said, "Maybe being barefoot is not your problem. Maybe you just need to be somewhere it's safe to walk."

The simple truth of that statement reverberated through my whole being, and in an instant I understood that I needed to stop telling myself the story of loss. I had a new reality, and it was vulnerable, but I needed to find a new way to walk with it in the world. Though my shoelessness was a defeat for my ego, it was a triumph for my soul. I never had another shoeless dream after that. But over the following months I felt like I was being dragged into the underworld, through gates of intensifying vulnerability, stripped of my outer world clothing, as if being prepared to make some kind of encounter. Finding the mythical thread of my story made that time of groundlessness bearable, because I knew that if I wanted to emerge in a new way, I needed to acquiesce to the initiation.

I defended that time with a tenacity I'd never had before. I realized that my severance from that life was a blessing. And while that year seemed primarily about confronting the patriarchal influences within my psyche, something holy was also gestating. During the following months, I had some of the most powerful, initiatory dreams of my life. Magic and synchronicity filled my days and pointed to my passion for dreamwork. And finally, with an overwhelming fervour to share what I was being taught, I birthed the Dream School! As grandiose as it sounds, the Dream School started as a humble series of talks in the local library and small circles of lovely misfits, but looking back on it almost two decades later, I recognize it as the pivotal chapter when I, the heroine of my own story, answered my vocation.

The dreams I received during that time showed me that I had been abandoning, neglecting, and even selling out my creativity. I needed to live and work in a way that was respectful of my gifts and abilities. I had been putting them in service to someone else's enterprise, which had very little vision beyond its own expansion. Meanwhile, my own scrappy, orphaned life was aching to be adopted. Finally under the roof of my belonging, it gave me more than I could have ever imagined.

Dignity is not something that can be given to you, it is the marrow-deep recognition of your own worth. To have dignity is to be comfortable in your own skin, unlike the person that lives so far outside themselves that they are always garnering appreciation and validation from others.

Dignity emerges in the way you finally carry your own story. Through your painstaking efforts to write yourself as the hero or heroine at the helm of your own life, your losses cease to consume you. They are not forgotten or made invisible but rather aggrandized in your telling, passed on through the line of mothers and daughters, fathers and sons, as the mythical 'obstacles to flight' that they were. Forgiveness is coming to a place of reconciliation within, where you no longer wish for things to have been different than they were. To choose things wholeheartedly as they were and are. But dignity also lives in your willingness to step wholly into a new life of love, even as its first strands are being woven together to create a shape that will warm you.

Spelling the Way

It isn't enough to hear the call of our destiny; we must also cast out a story for ourselves, lest we be swept along by the one the world casts for us. Getting caught up in the question, "What is my purpose?" is like looking for shoes instead of walking forward. While most people think of reality as something that happens to us, the shamanic approach is to 'get behind the creation' of your story. Life isn't only happening to us: we are happening to life.

I call this process Spelling the Way, because the original use of the word *spell* means to create an enchantment by speaking something out loud. Words have immense power. We can fall under the dark spells or enchantments of those more powerful than us. But just as some of us have been haunted by the words of others, an utterance made *by* us with equal conviction can bend the reality of our lives.

There is an old Aramaic word that I'm sure you're familiar with, *abracadabra*, which roughly translates as, "I create as was spoken." More than a mythological concept, it is the idea that the stories we tell, to ourselves and to others, have the power to conjure reality. Sometimes we get so swept along by the events of our lives that we forget to bring presence to the as-yet-unmanifest dream we have for our lives, and for the world. Magic doesn't require the world to act first, to prove itself, or miraculously appear. Magic is the act of behaving as if the thing we are becoming is guaranteed, speaking and moving as if it carries that secret in each step.

We tend to think of magic as something that, in times of doubt or lostness, might intervene on our behalf. We listen for its clarion call, an oracular declaration, the prophetic dream that sweeps us out of the stuckness of our lives. But if we take a more rigorous look at this way of thinking, it hinges on the belief that something knows better than we do what our vocation is, what our direction should be, where our people live, and so on. Certainly there are times in everyone's life when something greater pushes you in the direction of your destiny, but tsunamis can't exactly be sought out. If we want magic to come alive in our lives, we must tend to our everyday relationship with it.

We can use story to shape the future we are creating through imaginative journaling, writing in detail about the life we are stepping into. But we can also alter the past, or at least the way we perceive the past, by reframing the pivotal experiences in our lives as necessary to having shaped us. We can also play with changing the everyday language we use to shift our relationship to specific areas of our life. For instance, at a time when I was wanting to change my limited story around money, I decided to replace phrases like "I can't afford this," with "This is something I really value." Other story-based practices include art and movement as ways to reshape how we dance with difficulty. Of course, one of the most powerful restorying practices is to work with the symbols in our dreams.

We have been looking at waking and dreaming as an ongoing conversation between two worlds, but at the centre of this conversation is our free will. Dreams provide a wellspring of guidance—but once we receive a dream, we must take symbolic steps towards the life we are longing for. This might look like taking a leap in the direction of a dream's prompting, or it might be as simple as exalting in some physically symbolic way the life you are calling towards you. Like keeping a dream altar, where you honour the talismans from your visions, or buying a scarf in that vibrant, Grecian blue you saw in the previous night's dream, or planting a tree in the garden where you dreamed your ancestors' bones were buried. Symbolic gestures act as spells that reinforce the nascent energy which is seeking expression in your dreams. This gathering of evidence around you is what can tunnel you out of the ordinary into the world of magic.

Unlike the trendy *Law of Attraction*, Spelling the Way isn't about muscling against reality to achieve the ego's preferences, but a way of harmonizing with the nature coming through your instinctual yesses and noes.

We can think of our waking life as a response to the dream, and the dream a response to life. There is a dynamic reciprocity between the receptive and the active, each reflecting the other, and at the centre between them is our agency. Choice, and the lucidity to make choices, is where the real magic lives. First we are attentive to the ancient or ancestral story that is coming through us, or the land where we live, and then we practice Spelling the Way into alignment with it.

Restorying takes place along the living edge, where we are at once a disciple of the great story being born of our lives, but also the speller of the way. "In giving away the control," as Alan Watts says, "you've got it."[94] Mastery is found in spelling a good story out of the pieces you've been given, directing yourself as you're being inclined.

But restorying doesn't end at the level of the Self. When we get together in dream circles, for instance, we often find emerging storylines in our combined dreams. When we share our dreams in community, we are doing as our ancestors did, reinvolving ourselves and each other in the storying of culture. There is a wonderful Chinese aphorism: "Let us draw closer to the fire so that we may better see what we are saying."[95] When we gather in intimate community, we bring back the participatory element of storying itself, contributing to the creation of more sophisticated stories in our culture.

Seventeen
Tending a Village

The word 'community' is used often to describe the mashup of folks who have been thrown together by geography and milieu. But there is another version of the word which conjures an image of living in intimate communion with others for a unified purpose. A vibrant hamlet of land where we of like-hearts dwell together—but not too close—sharing our skills and splitting our yields. We laugh and make babies, fix each other's roofs, and gather around the fire with music to hear our elders tell stories. We long for this village life, in which everybody has a role to fill and all of our needs are met.

But for the many of us who don't have a sense of the village in our own lives, its very mention can be alienating. Community can feel like that oasis of hope that disappears the moment we get close to it. We speak about it yearningly, like a fairy tale we ache to find ourselves in. And its absence has a great presence in our lives.

When I lived in the city, I longed for village life. I wanted so much to be supported and valued, to be met in a way I'd never experienced with my own family. In my clumsy attempts to create a village from scratch, I would invite friends over for potluck gatherings, preparing days in advance by cleaning and making my home festive, cooking and sending out poetic invitations. And people would come, hungry for what gathering gives, but they would often show up empty-handed or bring convenience items like store-bought chips and salsa, and rarely offer help washing the dishes when all was said and done. When it was over, I'd be so tired that it would take me ages to do it again. Occasionally, the rare invitation was returned, but I was often too busy or tired from work to put in the effort to show up with a worthy contribution, if at all. It was as if community required some kind of momentum that none of us could get rolling. I don't think any of us were ungenerous, but rather unskilled at creating community, having never learned it. Without community as a shared way of life, no single one of us could conjure it.

It was a revelation to me when I moved to a small, rural mountain town and found that people knew how to tend a village much better than I. The potlucks were frequent through the winter, with voluptuous feasting tables of homemade food, dishes that glistened with the pride of making offerings worthy of our togetherness. Conversely, in times of crisis, everyone would mobilize to help the unfortunate ones. If someone had a fire or an accident, neighbours would get together to help them rebuild or to throw a fundraiser to support their medical bills. I met people whose entire lives and land were a dedicated refuge for community to gather.

Apart from a few generous friends, I'd never been exposed to this kind of living. And while I instantly knew that this kind of community was something I wanted to be a part of, it took me much longer to realize that community was something I needed to *practice*. Though in many ways I am still fledging the nest of individualism, here are some of things I'm learning are essential for making and tending to a village.

Reciprocity

A reciprocal roof is a self-supporting structure that can be made up of as few as three beams, up to any quantity, which are balanced on each other to create an extremely strong frame. You can make yourself a model of this by leaning three matchsticks on each others' shoulders. Because its centre is everywhere, if you remove even one of the beams, the roof will collapse.

In modern culture, we are so accustomed to the transactional, money-for-service relationship that characterizes our capitalist paradigm that, outside of our immediate families and close friendships, we rarely experience reciprocity at the community level. If there is something we need, we think of buying it before ever considering relying on each other for help. This framework of 'every individual for himself' is the enemy of community.

Before the invention of money, and in societies where consumerism has yet to dominate, trade, bartering, skill sharing, and collaboration are fundamental to village life. Like the reciprocal roof, every individual is recognized as having something to contribute to the whole, making everyone essential to its well-being while acting as a support upon which all can depend.

But as we grow in size from a village into a city, replacing reciprocity with capitalism, we lose the underlying indebtedness of the kin structure which keeps us beholden to each other. We lose the idea of a shared self. Instead we become strangers unto whom we owe nothing, and further, with whom we are in competition for resources.

There is a wonderful word in the Quechua language, *minga* or *mink'a*, which means 'collective work for the common good.'[96] Especially used in the agricultural sense, a *minga* is the reunion of friends and neighbours to collaborate in some shared work that will benefit the whole village. A day of work like this is usually celebrated with a feast, making it an opportunity for social bonding as well. The *minga* is based in the foundational practice of *ayni*, another word from the Andean people, which roughly translates into reciprocity, or mutuality—and it is the backbone of their way of life.

Ayni is a concept not limited to humans that extends to nature and the universe. For instance, a tree gives its fruits, shelter, and oxygen to humans— and in return, humans and other animals give back to the tree by spreading its seeds, converting oxygen back into carbon dioxide, maybe even watering it in the dry season. Practiced at the village level, this might look like a barn-raising, where helpers are recruited to build or restore a barn that is essential to the farmer's way of life. In return, the helpers are entitled to call upon the farmer when they are in need of food. *Ayni* might also look like giving circles, where groups of people come together to either offer their skills, time, or expertise to anyone in need, or petition the circle for support with childcare, graphic design, or borrowing tools. In a healthy community, all members are held essential and their gifts are valued, but *need* is the glue that binds us.

It may seem obvious, but two things are absolutely necessary to creating community over the long term: someone willing to take the lead and invite others to gather, and someone willing to answer that call. Taking the lead requires great risk because you are braving rejection. Whether it's a potluck, a book club, or a women's or men's circle, you may be opening your home or putting big effort into organizing an event, and there is no guarantee that others will come. So answering the call is also a kind of generosity. Beyond receiving what the other is offering, it is also a way of giving relevance to their efforts. It says that no matter how busy or tired I might be, community with you is important to me. Ideally it isn't just one or two people doing the organizing, because at different times we all need to be held. But with enough calls made, and enough answers to those calls, the fabric of community is eventually woven.

Leadership is essential to community, but in the reciprocal model, this role can rotate between members depending on the needs of the group. Unlike the way we normally think of leadership, as one person telling others what to do, reciprocal leadership is about engaging everyone to find the way forward. It is spherical in nature, rather than hierarchical. In this way of seeing things, a great leader is an expression of their collective, not its star. If done well, a leader should oversee, guide, and represent the collective's vision. But the right person for that role might also change as the group's needs change. At times, we may need a confident and outspoken leader to power us through a tangled passage, but other times we need the leader who quietly sees the network of connections within the whole. Sometimes we need a leader who hangs back so another may practice at stepping forward, challenging us to be better than we think possible. Reciprocal leadership ultimately recognizes the circle itself as the teacher.

There is a genius that can only be found in our coming together, and it's our combined abilities that elevate and strengthen us. True humility doesn't mean making yourself smaller, but recognizing that we are all the same size: necessary.

Reciprocity can also be an emotional back and forth, like coming together to pass the talking stick. When we share our stories and dreams, we are accepting help in the shouldering of grief and responsibility. By extension, our windfalls and triumphs belong to us all. In a sharing circle, we are cross-pollinating our wisdom and broadening our storylines, moving the locus of our attention from competition to collaboration. No longer governed by personal lack, we begin to make decisions as an ecosystem would, from the appreciation of our indivisibility.

Shared Values

One of the essential building blocks of community is a shared sense of values. Though we might be different in lots of ways, it's through our intersecting values that we create long-lasting connection and meaningful change. Before we can make the village we long for, we first have to name what we value most so that we can envision the tomorrow we want to create. Whether we're seeking certain personal qualities in our connections with others, wanting to meet people with common interests and perspectives, or joining together to build projects and take action, our shared values are the foundation of any community.

Once you have a clear idea of what you'd like to see more of in your life and in your neighbourhood, you have to engage in the conversation about it with others. Whether your vision is to welcome refugees, protect wild water, or address the wealth discrepancies in your town, it 'takes a village' to accomplish larger things. You need to rally together. Activism is a great way to meet like-minded folks, and odds are you won't have to start from scratch. Activists are notoriously good organizers, interested in the greater good, so it may be as simple as putting the word out on social media or plugging into a previously arranged event.

But if politics aren't your thing, you could join a dance class, hiking club, community garden, or singing circle. Festivals and fairs can also be a great way to meet and connect in deeper ways with community. Where I live, we have a weekly farmer's market, which is not only the best place to buy happy vegetables but a venue to connect with our neighbours and friends who value sustainable, local food.

Any time you're engaged in social contribution, you are strengthening community ties. Volunteering your skills, knowledge, or time is a great way to build rapport with others. It doesn't need to be an official volunteer position; it could be as simple as taking an interest in your neighbours and finding out what they need, endeavouring to fill that need, or simply offering them a listening ear. You might also choose to mentor someone in your chosen field, or become a big sister or brother to a young person. Enough kindnesses strung together like this eventually make a sturdy network.

Sometimes an issue of survival brings a community together. For example, the people of my adopted community have a powerful and abiding relationship with water. This may not seem consequential if you're used to getting endless water from taps, but when you live in a place where you can drink from mountain-fed rivers instead of bringing bottles on your walks, when you encounter the many wild creatures who do the same, or when you experience drought and watch as your garden suffers until the next rainfall, you become intimately linked with the health of your water. So you come together in droves to protect what you treasure.

As soon as you begin to move in the direction of what you value, participating in shared activities around those values, you begin to see that you aren't alone. When you're standing up with others, you can look around and see who you are belonging with and, by standing together, you fortify those values in the world.

Circles and Ritual

In order to strengthen the bonds of community, we need to make frequent excuses to gather in circle to celebrate, collaborate, and ceremonialize our rites of passage. More than a symbolic act, ritual is a powerful cultural technology that puts us into conversation with the invisible and holy elements of nature, creating occasions for us to express our feeling life in the open, weaving us deeper into togetherness.

Though we already observe certain conventional rituals such as weddings, birthdays, funerals, and holidays, many people feel an emptiness around these occasions because of how tied to consumerism and religion they have become. You may even feel a wariness or fearfulness around ritual because of how mishandled and appropriated these acts have been. But simultaneously, you may recognize a longing to be held in community during the many transitions of your life that others failed to recognize, like coming of age, entering parenthood, launching a creative endeavour, divorcing, death, abortion or miscarriage, and so on.

Ritual acts as a demarcation between the old way of life and the new one. When we recognize the potency of those transitions as a community, we have a much better chance of harnessing the personal and collective power available in those occasions.

A number of years ago I invited the women in my community into a red tent, an old tradition of gathering women during moontime, to speak about our menarche, or first menstrual experiences. The response was so overwhelming that we could barely fit so many women into my little living room. But more than that, I was amazed at how many women, like myself, felt their first blood went unrecognized and was shamed, leaving them with a lifelong trauma around their moontime.

Witnessing is one of the extraordinary powers of community. There are certain passages and initiations that require the presence of others to help hold the bigness of the new narrative while it stabilizes in our bodies, minds and hearts. When we leave behind an old identity for a new form of belonging, there are always moments when we are tempted to slip back into our old skin. Whether it is a grief that is too big to grieve alone, recovery from an illness that threatens to return, or stepping up to a new altitude of Self that's tough to acclimate to, community behaves like a broader leverage to bear the weight of transition. Friends remind us, simply by bearing witness, that we have become something new and, with the corroborative power of gathering in ceremony, we can never wholly unbecome it.

Bearing witness is also a privilege, as it awakens a symmetry of transition in our own becoming. After a beautiful woodland wedding, a friend turned to me and said, "It felt like we all got a bit married today." Indeed, the ritual feeds the yearning in all who attend it to be committed to something we cherish or, in the case of a grief ritual, given the invitation to touch our own ungrieved parts.

To be invited as a witness into the lives of others calls upon our accountability. The moment another opens an aperture into their secret hearts, we become each other's keepers. The strands of our stories are entwined in a shared tapestry of belonging unto which we become responsible.

The circle of belonging must be continuously attended to, woven outwards through our abiding curiosity in each other's expansions and contractions. It's important to invest ourselves in those moments that might otherwise go unnoticed: when a friend accomplishes something big, or perhaps suffers a loss they have no official way of acknowledging. If we can show up there with some symbolic gesture, it goes a great distance to making another feel at home in our hearts. The moment we stop making an offering of our presence to each other signals the end of our belonging together.

When a dear friend of mine took her own life and I was unable to attend her memorial because she lived a great distance away, my circle of sisters and I created a heart-shaped mandala out of flower petals from our gardens. It was so incredibly beautiful and allowed me to not only feel as if I'd honoured her impact on my life, but that the weight of my grief was being carried by more than myself alone. When another friend had a miscarriage, we brought her a basketful of treasures, including some Japanese paper for writing goodbyes, some rose oil and beeswax candles for a ritual bath, and wildflower seeds to plant in memory of the life that briefly visited her. These small but symbolic items invited her to befriend her loss, to be in conversation with it, and to feel the support of our community while doing so.

Beyond our personal transitions, it's also powerful to recognize transitions in nature like the important moons or events that mark the threshold between seasons, like spring and autumn equinoxes and winter and summer solstices. These rituals can be as often as a full or new moon. The ritual marking of seasonal thresholds takes us out of the human-centric drama and puts us into better relationship with nature and the elemental world from which we are wrought.

If you have no experience with ritual, or the ceremony you have experienced rubbed you the wrong way, how do you begin to include ritual in your life in a way that feels authentic? My suggestion would be to start simply. Reach out to a small group of friends who you would like to belong with, and invite them to commit to gathering a few times a year to create ritual together.

One of the greatest ways to begin is to gather around a fire pit. For as long as fire has existed, humans have belonged themselves to each other around it. Fire is that element which warms our centre and illuminates the dark, inclining us to storytelling, secrets, prayer, and song. By its very nature, it carries the teachings of transformation. Fire burns away the deadwood and decay, reinvigorating the soil with nutritious ash, preparing the ground for new life. Very little is needed beyond a few words brave enough to open the circle with the longing you have in your life to feel more connected to others and to the Creator. After that, you can simply pass the talking stick. Invite people to bring an object symbolic of their own longing, ask them to share its story or contribute a song that moves them. Or have everyone write down on paper what they're ready to leave behind, speak it out loud, and burn it in the fire.

Let yourselves be awkward together. We all have so much fear around groups, around sharing, around wanting to connect to the holy, that we invariably, and necessarily, feel like we're faking it at first. This is completely normal. We've been estranged from this way of life for so long. But when you think about it, all ritual was first invented by someone. Your longing to create and be held in ritual is the same longing your ancestors felt, under the same stars, the same moon, emergent from the same wellspring of dreams. So let us begin to weave that history now from scratch. All we need is the commitment to keep showing up, to keep holding the heartbeat call to gather, and slowly, imperceptibly, we'll begin to feel more natural with it. Even when we aren't entirely grounded in the experience, living partially in the mind which judges the ritual as trite or inconsequential, still we'll feel richer the next day. We'll walk by the ashes in the firepit, or notice the flowers someone put on the altar, or even see a blanket someone left behind, and we'll feel fattened with meaning, closer to love and belonging.

It's a good idea when starting a ritual circle to have a reciprocal leadership format and a rotating venue. If there is only one person holding this heartbeat of gathering for others, that person is in danger of burning out. If what you want is to build a village, then you must take up the heartbeat yourself. Look for ways to call people together, and then call on them to call each other together too.

The time of the lone wolf is over. Our future depends on us learning how to move as an ecosystem does, in harmony and collaboration. So look for any excuse to practice at being in circle; make every undertaking have some aspect that requires others.

Too often we focus on the deficits, absences, and needs of our own hearts. But sometimes the world needs us to be more to others, whether there is an overt reciprocity in the relationship or not. We may be called to give more than we receive, but in the giving we contribute to the archetype of the other's growing generosity. And while we may not see the private benefits of such a becoming, it will reinforce the greater web in which we belong.

Eldership

One of the worst griefs people feel is the longing for elders in their lives. How many times do we find ourselves in conflict, fear, or despair and wish we could receive guidance from someone who knows better? There is no shortage of *older* people in our communities, but what differentiates an *elder* from an *older* is not just age, but the wisdom they carry and the position they hold in their community. Among other qualities, an elder is someone who is committed to staying put, who has lived into the competencies of belonging and made an invitation of their lives to the young ones growing up around them. Less interested in the ambitions we associate with the first half of life, elders value inner development. They are curious about others, generous with their listening, and invested in helping young people stay on course to reach their potential.

But an elder can only exist within a community that values them. Elders need *youngers* in order to fulfil their purpose. If we deprive elders of our admiration, hiding them away in old folk's homes, we are in part responsible for their absence in our lives. Without the presence of elders in our becoming, we can lose our bearings in the continuum of that longer story. As civil rights activist Ruby Sales puts it, "There is a hunger that young people have, to be claimed, to be a part of an intergenerational—a trans-generational experience, because without knowing another generation, they feel incomplete, just like I feel incomplete without knowing younger people."[97]

An elder knows that without their staying put, you would have no home. There would be no boundary for your restless heart which, in all its wildness, actually wants nothing more than to belong to a greater purpose. The magic of the relationship between elder and younger is its mutuality. While the young person is given that sense of being cared for and looked after by someone who knows better than them, who expects them to grow into their best self, the elder is venerated as a carrier of wisdom at a time when they most long to be of service. They are given an important duty to guide young people on the course paved by their own lives, which was guided by the elders who came before them. There is an African proverb that says when an elder dies, a library burns down.[98] Indeed, there is much accumulated in a lifetime that goes to waste unless it can be passed along. The elder's greatest calling is to pass on the stories and teachings of their own lives, as well as those that they carry from previous generations, so the momentum of that legacy can be kept alive.

There is a sense in the word 'belonging' that an endurance has been paid, a distance travelled, a history shared. An elder knows that here, where the wound is deep with desertions of love and attentiveness, presence and endurance, is where we must remain. Here in the broken promises, we must keep to our word. Here we must put our breath on the flickering, tentative flame, letting the smoke carry our signature to the ancestors that might recognize us and lend us their strength. Here in this meagre corner entrusted to us, we must keep crafting the invisible masonry of our great temple of remembering.

If you are without elders in your life, or if the older people in your life aren't the wise ones you are longing for, consider befriending some in your community. Find those whose eyes still sparkle, who carry some gravitas, who are using their lives in service to something greater than themselves alone. Make a respectful courtship of them by showing up to support or keep them company in a consistent way. Listen to their stories, ask them for guidance, learn what they're willing to share with you.

But also know that it is never too early to practice at becoming an elder. Conscious eldering is about doing the inner work, attending to the soul life before it comes for you. So many people have what we call a 'mid-life crisis' in their fifties; suddenly they realize they have been living in false belonging their whole lives and have a desperate urge to scrap everything and start over. However, if we learn at an earlier age to attend to our longing, to take the risks necessary to live in alignment with our soul's calling, then we are preparing ourselves to be true elders in the second half of life.

Elder wisdom comes not from the accumulation of knowledge, but from reflecting on life; instead of living in a state of unworthiness and regret, we can grieve and forgive the past, find the redemption in our story, and recognize how it fits into our ancestral mythos. This work becomes our gift to the future.

Seeing and Being Seen

All of these things—reaching out to elders or youngers, participating in circles, showing up to an event or activity—require us to be seen. A sense of community really only develops the moment you feel your gifts being received. It may be as simple as someone knowing your name or seeing their face light up when you enter the room. We all need to feel as if our presence matters to others. As Henri Nouwen says, "The simple experience of being valuable and important to someone else has a tremendous recreative power."[99]

But mattering is only possible when we are contributing our presence, when we name our values, when we give our gifts. Where you long to be recognized, allow yourself to be seen. Can you risk being loved as you are, without the protections of distance? Can you surrender your control in order to be influenced, mixed with, and impressed upon?

By exposing our grief, fear, and anxiety to others, we are allowing it to commingle with new viewpoints, inducing change rather than remaining in stasis. Vicariously, we are also offering a validation towards what is hidden in the other, that they may brave it into view. In the many circles I've attended, it is only when one of us is brave enough to share a personal story that others begin to open up as well.

If you are doing your part to brave the beautiful values that are coursing through you into the world, then all that's left for you to do is to notice who notices. Don't dismiss the invitational presence in others. Keep these ones close by noticing their gifts in return. Practice at opening the heart, yours and theirs, through fierce inquiry and the expression of truth.

So many of us are out at sea, looking for home. We try this way and that way, battling the endless march of adversaries, led by cynicism and apathy. We fight them with every poetry we possess. We are gentle. We yield. We get back to navigating our crafts. But every once in a while, exhaustion can turn into despair. The tiny flame, which takes all our resources to shield, blows out in an unexpected gust. This is when it helps to think of more than ourselves. It helps to see the earth workers, the artists, the mothers, the lovers, the singers, the poets, and dreamers, as threads in a web. By ourselves we are fragile strands, songs with no listeners, but together we are a relentless network. Wherever there is depression there is colour made vivid by the grey.

When I feel this fog rolling in on me, I light fires of affection in the hearts of others. I tell them in tangible ways how the life they live makes me live mine differently, how precious and important they are to the rest of us. That fire then becomes a beacon, burning through the grey, that I can sail towards.

Becoming a Lowland

This being human is tough stuff, and one of the acute losses we all feel is that which our great ancestors took as certain: when one of us is wounded, we are all implicated. So we shoulder our unbearable questions together. We honour with ritual the devastating requirements and initiations that being alive asks of us. But in the impoverished condition of modern culture, we are taught to feel ashamed of our weakness and to deny our own suffering, never mind share its burden. We've grown a thorny hedge around the very places where we should be depending on each other.

And then it's hard to reach out. It's hard to be seen with your messy lostness, exhaustion, and overwhelm as you stumble through the complexities of life. But how else can someone become trustworthy unless you allow them to share in your hardship? How can we form the village we ache for unless we allow ourselves to wrestle with these things together?

If you are well, consider being the medicine for someone else's pain. Rumi says, "Where lowland is, that's where water goes. All medicine wants is pain to cure."[100] But if you are unwell, consider asking a friend you want to trust for help. Consider that to be invited behind your hedge is a privilege, and it calls upon the lovewater in all of us that yearns to flow into a lowland.

Sometimes the person you call upon may not have the capacity to meet your vulnerability—and there is terrible grief in this. You might be tempted to grow your hedge even higher and swear off this 'reaching out' stuff. But perhaps there is a greater attrition taking place. Perhaps you already knew you were calling upon the wrong person. And perhaps there's someone unexpected in your midst who keeps showing up and challenging you to receive their support.

You, who would normally bear it alone: yours is a necessary yielding. Your asking is the invitation that may keep us bound in place and memory together. Yours are the first threads of a village in the making.

Reaching out can be enormously difficult for a heart that has been wounded in the act. But it helps to remember that reaching out is actually an offering of generosity, the invitation which allows the other to contribute their gifts into our shortfall. It is an act of recognition of the other's necessity which, to an ecosystem, is the joining process itself.

We have a friend who underwent a serious operation who typically has a hard time asking for help. Despite her discomfort, she decided to reach out to us and ask if we could buy her some groceries. We were so honoured to be asked that we also made her a pot of homemade soup and showed up with some wildflowers. She was so grateful that she asked because, as it turned out, she also really needed someone to split some kindling for her. She was moved to tears by our simple generosity, and we had one of the loveliest afternoons of that winter. Fast forward to a year or so later, when we were high and dry for firewood late in the season, and it was she who offered us an excellent connection. As it turns out, not only did she do us a great favour, but the lovely fellow whose firewood we bought was in desperate need of the money. So there is a cascade of abundance that thrives when we ask for help.

Far from the cultural notion that to be dependent is feeble, it is the fortifying activity of our interdependence. We know that when we lean in to support another, we are sustaining our own circle of belonging.

If a person's heart has been shut down or denied, they might develop a fierce self-reliance that prevents them from reaching out. But while this independence may look outwardly impressive, at its core there may be a deficiency of trust in others, which is the great glue of our belonging. The more we reward this image in others, by praising them at a distance, the greater the difficulty they'll have in contacting the hidden gems of their own heart. While we cannot force someone to receive, we can make ourselves useful to them without them asking. It is often the most resilient and generous among us who are longing for support.

Leaving Well

Belonging is a dynamic process that requires alternating periods of separation and togetherness. As we develop the capacity for tending a village, so too must we develop skillfulness with leaving. Unlike *ghosting*, which is the growing modern phenomenon of ending all communication in a relationship without explanation, leaving well means acknowledging all that relationship has given you while still honouring the onward call.

Closure normally requires two or more people coming together to consider each other's points of view and come to a consensual agreement for how to move forward, together or separately. But if one or more people are unwilling or unable to undergo this ritual, we can be left with a lack of closure.

When someone has ghosted on a conversation, commitment or conflict, it's important to realize this as an act of indifference that counters belonging. Ghosting is all we believe we owe to a world on which we don't feel we've made an impact. In a sense, it is to make yourself a ghost in your own life, dissociating from the importance of your presence in others' lives. It is to withhold your disagreements, your longing to be seen, and to make yourself and others around you disposable. Unless someone is willing to hold you accountable, and be accountable themselves, they can never take a seat at the table of belonging.

We need to show each other that love is worth wrestling for, braving ourselves into the fires of intimacy. We are not expendable. And we shall know each other every time we show up for conflict, hurt, and confusion.

This state of limbo can be an enormous drain on our energy, even unconsciously, as we keep returning to the moment, wondering if we handled things well enough, imagining the other's reaction, or lack of reaction, unable to move forward without their acknowledgment. In these situations, it's important to make an act of closure, even symbolically. This begins with forgiving both yourself and the other for your limitations.

If you have invited such a person or group to move consciously through conflict, and they've refused you, first you must give yourself wholeheartedly to grief. In French, instead of "I miss you," we say, "*Tu me manques*" which means "you are missing from me." In your grief, you are valuing the impact of your separation, the missing they've left behind.

When you're ready, find or create an object that symbolizes the closure you seek, and consider imbuing it with your prayers:

> *I bless your absence, your silence, your disappearance from me with this grief. May the echo of your going missing reach back to you one day, so you know your own substantiality. May I know my grief as a measure of my willingness to devotion, and may I trust that I've been spared from halfway love. May this and all disappearances inspire me to become ever more scrappy and tenacious in love. May I know with greater clarity others who are the same. And when I meet them, may I redouble my commitment to the craft of belonging.*

Once you've given thanks and made your intent, throw your symbolic object off a bridge, burn it in a fire, bury it in a grave—but dispose of it and let it be final. There are a million tiny heartbreaks in every failed friendship, every disappointed hope, every extended hand denied, and we must grieve them all. But at a certain point, we also must stop carrying them with us. We must declare what's done was all that could be done. We have to sever those subtle ties that keep us hoping for a response to spring from the ashes.

Every separation you make from a person or place that cannot meet you where you stand is a step towards the community of your true belonging. In as much as you have grown your capacity for inclusiveness, so too will you be challenged to hold protective boundaries around the village you are building. Not everyone will share your values, but in the act of turning *away* from those that don't, you are also turning *towards* those that do.

Be the Longing

Instead of always asking, "Where do I belong?"—a question that is based in shortage—consider reversing your definition of the word from a noun to a verb, in which belonging becomes a practice of generosity as in, "I belong myself to that which I love." A wise teacher once told me that the greatest spiritual practice he knows is to discover what you are most missing in your life...and then give that thing away. In other words, take what little you have, which knows too little about everything big, and make of it an offering.

Belong yourself to those who need you. Find those, human and other than human, who are drifting to the fringes, who are the least valued or most unexpected to have something to offer; look for those without a voice, and draw them in closer. When you go to a party, instead of letting the fear of fitting in overcome you, practice wondering instead if anyone you meet might need belonging. The recognition that everyone around you is just as afraid of not-belonging is a revelation. We are all looking for that presence in another which can shelter us, educe our own stories, make us feel through their engagement that we are necessary in this life. At some point we must come down off those waiting stairs and begin to act as if we are necessary. Whether it is reflected in our world yet or not, we must assume our own importance and begin to give the gifts which we possess and which are desperately needed.

Where you long for the friend who calls only to find out if you're well, be that caller for another. Where you long for eloquent prayers to be made of everyday things, let your own clumsy words bless your meals out loud. Where you wish for ritual under the moons, be the one who holds the heartbeat of gathering. Where you ache to be recognized, allow yourself to be seen. Where you long to be known, sit next to someone and listen for insight into what they love. Where you wish you felt necessary, give those gifts away.

Rather than a disappointed wanting to belong, this is the practice to Be the Longing. Maybe it will take a lifetime, or maybe only the young ones who come up around you will feel the benefits, or maybe it will sneak up on you in a sudden moment as you sit feasting with your loved ones: that you belong to this beautiful village you've made with your life.

I Want to Be Alive with You

I want to be guided by older-ups. I want babies to be born where old people die. I want to be sandwiched in the middle of a messy togetherness. I want to be warned before I do something stupid. I want to be forgiven when I do it anyway. I want wisdoms to be tapped out on my eardrums and not Googled. I want transitions to be recognized by fire. I want gifts to be educed from children. And teenagers and adults. I want to mean something to my community. I want to get drunk on substance morning and night. I want to hear your dreams. I want to raise a revolution for gentleness. I want to call bullshit on consensus reality. I want to get rich only so I can billboard the highways with validations.

I don't want to be another faker. I don't want to show you my good side and hide my humanity. I don't want to dole out my self in digestible status-chunks. I want to challenge you in long, drawn-out rituals and still find you interested. I want to feed you seventeen-course meals made with spices I crushed. I want to recite you circular poems, each beginning cutting a deeper grasp. I want to make you feel something, even if it's awkward. I want to sing you songs which are ancient and new. I want to carve stories in trees with tools my elders fashioned. I want to keep sharpening them. I want to find places we've never been. And then, I want to return there, but backwards.

I want to shuffle up words so we don't sleep through them. I want to learn things and then be splashed into never forgetting. I want to make you feel seen. I want to hold your pounding heart in my gentlest of hands. I want to make your piece feel like my piece. I don't want to miss a moment. I want to dig at the bottom and find it false. I want to turn up unknown depths. I want to stand in this hurricane and sing the sweetest, most naked song you can bear. I want to be alive with you.

Eighteen

Reciprocity with Nature

When I was a little girl I used to lose myself in the woods behind our house, making up songs and stories with my imaginary forest friends. There was a particular grove of maples where I would gather my loot at the end of a day well-spent. Stones and leaves from the dark gorge filled with clay, bulrushes from the pond where I watched tiny tadpoles grow into frogs over the summer, or wildflowers from the meadow where I'd hear snakes slithering through the tall, dry grass. Nature was for me the great mother who, in times of growing turbulence in my family, always welcomed me into belonging with her.

I returned to that beautiful woods some twenty years later only to find a crowded housing development as far as the eye could see. Gone was the treeline which marked the end of human-centricity, gone was the path that connected meadow and gorge and forest, gone too were the unseen snakes and frogs and evening songbirds. I remember being disoriented for a long moment, sure that I was in the wrong place, unable to locate myself without those important natural features.

Reflecting on our present-day relationship with nature, you could say that we are collectively and chronically disoriented. I believe a great deal of the lostness we feel as a culture is a result of how alienated from the natural world we've become. Not only are we disconnected from nature but anaesthetized to the enormity of that loss. Many people don't even realize what is missing because they've never known it, but underneath our preoccupations with getting ahead and being accepted, there is a deep well of pain: our unbelonging to the earth herself.

Of course, we can never truly be separated from the natural world because, like every other living being, we are quite literally expressions of the earth. But in the grandness of what we as a species have created and called civilization, we have come to think of ourselves as conquerors of the wild. Forgetting, in some pandemic amnesia, the true origins that make any of it possible.

Our consciousness is so disconnected from the web of life that we have come to think of the earth's generosities as our own resources to privatize and commodify for profit. We are so enamoured with the construction of our own endless, narrow tunnels of productivity that we have become alienated from the very body that supports and sustains us. We no longer see how it is through the sacrificed life of others that we are sheltered and nourished every day.

Now we are faced with the consequences of that one-sided ideology. Along with climate change, the pollution of our oceans and air, and the dwindling of natural resources, we are, as Joanna Macy describes, facing the sixth mass extinction on our planet.[101] Even with the rapid decline of species and the growing number of ecological disasters that are the direct result of human greed and intervention, amazingly, there are still people who deny our responsibility in this slow apocalypse.

How did we go from being *a part* of this greater earthbody to feeling *apart* from her? And how might we practice belonging ourselves back to the ecosystem?

Our overemphasis on rationalism has sent the feeling life into atrophy, but it is the feeling capacity which connects us to empathy. This empathy is essential to our interrelatedness with each other and all living beings. It is the sense of interbeing with a group or place that makes us feel cheerfully responsible for it. We are called to serve it with our lives. Without feeling connected to other forms of life, they become expendable. And isn't that feeling of being expendable at the root of our personal exile as well?

We've spoken about our focus on materialism, and how it has resulted in the loss of the mythic life. But without the wisdom of the earth, as transmitted through the stories of our elders, we have ended up in an evolutionary cul-de-sac. Instead of being in daily communion with the teaching stories that come from plants and dreams, animal spirits and ancestors, our next generations are being raised on increasingly empty images.

When we are not guided by a mythic perspective, our individual and collective lives cease to have meaning. Our goals are no longer governed by a larger quest for the good of all, but by the empire's competitive system focused on the dominance of the individual over others, and the species over nature. It isn't difficult to see why we bully each other out of belonging, because such a mindset requires us to isolate and serve ourselves alone.

Which brings us to narcissism. I believe a huge part of our collective feeling of emptiness comes from living in this self-centred phase of our evolution as a species, where everything begins with *I*. *I* want this object, *I* want to succeed. *I* want to improve myself. Even: *I* want to belong. But true happiness depends upon our reciprocity with the environment in which we are embedded, and unto which we are indebted. In the same way that mitochondria work to break down nutrients and turn it into energy for our bodies, we too are but a single component of a greater biosphere that sees no hierarchy between ferns and redwoods, worms and eagles.

If we imagine an invisible mycelial network under the visible surface of things, of which we are but fruiting bodies, then we see how our lives should be in service to feeding the whole forest together. Our negligence of that reciprocity is, more than any other factor, what fosters unbelonging. It is at the root of loneliness, because without the greater intelligence of the mission coursing through our veins, making our purpose meaningful, we are but isolated bodies going through empty motions. This is why people who experience tremendous success can still feel lonely and unhappy.

The word 'animism' refers to something so commonplace, so taken for granted in tribal cultures, that most don't even have a word for it—it is the foundational belief that spirit and matter are one. That all things are imbued with a soul; not just humans and animals, but mountains, thunder, shadows, and even the wind. If we learn to listen to and engage in a dialogue with that diversity of voices, we begin to see how there is a constant dynamism taking place between waking and dreaming, seen and unseen, mundane and holy. Like a tree whose roots are hidden in the rich darkness of the soil, human beings are meant to take our cues from the inner life—not the other way around.

Following on this idea that there is a symmetry between the inner and outer worlds, we might begin to see our global crisis as a collective initiation which each of us must, reluctantly, go through alone. As we explored, initiation has several distinct phases. First we become separated from false belonging, which is a kind of awakening when the wool is pulled from our eyes. Then we must wholeheartedly grieve the losses we have sustained in exile. And if we grieve well, we come into conversation with our true values, listening for the call to act. If we rise to the challenge, we'll bring back the medicine we've retrieved from our descent, and become contributing agents to global transformation. What sets us apart from all other species is that we have the free will to choose how to move across this frightening threshold. As evolutionary biologist Andrew Cohen puts it, "We must liberate the power of choice from unconsciousness."[102]

Instead of being swept up in the urgency to attend to the world 'before it's too late,' let the way that we walk be slow. Let us listen to the pleas of our surrounding thirsts. Let us acknowledge the forgetting that drifted us onto this terrifying precipice. Let the grief of it all make its encounter with us through our remembering. And may beauty come alive then, under our feet.

As we learn to listen to our bodies and honour the intelligence of our feelings and dreams, we are contributing to the awakening of what some call Gaia Consciousness. Our personal embodiment practice reverberates at the level of the whole. The cues we are taking from our inner nature are the cues of our greater dreambody, calling us to make choices that result in collective harmony and sustainability.

We are remembering how to be an ecosystem. As sustainable living writer Vicki Robin suggests, "Treat everyone within fifty miles like you love them."[103] I would add that we include in our image of 'everyone' the standing people, the feathered people, the rock people, the water bodies, and so on. We must reconstitute the world through our many small contributions, collaborations, and togetherness. As we work to protect the last stands of wilderness around and within us, creating beauty from loss and heartbreak, we will meet each other: those with no extraordinary power but the devotion to do what we know we must do—and look after each other. We include each other whenever we can by doing things in pairs or circles and groups, like work parties and generosity circles, clothing swaps and protests, practicing at the power of our belonging together. Because as times get tougher, we will need a strong, reciprocal web of skills and attributes to be called upon.

When I moved to the country, I was thrust into a sudden relationship with the sun and the moon, the stars and the landscape, where the most impressive thing on the horizon was trees. In a city, the greatest things on our horizon are towers made of glass and steel, man-made testaments to our dominance and virility. Only taller than trees are mountains. And only wider than mountains is the sky, and pastures spread out as far as the eye can see. It alters the psyche entirely to be in a place where nature prevails in that it relativizes our importance in the larger family of things.

Nobody knows if humans will survive this crossing, if we'll leave anything habitable behind for future generations, but I believe our global catastrophe is a clarion call to our highest abilities. Whether we'll be successful or not, we must give everything we have to doing what we believe is right. We are but disappearing comets who must summon the grace to accept our fate while working to leave an elegant and contributive streak behind us as we go.

Restoring Temenos

Just as we practice at belonging ourselves to community through a listening presence, so too must we devote ourselves to our place. As uprooted people, so many of us are in a place for the first or second generation. Though we often think of our unbelonging as a personal quandary, our displacement from our people's place of origin is a huge contributor to the ancestral archetype of exile that we carry.

We have discovered that we are quite literally made of the earth. Just as the earth is 70% covered in water, our bodies are made up of 70% water. The elementary compounds of the earth, including oxygen, carbon, hydrogen, nitrogen, calcium, and phosphorus, also make up 99% of the human body. Our bones, teeth, breath, and blood are made of the same minerals, air, and water as the earth. It isn't difficult then, to make the leap into how the specificity of a geography, its quality of soil and water, climate and altitude, would change the evolutionary makeup of a people quite dramatically. For instance, how the wind in the mountains might broaden the shape of one's face, or how being closer to the sun might darken the skin, how constant cold might shape a nose to be long and narrow, to conserve heat. Just as land is shaped by the conditions of its place, we too are similarly landscaped.

To belong to a place is to be embedded in it. Its struggles are your contentions, its harvests your wealth, its needs your purpose. Your place's history is the story of your own becoming. If the cloud gods move in, your own mood is grey. If the year suffers with drought, you feel the desperation of thirst in your own skin. There is no separation from the place where we live, except for the one made by our own forgetting.

It's said that after arriving in a new place, we will have replaced the entirety of the water in our bodies with that of the local watershed in just a few days. Though these adaptations happen at a biological level, we are vastly unconscious of the implications a place has on our psyche. Just as humans carry an energetic signature, so too do geographies. However, like fish swimming in water, we are rarely aware of what energy a place holds until we leave it, or return to it after time away.

I remember a number of years ago travelling from the city where I'd been living for fifteen years to spend time with friends in the country. It was a very heart-opening visit, which must have contributed to my porousness upon returning, because I distinctly remember getting onto a streetcar and feeling a very familiar, yet subtle, quality of resignation enter my body. That was a revelation for me, because I'd always just assumed that quality was my own— and in this tiny interstitial moment of awareness, I saw that it belonged to this place. When I finally moved away, some years later, I never experienced that feeling again.

You might ask, "How do you know that quality of resignation wasn't a cultural energy rather than a geographical one?" And it certainly could have been. But when we look through the lens of reciprocity between culture and place, between body and earth, then the distinction falls away. If we are made of the same stuff as our place, then we are expressions of that place, but the reverse is also true. What we bring, or don't bring, to the tending of a place is also part of how that place is shaped. If you've ever tended a garden, you know exactly what I mean. When you sit with a patch of land long enough, listening to its needs and learning from its habits, you can eventually grow something very beautiful there. Conversely, if you neglect it in your thoughts, your little garden patch may become arid and fallow.

On one hand, we are missing from our place of origin. If we want to grieve it well, we must return to it physically or psychically so that we can consciously understand how it has shaped us. But on the other hand, we must re-embed ourselves, tending to the place where we have arrived. Simply moving somewhere isn't enough to make a place home. Similarly, it isn't enough to work at finding vocation and creating community. We must also become skillful with the land upon which we live, creating through the reciprocity of listening and responding, a holy grove in which to dwell.

I have a dear friend named Terence who, after thirty years of living in an ashram, decided to leave and enter the world with his gifts. With nothing more than a piece of gold he'd inherited from his teacher, he moved to Toronto and rented himself a tiny flat and began to look for a job. He soon got an entry-level position working for an investment company and applied himself, as he had in the ashram, with great discipline to the craft of financial management. Over the next ten years he became incredibly skillful with money, so much so that he went on to become the CEO of this prestigious financial institution, making a six-figure-income while still living in his tiny apartment and biking to work.

At a certain point, Terence was no longer challenged by the work and felt the inclination to travel, so he announced to his board of directors that he was leaving. Shocked that at the top of his game he would leave everything behind, and assuming it was a matter of money, the board offered him millions of dollars to stay in the job as CEO. He refused and went on to hike in the Himalayas.

Eventually, Terence came back to the place he'd lived most of his life, where the ashram was located, and decided to buy a piece of land in those same mountains. Every day for the next five years, he visited that empty acreage just to sit and listen for the invitation to build something there. He wanted to feel as if the land wanted to be developed, rather than asserting his control upon it. One day, he heard the clear call to build a home that could act as a hub of healing and togetherness for the community. The next day, he began to do just that. Using many materials indigenous to the land itself, he built a beautiful home around the particular bends and curves of that mountain spot. Careful to cut down as few trees as possible, Terence also built his foundations around a giant grandfather boulder which, to this day, emerges from his basement walls.

Out of respect for what the land had asked of him, he also erected a tipi, a sweat lodge, and a garden, all of which are now places of *temenos* for the people of his village. Over the years, Terence's land has held innumerable sweat lodges, *despacho* ceremonies, potlucks and sacred rituals in which the land has been continuously tended, thanked, and cultivated. And you can feel it when you walk there, how the earth guides your feet around its intentional paths, how the birds are settled in their tree-homes for generations to come, how there is a combined beauty of nature and humanity everywhere the eye falls. As one of my dear friends says, the earth gives back so much when you tend to it.

This reciprocal relationship with the land upon which we dwell is so essential to our practice of belonging. For those who live in urban centres, it is important to adopt even a small patch of green, whether it's on a balcony or rooftop or in a community garden plot, and begin to learn its ways. Learning might even begin with something as quiet as a houseplant which, if you listen, will eventually begin speaking to you. It will tell you when it's thirsty, wilt when it needs your attention—or, if it likes what you're giving it, demand bigger and bigger pots. In return it will offer you its beauty and patience and help you calibrate your ear. Eventually, it's good to expand your reciprocal relationship to the land around you. If it is a place devoid of nature, consider learning what used to be there. Learn where your water comes from and if there was once a forest where your building stands. What species of trees and animals have survived the paving? Which have not? Have they been properly grieved? Is there some way you can honour them? If you need to go further afield, find a park or a forest, some stand of wilderness nearby where you can apprentice yourself to the natural mysteries.

If you're lucky enough to live in a place surrounded by nature, you are blessed with a lifetime of learning ahead of you. There are some things which, if they aren't passed down from your elders, can only be taught over the course of years. You can become like the woman who has lived with her land for more than twenty years and can tell you what month it is based solely on the quality of light reflecting on the lake. Or which flowers lead the slow-motion parade of springtime. Or how long you can procrastinate harvesting the nettles before they go to seed. Or which tree is the family home to generations of ravens, and when to expect the annual visit of their noisy relatives. The greatest joy of any apprentice is to find a question that will engage them for a lifetime. If the edges of knowledge are always beyond her reach, she can rest in the sweet humility of not-knowing while being continually enriched by the gifts of discovery.

The reciprocity that makes land sacred, that creates a *temenos* or temple of worship in the ordinary places we live, requires more than our receiving of its gifts. We must contribute to its ability to be generous. Whether it is to weed around a magnolia tree so that it may flower more freely, or to prune the young apple maiden to sturdy her posture to carry heavier fruits, or to hang a birdhouse high enough that nesting wrens are out of a covetous cat's reach—we must contribute to the conversation with the holy in nature. Your contribution to that conversation might also be to protect a piece of land, beyond your own borders, which you love. To make a promise that when the time comes, you will use your voice for the voiceless. To rally with others like yourself, who understand that a life worth living is one in chorus with nature.

Developing this response-ability is what attunes us to magic. It is what puts us into that no-time, where all eternity dwells. As anyone who has played an instrument at dawn or dusk knows, the birds and insects, and sometimes even frogs, are eager to sing with you. It isn't unusual, though it is always astonishing, how harmoniously and in rhythm the animals will sing with your song. In the same way that all these species join in a wild chorus to celebrate the rising sun and the dusking of night, we too are invited into the song of things. For several hours every day, we are in unison. We calibrate as a community, expressing our unique but equally necessary voice into the swell of life. We sing to remember that we are in this together.

Nineteen

Conclusion

am filled with awe at the lengths my apprenticeship to belonging has taken me. Though I am grateful for the wisdom wrought of this long and often treacherous journey, there were many times when it seemed I'd climbed a whole mountain only to find another mountain at the top. Yet turning back was never an option. I was in its possession, and it intended to fundamentally change me.

From the initial heartbreak that took me down fast and hard into my core wounding, I never could have known how deeply I was yet to be schooled. During the long and isolating depths of physical pain, I learned how to inhabit my aloneness. Rather than unconsciously avoiding that terrifying tundra, I was cast into a sudden intimacy with it.

In illness, my identity as a capable, independent woman was stripped away. And when nothing was left, difficult questions arose: "If I have nothing to offer this world, how can I be of value? How can I be lovable? How can I belong?"

Though it didn't feel like it at the time, it was a hidden blessing to meet these questions living in my bottommost depths—because they'd been there all along, shaping the way I behaved to avoid ever having to ask or be asked by them. But there in my desolation the questions emerged ripe and ready to be asked, and asked again.

When I could do so little for myself and Craig prepared beautiful, nourishing meal after meal for me, the questions confronted me. "How can you be lovable, if you offer nothing in return?" Friends came over and worried about my health as if it were their own, and the questions asked, "Are you of value if you can't mother others?" And when many friends fell away because they couldn't deal with the gravity of my disease, they asked again, "Have you run them off with your grief and neediness?"

Every generosity brought tears to my eyes. I was being constantly humbled by life's provisions, even when I was at my lowest. And perhaps those generosities had always been there, but I was under the false impression that I'd been earning them. As if there were a penance to deserve goodness.

242

From this perspective, I never fully received what I was being given, because I believed it was contingent on my wellness, my capability, my independence, my contributions. It's like when someone gives you a compliment and you bounce it right back off a closed heart because you secretly believe it's transactional, with a hidden motivation lurking behind it. But the truth is you can't receive it because you can't give it to yourself. The aperture of your heart is tightly closed so that you don't have to face the grief of your unworthiness to love and belonging.

But I had no choice, day and night, to receive those artful meals, to watch as my husband also did the dishes, cleaned the house, shopped for the food. I had no choice but to receive the gifts of certain friends who, instead of abandoning me as I feared, loved me more sweetly. In their staying put, enduring the drudgery of illness, taking up the load I couldn't carry, I found my answer. Yes, I am still lovable when I offer nothing in return. Yes, I can have all the feelings in the room and still be valued. Yes, I can be this needy and still belong. My husband, my friends, and nature itself, became the mirror for how I needed to cherish myself.

The turning point in healing my own belonging was the moment when I finally dropped my resistance to pain, against which I had mounted a full-scale opposition, and began to see it as a beggar who'd arrived on my doorstep who I'd been treating as an unwelcome guest. But it was because the conditions of my life were so sweet that this friend finally—perhaps after generations of being outcast—felt safe enough to raise its voice and ask to be welcomed into belonging with me.

One after the other, new guests related to my friend arrived on my steps. Anger, resentment, anxiety and depression—each one asking, in turn, to be let into my house of acceptance. This confrontation with my unconscious was the attrition of the false identity that had been keeping me from knowing my innate goodness. As Jung describes it, "God is the name by which I designate all things which cross my willful path violently and recklessly, all things which upset my subjective views, plans and intentions and change the course of my life for better or worse."[104]

There were times, of course, when all I wanted was for my house guests to leave, to give me back my life again. But the longer my friends stayed, the deeper I was brought into compassion for myself and into presence with life. Dear beggar, come closer, I prayed. Tell me how I can care for you, I asked. Rest here and let me wash your feet, let me anoint you with healing balms. Let me listen to the story of your long wandering homelessness.

243

As I listened, I found my own story emerging, the one I'd worked so hard to leave behind. The story of being an orphan, with no credibility, rejected from my family of origin. The grief of this, I have come to know, will never disappear. But in my deep acknowledgment of it, the losses are finally coming to live under my roof.

In reclaiming my story, I recovered the story of my ancestors, who had been sent into an exile so complete that it ended in their deaths and the genocide of our people. I allowed myself to touch the rapacious grief that comes with being an outcast from the whole human race. And in my ancestral story, I found a universal one: the great terror of *otherness*, which is so malignant in our world that it drives us to tribalism, xenophobia, nationalism, and war.

As I was taken into these broadening levels of understanding, I could see how my story was a microcosmic expression of the millions of displaced people in the world. Unaware of our unmetabolized pain, our ancestral grief, we live split-off from the vulnerability which threatens to awaken it. The anesthetized heart is capable of great cruelty, war, and the objectification of others including, and especially, the natural world.

In the breaking open of my heart I am learning to make a true encounter with life. The more I fall in love with it, the sharper the pain of witnessing it becomes. As Arthur Miller once wrote, "I dreamed I had a child, and even in the dream I saw it was my life, and it was an idiot, and I ran away. But it always crept onto my lap again, clutched at my clothes. Until I thought, if I could kiss it, whatever in it was my own, perhaps I could sleep. And I bent to its broken face, and it was horrible...but I kissed it. I think one must finally take one's life in one's arms."[105]

In kissing our own beautiful idiot lives, I believe we are contributing to the larger presence we need to cross the threshold of our collective initiation. We are being called to stop turning away from ugliness, to witness the shattering, so that we can consciously participate in the reconstitution of a new world. It's only in re-membering our wounded, outcast selves that we can belong our world back together.

Through the practice of dreamwork I have been able to see through a mythic lens the meaningfulness of my own descent into, and emergence from exile. And to complete the classical heroic cycle, I had to bring an elixir back from the underworld, so I decided to write this book as an offering of beauty to our shared grief and estrangement.

As I sit in a hand-built cottage tucked in the foothills of Chirripó mountain in Costa Rica, where I've come to finish the writing of this book, I am struck with an embodied awareness that psyche and nature are reflections of one another. As I look out onto this lush and majestic valley filled with life, I can feel how widely my heart has been opened through grief to receive more beauty, more love, and more belonging to life. This place, for me, personifies that something greater that lies on the other side of the living bridge we've been weaving.

It is my hope that you will be turned upside down, as I have, in your reclamation of the language and competencies of belonging. Where once it was a noun, an elusive object always beyond my grasp, it has become a verb for me: the living practice focused no longer on attainment or possession, but on the deep attending and weaving into love. May it become a verb in your life as well.

Like an idyllic valley cradled on all sides by mountains who protect it from influence and encroachment, there is a place within each of us that is in a continual dance of belonging together. All of the species of trees and birds, insects, frogs, fungi, and soil are necessary ingredients in this exquisite blend of chaotic integrity.

Similarly, there is a place within us where everything should be allowed to flower in its own time and way. The way of nature is to accept everything just as it is. Whether with fruits or blossoms, compost or storms, everything has something to contribute to the whole. All of the tributaries from above trickle down into a gathering river that, wild and clean, rushes through our centre in a ceaseless baptism of *this too belongs*.

After all this time searching for a mysterious place in union with others and out in the world, may you find there was a home you've always-never known waiting within. Unaware as you may have been, it has gone on chirping and creaking and mutually flourishing, waiting for you to stop seeking and allow yourself to belong.

As you learn to walk with this ever-allowing, others catch glimpses of their intactness in your mirror. This is the great irony of belonging: that in all your searching for a home of love, it was yours to give away all along. And the real reward of your quest is to fling your doors open and let your life become a shelter of belonging for others.

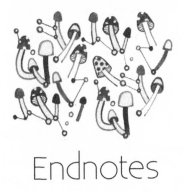

Endnotes

ONE
Something Greater

[1] *Human Planet*, "Rivers: friend and foe," (2011), BBC One

TWO
Origins of Estrangement

[2] Ngubeni, Agnes (Kabwe, Zambia) interviewed by IRIN, http://www.irinnews.org/report/87056/zambia-orphans-grow-without-cultural-identity

[3] Abraham Adzenyah, et al., "Let Your Voice Be Heard! Songs from Ghana and Zimbabwe," (World Music Press, 1997), 43

[4] Kimball, Melanie A., "From Folktalkes to Fiction: Orphan Characters in Children's Literature," *Library Trends* 47.3 (1999), 599

[5] Paraphrasing Carl Jung, Ulanov, Ann Belford, *The Feminine: In Jungian Psychology and in Christian Theology*, Northwestern University Press (1971), 48

THREE
The Death Mother

[6] von Franz, Marie-Louise, *The problem of the puer aeternus*, Toronto, Canada: Inner City Books. Original edition, Spring

Publications, Zurich (1970), 23

[7] Sieff, Daniela F., "Confronting the Death Mother. The Psychology of Violence," *A Journal of Archetype and Culture*, Spring (2009), 177

[8] Sieff, Daniela F., "Trauma-worlds and the wisdom of Marion Woodman," *Psychological Perspectives* Issue 60(2) In press (2017)

[9] Marion Woodman interviewed by Sieff, Daniela F., *Understanding and Healing Emotional Trauma*, London and New York: Routledge, Taylor & Francis Group (2015), 66

[10] Ibid, Sieff, Daniela F., "Trauma-Worlds"

[11] Ibid, Sieff, Daniela F., "Trauma-Worlds"

[12] Sieff, Daniela F., *The Death Mother as Nature's Shadow: Infanticide and the Deep History of Humankind*, Manuscript submitted for publication, (2017)

[13] Ibid, Sieff, Daniela F., *The Death Mother as Nature's Shadow*

[14] Walker, Alice, *The Temple of My Familiar*, Harcourt (1989), 287-289

FOUR

False Belonging

[15] O'Donohue, John, *Anam Cara*, New York, NY: Cliff Street Books, an imprint of Harper Collins Publishers, (1997), 143-144

[16] Williamson, Marianne, *A Return to Love: Reflections on the Principles of A Course in Miracles*, Harper Collins (1992), 190

FIVE

The Inner Marriage

[17] Federici, Silvia, *Caliban and the Witch: Women, The Body, and Primitive Accumulation*, Brooklyn, NY: Autonomedia (2004), 164

[18] Ibid, Federici, Silvia, *Caliban and the Witch*, pp. 115, 170

[19] Paraphrasing Jung, Ulanov, Ann Belford; Dueck, Alvin, *The Living God and Our Living Psyche: What Christians Can Learn from Carl Jung*, Grand Rapids, Mich.: William B. Eerdmans Pub., (2008), 98

SIX
Initiations by Exile

[20] Jung, Carl, *Collected Works*, 9i, Para 126

[21] Halifax, Joan, *Shamanic Voices*, New York: Dutton, (1979) paraphrased by The Spiritual Competency Resource Center (spiritualcompetency.com)

[22] Jung, Carl, CW 10, Para 33i

[23] Ladinsky, Daniel, "Eyes So Soft," from *The Gift, Poems by Hafiz*, Penguin publications, (1999)

SEVEN
The Symbolic Life

[24] Barks, Coleman and Moyne, John, *Quatrains of Rumi*, Threshold Books (1986)

[25] Sobol, Joseph, *The Storytellers' Journey: An American Revival*, University of Illinois Press (1999)

EIGHT
Trekking the Creative Wild

[26] Estés, Clarissa Pinkola, *In the House of the Riddle Mother: The Most Common Archetypal Motifs in Women's Dreams*, Sounds True (2005)

[27] Hillman, James, "The Animal", 320. Quoted by Fisher, Andy, *Radical Ecopsychology*, Suny Press (2013)

[28] Gibran, Khalil, from "Giving" in *The Prophet*, (1923)

[29] Stein, Gertrude, *Everybody's Autobiography*, Random House, New York (1937)

[30] García Lorca, Federico; Christopher Maurer, ed. and trans. "Play and Theory of the Duende," *In Search of Duende*, (New York: New Directions, 2010), 49

[31] Powell, Richard R., *Wabi Sabi Simple*, Adams Media (2004)

[32] Cave, Nick, "The Secret Life Of The Love Song," Vienna Poetry Festival (1998)

[33] Cocteau, Jean, *Le Rappel á l'ordre*, (1926)

NINE

The Dark Guests

[34] Bly, Robert, *A Little Book on the Human Shadow*, HarperOne (1988)

[35] Walker, Alice, *The Temple of My Familiar*, Harcourt (1989), 393

[36] Angelou, Maya, "Iconoclasts," Sundance Channel (2006)

[37] Ronnberg, Ami; Martin, Kathleen, *The Book of Symbols*, Taschen (2010), 6

[38] von Franz, Marie-Louise, *Way of the Dream: Marie-Louise von Franz in Conversation with Fraser Boa*, Windrose Films (1988)

[39] Castaneda, Carlos, *The Eagles Gift*, Washington Square Press (1991)

[40] Rumi, Jelaluddin; Whinfield, *Masnavi i Ma'navi: The Spiritual Couplets of Maulána Jalálu-'d-Dín Muhammad Rúmí*, Routledge (2000)

[41] Walker, Brian Browne, *The I Ching, Or Book of Changes*, St. Martin's Press (1993)

[42] Prechtel, Martín, *The Smell of Rain on Dust*, North Atlantic Books (2015)

[43] Macy, Joanna, "New Morning," Hallmark TV (2006)

[44] Ibid, Prechtel, Martín, *The Smell of Rain on Dust*

[45] Somé, Malidoma, *Ritual: Power, Healing and Community*, Penguin (1997)

TEN
Pain as Sacred Alley

[46] Scarry, Elaine, *The Body in Pain*, Oxford University Press (1985)

[47] Glucklich, Ariel, *Sacred Pain*, Oxford University Press (2003)

[48] Ibid, Glucklich, Ariel, Sacred Pain

[49] Hedva, Johanna, "Sick Woman Theory" *Mask Magazine* (2015)

[50] Woodman, Marion, keynote address for Civilization in Transition Conference, Chicago (1987)

[51] Edinger, Edward, "Archetype of the Apocalypse" Open Court Pub Co (1999), 58, 5

[52] Jung, Carl, CW V17, Princeton University Press (1972), 77

[53] Jung, Carl CW V17, Princeton University Press (1924/1981), 124

[54] Levy, Paul, "Unlived Lives" www.awakeninthedream.com/unlived-lives/

[55] Rumi, Jelaluddin, *The Essential Rumi*, trans. by Coleman Barks, HarperOne (1961) "Cry Out in Your Weakness"

ELEVEN
Holy Longing

[56] Ibid, Rumi, Jelaluddin, "The Reedbed"

[57] Ibid, Rumi, Jelaluddin, "Song of the Reed"

[58] Hillman, James, *A Terrible Love of War*, New York: Penguin Press (2004),133

[59] Rumi, Jelaluddin, A Garden Beyond Paradise, trans, by Jonathan Star, Bantam Books, NY (1992), 148-149

[60] Dollard-Leplomb, Christine, Sauveteurs d'étoiles en Ardennes, (2006)

TWELVE
Handmaking A Life

[61] Walker, Alice, *The Temple of My Familiar*, from "The Gospel According to Shug," Harcourt (1989)

[62] Estés, Clarissa Pinkola, "A Life Made by Hand," (A Sounds True interview) via http://www.biospiritual-energy-healing.com/a-life-made-by-hand-interview.html

[63] Suzuki, Shunryu, *Zen Mind, Beginner's Mind*, Weatherhill (1970)

[64] Prechtel, Martín, *The Unlikely Peace at Cuchumaquic*, North Atlantic Books (2012) p. 398

[65] Shakespeare, William, from *Measure for Measure*, Act 1, Scene 4 (1603)

[66] Maslow, Abraham H., *The Psychology of Science* (1966)

THIRTEEN
Bearing the Pleasure

[67] Giovanni, Nikki, "Mothers" from *My House*, William Morrow (1972)

[68] Ibid Gibran, Kahlil, *The Prophet*

[69] Wordsworth, William, *Lyrical Ballads* (1798)

[70] Rumi, Jelalludin, "The Guest House" from *The Essential Rumi*, HarperOne (1961), translation by Coleman Barks

FOURTEEN
The Invitational Presence

[71] O'Donohue, John, *Eternal Echoes: Celtic Reflections on Our Yearning to Belong*, A Cliff Street Book, Harper Collins (1999)

[72] McDougall, Leonard Sonny, "Introducing Yourself in Ojibwe," from anishinaabemodaa.com

[73] "Introducing Yourself in Navajo," NavajoWOTD.com

[74] Kozlov, Archimandrite Mikhail (1826–1884) and Troepolski, Arsenii (1804–1870)

[75] Cohen, Leonard, from "How to Speak Poetry," from *Death of a Ladies' Man*, Warner Bros (1979)

[76] "History of timekeeping devices," Wikipedia (https://en.wikipedia.org/wiki/History_of_timekeeping_devices)

[77] Lombardi, Michael A., "Why is a minute divided into 60 seconds, an hour into 60 minutes, yet there are only 24 hours in a day?" *Scientific American*, (Mar 5, 2007)

[78] "Standard time," Wikipedia (https://en.wikipedia.org/wiki/Standard_time)

[79] Janca, Aleksandar; Bullen, Clothilde, "The Aboriginal Concept of Time and its Mental Health Implications," *Australasian Psychiatry*, Vol. 11 (2003)

SIXTEEN
Storywells and Songlines

[80] "Sleep Deprivation," Wikipedia https://en.wikipedia.org/wiki/Sleep_deprivation

[81] Houston, Pam, *Contents May Have Shifted*, WW Norton (2012)

[82] "List of creation myths," Wikipedia http://en.wikipedia.org/wiki/List_of_creation_myths

[83] Nettle, Daniel; Romaine, Suzanne, *Vanishing Voices: The Extinction of the World's Languages*, Oxford University Press (2002)

[84] Basso, Keith, *Wisdom Sits in Places: Landscape and Language Among the Western Apache*, University of New Mexico Press (1996)

[85] Permission for use has been granted by Ngan'gikurunggurr Elder Miriam-Rose Ungunmerr, Miriam Rose Foundation

[86] Chatwin, Bruce, *Songlines*, Penguin (1987)

[87] Bradley, John, "Ancient knowledge given life in a virtual world" (http://www.monash.edu/monashmag/articles/issue2/ancient-knowledge-given-life-in-a-virtual-world.html)

[88] Prodanovic, Konstantin, "The Silent Genocide: Aboriginal Language Loss FAQ" (2013) http://www.terry.ubc.ca/2013/10/16/the-silent-genocide-aboriginal-language-loss-faq/

[89] Leonard, Stephen, "Death by monoculture" (2011) http://www.cam.ac.uk/research/discussion/death-by-monoculture

[90] Ibid, Leonard, Stephen, "Death by monoculture"

[91] Adichie, Chimamanda Ngozi, "The Danger of a Single Story," Ted Talk (2009) https://www.ted.com/talks/chimamanda_adichie_the_danger_of_a_single_story

[92] Tocher, Michelle, "Breaking Spells in Life and Fairytales," *Immanence Journal*, (Spring 2017), 56

[93] Morrison, Toni, *Beloved*, New York: Vintage Books (2004)

[94] Watts, Alan, "Gaining Control by Letting Go," (2016) https://youtu.be/RQfzwinDrrQ

[95] Shlain, Leonard, *The Alphabet Versus the Goddess: The Conflict Between Word and Image*, Penguin Books (1999)

SEVENTEEN

Tending A Village

[96] Definition of "Minga" from http://etimologias.dechile.net

[97] Sales, Ruby, from "Where Does it Hurt," *On Being* with Krista Tippett (Sept 15, 2016 episode)

[98] Hampâté Bâ, Amadou at L'UNESCO (1960)

[99] McNeill, Donald P.; Morrison, Douglas A.; Nouwen, , *Compassion: A Reflection on the Christian Life*, (1983) 80

[100] Rumi, Jelalludin, "Cry Out in your Weakness" from *The Essential Rumi* (1961), translation by Coleman Barks

EIGHTEEN

Reciprocity With Nature

[101] Macy, Joanna and Johnstone, Chris, *Active Hope: How to Face the Mess We're in Without Going Crazy*, New World Library (2012)

[102] Keogh, Martin, *Hope Beneath Our Feet*, North Atlantic Books (2010)

[103] Ibid, Robin, Vicki "Letter from the Future," ed. Keogh, Martin, *Hope Beneath our Feet*, 44

NINETEEN
Conclusion

[104] Edinger, Edward, *Transformation of the God-Image*, Inner City Books (1992)

[105] Miller, Arthur, *After the Fall*, (First Performance 1964)

Author's Note

My name was given to me by my parents. They chose it from a book of poems called *Technicians of the Sacred*, by Jerome Rothenberg. Toko-pa is a deity in the Māori creation myth, known as the "Parent of the Mist." Over the years, I've come to think of that mist as the realm between worlds, waking and dreaming. Indeed, my life is a devotion to repairing the bridge between them.

I was born on a farm in Devon, in the south of England, and came to Canada at the age of four, where my maternal grandparents took refuge after the war in Poland. I was raised in a Sufi community in Montreal.

My greatest love has always been music. I play the guitar and sing, and in my early twenties I even toured with a band and recorded an album of original music. I strayed for a while into the music business, becoming an A&R executive for a record company.

Thanks to a dark-night-of-the-soul, I left that life and returned to the mystical teachings of Sufism and the study of dreams. I became deeply interested in Analytical Psychology and did a three-year internship at the Jung Foundation of Ontario. In exchange for making tea and taking registration, I got to sit at the feet of teachers like Marion Woodman, James Hollis, J. Gary Sparks, and other great Jungians.

Blending the mystical tradition of Sufism with a Jungian approach to dreamwork, in 2001 I went rogue and founded the Dream School. Out of the humble longing to share what I was learning, I began to teach and support others with their dreams in my private practice. Now, almost 17 years later, we have grown a network of more than a hundred thousand dreamers all over the world. In addition to tending dreams, my work focuses on restoring the feminine, reconciling paradox, elevating grief, and facilitating ritual.

Belonging is my first book.